Mastering 3D Animation

TEXT AND ILLUSTRATION BY

PETER RATNER

ALLWORTH PRESS
NEW YORK

05 04 03 02 01 00   5 4 3 2 1

Published by Allworth Press
An imprint of Allworth Communications
10 East 23rd Street, New York, NY 10010

Cover design by Douglas Design Associates, New York, NY
Cover illustration by Peter Ratner, Penn Laird, VA
Page composition/typography by Sharp Des!gns, Inc., Lansing, MI

ISBN: 1-58115-068-7

LIBRARY OF CONGRESS CATALOGING-IN-PUBLICATION DATA
Ratner, Peter
      Mastering 3D animation / Peter Ratner.
          p. cm.
      Includes index.
      ISBN 1-58115-068-7
      1. Computer animation. 2. Three-dimensional display systems.
      I. Title.
TR 897.7 .R39 2000
006.6'96—dc21   00-59392

Printed in Canada

Dedicated to Sharon,
Ori, and the ECK

Contents

Foreword

You now hold in your hands the proof that there is no "Make Dinosaur" button. This mythical button stems back to the time when the movie *Jurassic Park* was released. Many people thought that the artists who created the digital dinosaurs had a button on their computer screens that would allow them to create a dinosaur with the click of a mouse. This was easier to comprehend than the fact that it took a lot of time and artistic and technical talent to make a digital character.

Today, 3D animation is one of the least understood disciplines. Due to the complexity of the software, most people are not motivated to learn about computer animation. Aside from the technical difficulties, there are many other skills animators have to learn. Some of these are drawing, painting, modeling in three dimensions, lighting, texturing, cinematography, sound syncing, and animating. One would be hard-pressed to find any other art field that requires such a broad range of creativity, knowledge, and technical skill.

Most animation studios appreciate the overwhelming burden that one person would have to carry to know everything about 3D. This is one of the reasons why studios split the tasks up among lighting specialists, modelers, texture artists, render wranglers, animators, and so on. However, to reach that level, aspiring artists have to produce an animation tape, and this often requires the application of every 3D animation skill.

The purpose of this book is to provide readers with a set of learning tools to help them create a respectable animation. Many 3D modeling and animation essentials have been outlined in various formats. Some are presented in tutorial form while others are in an explanatory discussion. Since most artists are visually oriented, numerous illustrations have been provided along with models and sample animations on the CD-ROM. It is recommended that you copy the QuickTime animation movies to your hard drive so that they will play in real time.

As an animation teacher at the university, I have been able to try out and refine most of the written and illustrated material in my introductory, intermediate, and advanced classes. The results have been positive and it has been gratifying to see so many of my students find work in large and small animation companies, gaming studios, and multimedia firms.

This book does not concern itself with the type of software or hardware available to the reader. Its purpose is not to create button pushers who can boast about megahertz, abundant RAM, big monitors, and software with all kinds of bells and whistles. It is hoped that aspiring 3D artists will learn some valuable lessons from the great art geniuses that have preceded them. Some struggled to create works with meager resources under the most dismal conditions. By applying their creativity, skills, and discipline, they were able to produce the magical alchemy that transforms the mundane into the extraordinary. Perhaps the most important lesson one can learn is humility in the presence of their accomplishments.

Although I have tried to keep this book as non-software-specific as possible, it was often difficult not to mention certain software. Some procedures are highly dependent on the kind of software used. In those cases, I tried to show at least several software approaches. I hope that this book will prove to be a useful resource for most readers, no matter what platform or software they are using. Software changes often, and focusing too much attention on it detracts from the attention that should be paid to the key principles of 3D animation. Books overly dependent on specific software frequently become dated and sometimes have a very narrow focus.

Before using this book, you should know how to operate your particular 3D software package. Most have good manuals that make it possible to learn a great deal in a fairly short time. Although these software texts teach how to use animation tools, they usually do not dwell on applying them in a certain style. Space and time constraints prevent software writers from dwelling too long on these principles of modeling and animation.

I would like to acknowledge SGI's Alias/Wavefront software division for providing me with its outstanding 3D package, Maya. Its impressive tool sets and revolutionary workflow have had a direct influence on the development of other major software packages.

I am also grateful to Patrick Wilson, a former student who now works on PIXAR's lighting team. His expertise has helped me a great deal when writing about lighting.

Another invaluable contributor to the lighting chapter was Avi Das, a color and lighting artist at Digital Domain. Avi brims with ideas and interesting facts about lighting. I owe him a great debt.

This book would be incomplete without mentioning the efforts of some of my former students. One of these, Sharon Bilyj, adopted one of my methods for building a human head and then proceeded to take it a step further. After some experimentation, she was able to model not only the head seamlessly, but also the entire body. I consider her accomplishment one of the most ingenious techniques I have seen in 3D modeling. Another student, Andy Higgins, showed me his style of building a character with polygon bevel tools. It appears to be an interesting approach to subdivision-mesh modeling familiar to many 3D artists.

I would be remiss not to mention the contributions of my brilliant seventeen-year-old son, Ori. One of his many gifts is his ability to surface objects creatively. He thought up the technique for creating a pinhead with displacement mapping.

A final thank you goes to my wife, Sharon, who has been very patient and supportive during the time of this project.

Create and take some delight in it. The journey is more important than the outcome. Best wishes on your endeavors.

PETER RATNER

About the CD-ROM

Thank you for purchasing this book. Although this CD-ROM does not contain any software programs, it does include useful models and examples in a variety of formats to help you work your way through the book. As you read the book, you will be directed to view specific images and animations that illustrate the technique or instructions being discussed. This CD-ROM is also intended to be a resource even when you are not using the text, by providing you with some useful tools, images, and models that you can apply to your own animation projects.

Technical Requirements

Mastering 3D Animation should work with most high-end software. These are:

- Maya (Alias/Wavefront)
- LightWave (NewTek)
- 3D Studio Max (Discreet)
- Softimage (Avid)
- Houdini (Side Effects)

Mid-range software packages will work for some of the exercises but may lack the capabilities required for character animation. Before purchasing mid-range software make sure that it has the capabilities to create skeletons and shape shift.

Skeletons are essential when animating characters. Shape shifting (morphing) is important when you want your characters to show facial expressions. Some mid-range packages are:

- Animation Master (Martin Hash)
- TrueSpace (Caligari)
- Inspire 3D (NewTek)

The movies on the CD-ROM are in QuickTime format. If you do not have QuickTime on your computer, you can go to the Apple site to download it, *http://www.apple.com*.

To play the movies in real time, you should copy them to your hard drive.

Images that are cited in the text as well as textures have been saved as JPEGs (.jpg). Most image browsers should be able to open these.

Organization

The folders or directories are arranged by chapters. Each folder contains the materials for one chapter, except for chapters 06, 07, and 08, which have been placed in one folder since they contain support materials for Part 2 of the book titled Advanced 3D Modeling. The models in the Chapters 06, 07, 08 folder can be used as either 3D templates or reference materials. The models in the various folders are saved in a format compatible with the specific software that is referred to in the lesson. Most models are saved in Maya (.mb) or LightWave (.lwo) format. The templates have also been saved in Wavefront (.obj) and AutoDesk (.dxf) format. In any case, most mid- to high-level modeling programs should be able to open the files in one form or another. Nowadays, nearly all low level modeling software can read the .dxf format. Check your software manual to find out which formats it can import.

If you want to use templates of generic 3D male and female models, you will find some that I modeled for you in the folder labeled "Chapter06, 07, 08." These models are without detail and are meant to be used as proportion guides. I also included some detailed parts of the male and female for you to use as final finishing touches templates. You can find these in the Chptrs6,7,8 > Templates > DetailedParts folder. Some LightWave model detail parts can also be found in:

- Chapter06,07,08 > Templates > Female > LWOFemModelSteps > FinalSplSteps

and

- Chapter06,07,08 > Templates > Male > LWOMaleModelSteps > FinalSplSteps > Male1orMale2.

You can also view some of my students' models on the CD. Most of them are from my beginning courses on modeling and animating. The advanced students generally do not like giving out their models because they worry people will appropriate them. However, you can find a few in the "StudentModels" folder. I hope you will not utilize any of these models for your own animations or for commercial uses. The purpose of this book is to help you create and animate your own models. Using someone else's defeats that purpose.

The contents of the folder labeled Textures can be used for various surfacing projects. Many 3D artists are interested in finding and making new textures. Maybe you can find new ways to use the ones included here. The Photoshop brush file (.abr) in the Chapter 10 folder can be utilized for creating grime textures. Perhaps it will serve as a starting point for the development of your own unique brush styles.

Finally, the folder titled Gallery has some images for you to browse through. The gallery also contains some of my students' renderings from various animations.

Like all good art, good animation makes it look easy. As this book makes clear, that ease is one of animation's best illusions. However, if you find 3D animation as fascinating as I do, it will be well worth the effort. Best wishes on your endeavors.

PETER RATNER

PART I

3D Modeling and Animation Fundamentals

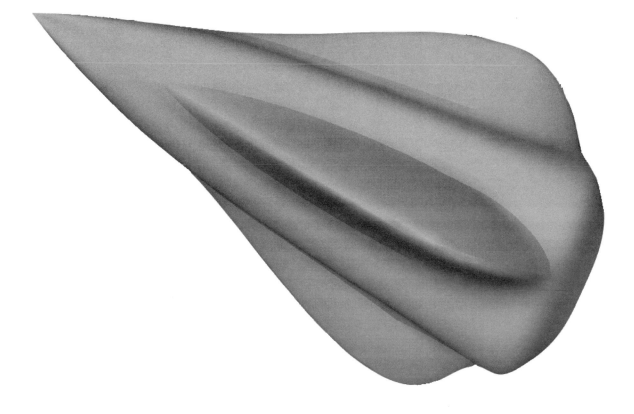

CHAPTER 1

The Fundamentals
of 3D Modeling

Currently, there are two methods employed in 3D modeling: polygon and spline-based. Polygons are composed of two-dimensional shapes made from a sequence of line segments. These can be any amount, which means polygons can have any number of sides. Polygons are named according to the number of sides they possess. Among them are triangles (three sides), quadrilaterals (four sides), pentagons (five sides), hexagons (six sides), heptagons (seven sides), and so on. In computer graphics, polygons with more than four sides are referred to as ngons or *n*-sided polygons. A polygon mesh is composed of a series of various sized polygons, each one having three or more points. The polygons in a mesh share adjoining points and sides.

Splines are flexible line segments defined by edit points called vertices. Splines require very few points to make a curve whereas polygons require many vertices and edges. Thus, spline-based models often contain less data than polygon models. In polygons, each vertex contains a value for the *x*-, *y*-, and *z*-axes. Figure 1-1 illustrates some of the best-known spline types.

Non-uniform, rational b-splines, affectionately known as NURBS, are flexible lines used to create smooth curves and surfaces. These curves and surfaces are defined by a set of control vertices (CVs) that influence the object or shape in their vicinity. The overall form of the object is determined by the location of the control points in space (Figure 1-2). When these vertices are moved, the shape bends accordingly. NURBS are defined by very complicated mathematical formulas. Of all the splines, they are the most complex. They are non-uniform because knots connecting the line segments can be spaced in any number of ways to yield a variety of different curves. They are also rational because

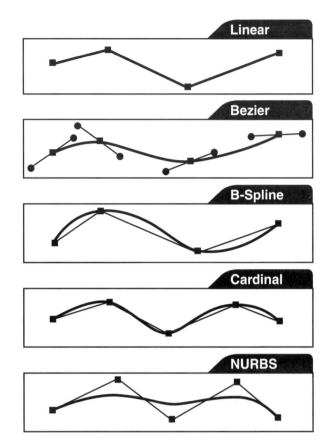

Fig. 1-1 Five commonly known spline types.

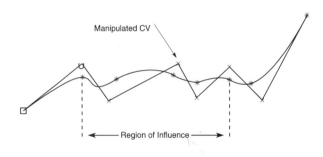

Fig. 1-2 The control vertices influence the shape and size of the NURBS mesh.

points can be weighted unequally. One point can influence a curve more than others. Unlike other curves, which can only be cut at their control points, NURBS can be trimmed anywhere along the line. The end knots on a NURBS curve can be put anyplace.

Some of the more useful software packages combine NURBS and polygon modeling. A few of them have the capability to create spline-based models, which can then be surfaced with polygons or transformed into polygon models. After being converted, polygon tools can be used to refine and complete them.

Polygon Modeling

Three or more points can be connected by a line to form a closed loop. This closed loop is a poly-

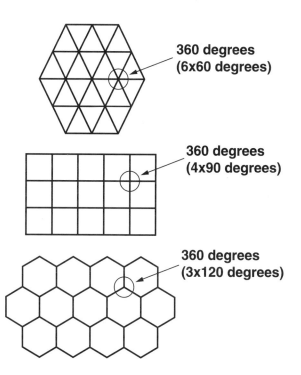

360 degrees
(6x60 degrees)

360 degrees
(4x90 degrees)

360 degrees
(3x120 degrees)

Fig. 1-3 The three regular tessellations.

gon. A polygon is a portion of a plane bounded by three or more lines or segments. A polygon can be planar, non-planar, convex, or concave. Non-planar means that one or more vertices do not lie on the same plane. For example, if you lay a square down on a flat surface and pull up one of its points, it becomes non-planar. This results in an impossible situation because polygons can only have flat and not curved surfaces. Unless a polygon is split, it cannot curl up on one corner. As a result, non-planar polygons can cause rendering problems. Parts of the polygon mesh may look dark or flicker during an animation.

It is usually recommended that before rendering, all polygons be tripled. A triangle cannot be non-planar because its three points are always on the same plane. It is a good idea to save the original model separately from the tripled version because you may have to go back and change parts of it. It is easier to make changes on a model with square polygons.

A series of joined polygons are referred to as tessellations. A regular tessellation is a tiling pattern made up of regular polygons. There are only three regular tessellations because there are only three regular polygons whose face angles divide evenly into 360 degrees: triangles, squares, and hexagons (Figure 1-3).

Semi-regular tessellations are tiling patterns composed of a combination of regular and semi-regular polygons. When joining a square, equilateral triangle, and hexagon, two semi-regular polygons may be formed: the octagon (eight sides) and the dodecagon (twelve sides). Only these five polygons can be constructed so that all angles add up to 360 degrees (Figure 1-4). Although there are only fourteen common vertices of these polygons, there is an infinite number of ways to combine them.

Adjoining groups of polygons form polyhedra. The first five, regular uniform polyhedra are known as regular convex uniform polyhedra or Platonic solids (Figure 1-5). The remaining four, regular uni-form polyhedra are called regular non-convex uniform polyhedra or Kepler-Poinsot solids.

Polyhedra, which have a similar arrangement of polygons of two or more different types, are called semi-regular polyhedra or Archimedean solids. They are distinguished from prisms, antiprisms, and elongated square gyrobicupola by their spherical symmetry. The others have dihedral symmetry. There are thirteen semi-regular polyhedra, two of which can be seen in Figure 1-6.

Polygons can be arrayed into innumerable convex and non-convex polyhedral structures. Many artists like Leonardo daVinci, M. C. Escher, Sol LeWit, and Don Judd have been fascinated with polygon-based structures. It is a rich field of study worthy of investigation.

Aside from the fact that polygons can be joined in so many ways, they also have a few other distinguishing characteristics. They can be convex, concave, have holes in them, and their vertices can even double back so that a surface intersects itself. The ability to easily join polygons at their vertices and to split them anywhere makes this a very flexible system of modeling. Polygon modeling is well-suited to objects that have varying degrees of detail. For example, when modeling a human, you can use more polygons in parts of the face and fewer for the torso, arms, and legs. The only drawback to polygons is that their edges are straight, which means that many have to be laid end-to-end to make an object appear curved.

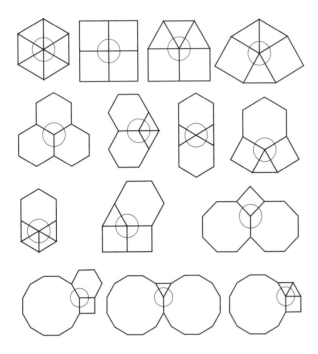

Fig. 1-4 Of the regular and semi-regular polygons, only triangles, squares, hexagons, octagons, and dodecagons can tile in various combinations around a common vertex. As shown above, there are only 14 such combinations.

Fig. 1-5 Regular polyhedra are made from polygons with the same faces. These are the dodecahedron, icosahedron, cube, octahedron, and tetrahedron.

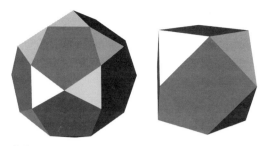

Fig. 1-6. Semi-regular polyhedra are made up of two or more different types. Pictured above are two out of the 13; the icosidodecahedron and the cubeoctahedron.

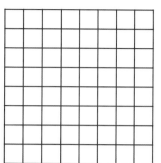

Fig. 1-7 A square divided by 8 segments.

Fig. 1-8 A curved spline placed on top of the rectangular mesh.

Creating Areas of Detail on a Polygon Mesh

The following tutorial shows you how polygons can be split and specific points moved to create areas of detail. In this lesson, you will make a slight depression in a smooth surface to produce a crease or wrinkle.

Start by making a rectangle on the *z*-axis (front view). It should be split into eight segments on the *x*- and *y*-axes (Figure 1-7). There is no need to give it any depth on the *z*-axis. Now sketch a curving spline (line) that sits on top of the rectangle (Figure 1-8). If you have a layers option, create the spline in the second layer.

The next step is to make the curve a part of the rectangular mesh. Depending on your software, you can project the curve or stencil it on with a drill operation. If you can name the curve, do so and be sure to stencil it on the *z*-axis.

If you end up with extra points, you can delete some and merge the ones closest to each other. Leave just enough points to maintain the curve of the line (Figure 1-9).

Another approach to making a curve on the mesh is to use the spline as a guide or template and then select an "add points" tool to insert points that follow the template curve (Figure 1-10). After

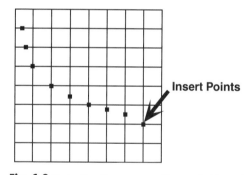

Insert Points

Fig. 1-9 Projecting the curve on the mesh. Note the location of the extra points in order to bend the curve more.

Fig. 1-10 A curve on mesh can also be created by inserting individual points.

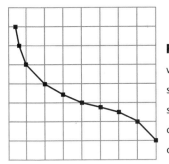

Fig. 1-11 The points that will form the line are selected in order and a split polygon command creates the rough curve on the mesh.

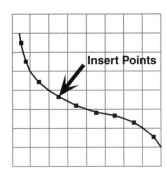

Fig. 1-12 More points are inserted along the line for extra control.

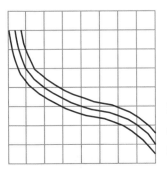

Fig. 1-13 Two more curves are made on both sides of the original.

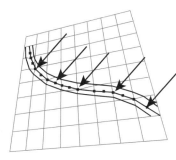

Fig. 1-14 All the points are selected along the middle curve and pulled back.

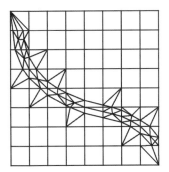

Fig. 1-15 Polygons with more than four sides can be split into three- and four-sided ones.

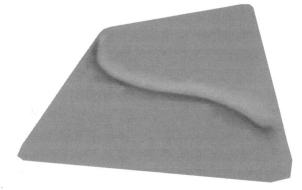

Fig. 1-16 A shaded view of the final rectangle and the groove.

selecting all the polygons, the newly inserted points are then chosen in order, and a "split polygon" command will subdivide the polygons along the inserted points (Figure 1-11). The result will be a rough curve that can be modified by inserting extra points along the line (Figure 1-12). Moving the extra points according to the template completes the process.

Once you have completed the curve on the mesh, repeat the above steps to create two more curves on both sides (Figure 1-13). Select all the points except the two end points along the middle curve and pull them back on the z-axis (Figure 1-14). This will create a groove in the polygon mesh.

You may want to clean up some of the polygons by splitting them so that you only have three- or four-sided versions in your mesh (Figure 1-15). Smoothing can also be applied to refine the final crease or wrinkle (Figure 1-16). Later, you can use this method on your polygon models to add wrinkles to the skin, grooves in the hair, wrinkles in clothes, and so on. Usually, three curves should be enough, but some people prefer to use four and then pull the two middle ones back. This yields a kind of box canyon effect.

Joining Two Polygon Objects Seamlessly

Another important polygon modeling skill is the ability to join two separate objects in a way that makes them appear as one. This is useful for tasks such as joining an arm to a torso, a head to a neck, and so on.

In this exercise, two differently shaped spheres or balls are joined. Often, Boolean operations can be used to unify separate objects like these. However, the problem with using an automatic method like Booleans is that they often create too many extra points. Polygons are also not joined in the cleanest way possible. The cleanup after Booleans can be more time consuming than if you had completed the task manually. The beauty of polygon modeling is that with the right tools, one controls the most minute parts of a model. This means every single point. The following technique shows how this works.

Create a simple sphere or ball with eight sides and four segments. Rotate the sphere so that its poles are no longer on the *y*-axis (top) but on the *x*-axis (side). Stretch the sphere on the *x*-axis. Make another sphere that is larger with the same settings. Leave this one in its original form. Move them together so that they overlap slightly like the ones in Figure 1-17.

Select the polygons at the end of the elongated sphere. These are the ones that are penetrating the round sphere. Delete them so that your spheres look somewhat like the ones shown in Figure 1-18.

Select the end points on the elongated sphere.

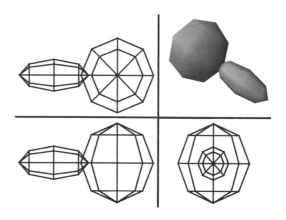

Fig. 1-17 An elongated and a regular sphere are placed next to each other.

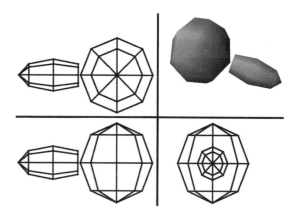

Fig. 1-18 The overlapping polygons on the elongated sphere are cut away.

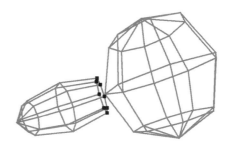

Fig. 1-19 The 8 points along the end of the cut polygon are selected and copied.

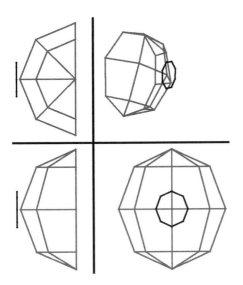

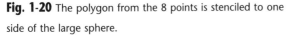

Fig. 1-20 The polygon from the 8 points is stenciled to one side of the large sphere.

Fig. 1-21 The stenciled polygon on the sphere.

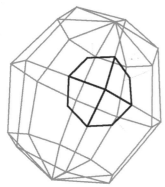

Fig. 1-22 The stenciled polygons are deleted leaving a hole in the sphere.

This is the section from which you deleted polygons. There should be eight points (Figure 1-19). Copy and paste them into another layer. If your software does not have layers, then paste them but do not move the points. Pick each point in order, moving in a clockwise or counterclockwise direction. Once all of the points are selected, make a polygon out of them.

Hide everything except the newly made polygon and the polygons on the large sphere that are closest to it (Figure 1-20). Using a drill operation, stencil the polygon with eight vertices to one side of the large sphere. This should be done on the *x*-axis and, if possible, name the stencil surface. This will make it easier to select the polygons later. Figure 1-21 shows the large sphere with the stenciled polygon on its surface.

Choose the stenciled polygons and delete them. This will leave a hole in the large sphere (Figure 1-22). You may need to select points that have been stenciled onto the surface and are near the original points of the sphere, and merge them. In other words, if you see any points close to each other, select and merge them. You should end up with only eight points around the hole.

Make both spheres visible. You can now select corresponding points on the two spheres and weld them together, or create new polygons by selecting four points closest to each other. Figure 1-23 shows corresponding points selected in pairs to be merged. Figure 1-24 illustrates the selection of four nearby points to make a polygon. If you are making polygons out of points, then simply go around the hole until you have a set of eight connecting polygons.

Figure 1-25 shows the merged spheres. To make the area around the joined surfaces smoother, you can subdivide that area or apply a "smoothing" command for the entire unified object (Figure

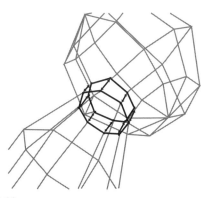

Fig. 1-23 The arrows point to the corresponding points which are selected one pair at a time and welded.

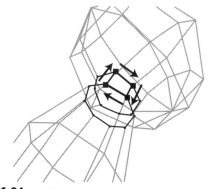

Fig. 1-24 Another approach to connecting the two objects. Four points are selected in order (arrows) and made into a polygon.

1-26). If you are using a program such as Lightwave 3D, then you can either metaform the objects or turn them into MetaNURBS and freeze them.

Working with Spline Cages

Although a variety of modeling techniques can be adapted to polygon modeling, polygons nevertheless are subject to one general weakness: their inability to bend. Unlike NURBS or splines, the line that connects a polygon from one point to another is always straight. Subdividing polygons into smaller

ones usually solves facet problems making them similar to a cut gemstone. However, when it comes to modeling, it is very difficult to work with subdivided surfaces containing many polygons.

Splines and NURBS, on the other hand, do not require a complex wire mesh to make a surface appear smooth. This simplifies the modeler's work because there are fewer points and lines to contend with.

When it comes to the organic modeling of humans and animals, it is often best to start with splines and end with polygons. The most advanced

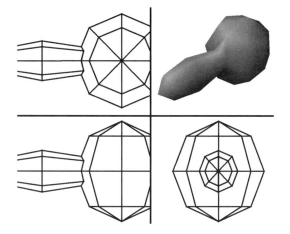

Fig. 1-25 The two spheres welded together.

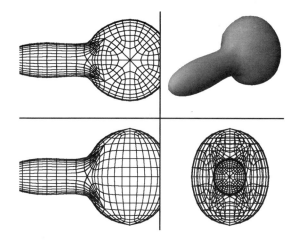

Fig. 1-26 Smoothing the spheres.

11

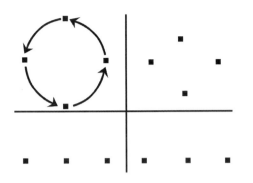

Fig. 1-27 Four points are made in the top view and selected in order.

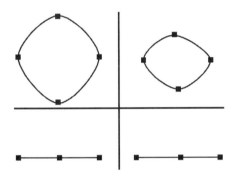

Fig. 1-28 The points are connected with a closed curve or spline.

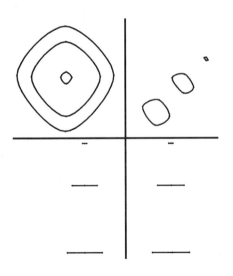

Fig. 1-29 The closed curve is duplicated twice and scaled.

modeling programs combine spline and polygon modeling. Some proprietary software even allows models to be composed of both NURBS and polygons. Usually a spline or NURBS object has to be converted totally to a polygon. Unfortunately, this is a one-way street because polygon models normally cannot be converted into NURBS objects.

If your software supports spline and polygon modeling, then you may decide on the following directions, which will prepare you for more advanced organic modeling in later chapters. Your software should have the capabilities to create open and closed splines, add points on splines, connect one spline to another, and finally, convert the spline mesh to one made of polygons.

Create four points in the top view. Imagine a clock and place the points at twelve, nine, six, and three o'clock. Select all four points in order, either clockwise or counterclockwise (Figure 1-27). Connect all the selected points with a closed curve or spline (Figure 1-28).

Select the closed curve (oval) and duplicate it twice. Move each copy above the other in the front view. Scale each of the two top copies so that they look somewhat like the ones shown in Figure 1-29.

Now connect the points from one closed curve to the second and then to the third. This will result in a spline cage. Corresponding points will have to be selected in the right order, that is, points that are duplicates of each other. Figure 1-30 shows the completed spline cage. Select the top point first on the smallest oval, then the next point on the middle oval, and finally, the third point on the large bottom oval. Connect the three selected points with an open curve. Do the same with the rest of the points.

Note the resulting spline cage. Every section has four points. This is very important. Each spline must intersect in a way that forms a four-sided

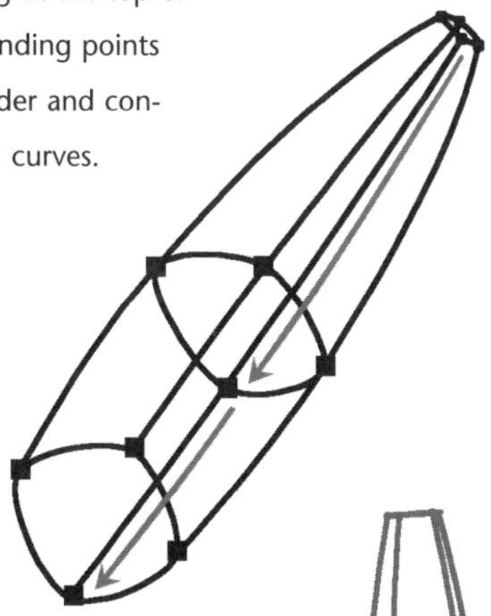

Fig. 1-30 Starting at the top or bottom, corresponding points are selected in order and connected with open curves.

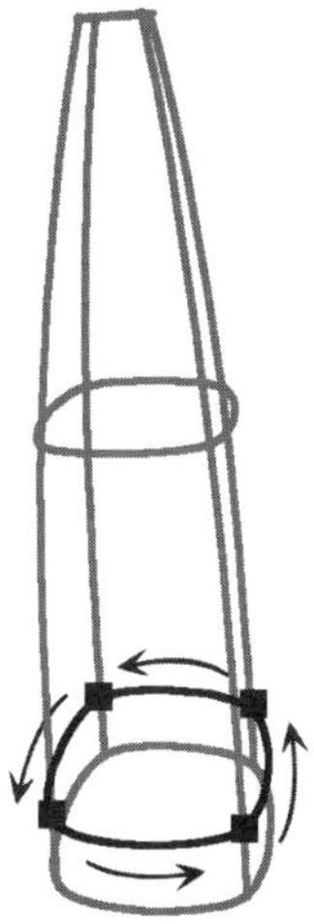

Fig. 1-31 Four extra points are inserted near the bottom and made into a closed curve.

shape. You can also have three-sided shapes, but sometimes these can result in flipped polygons. The AutoPatcher plug-in in Lightwave 3D, which is used to create polygons over a spline cage, works best with four-sided shapes.

Before proceeding to the next step, you may want to try covering or patching your spline cage with polygons to see how it works. When you are finished testing, undo or delete the polygons to return the model to its original spline cage.

Figure 1-31 shows where you should insert four extra points. Line them up in the front or side views so that they are straight across. Select the points in order and make a closed curve out of them.

Starting with the top oval and ending at the bottom oval, insert one point on each. Connect the points with an open curve. From these new points, select the third one down from the top and pull it out (Figure 1-32).

Figure 1-33 shows the location where you will now add two more points. Four of the points, as

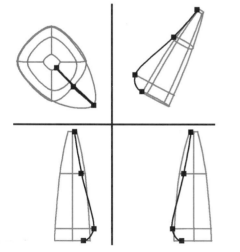

Fig. 1-32 Four more points are inserted along the *y*-axis between two of the splines and connected with an open curve. Of these, the second from the bottom is pulled out.

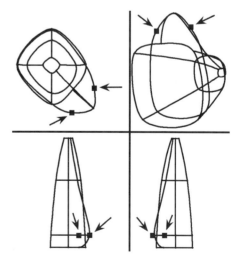

Fig. 1-33 Two new points are inserted on the third oval between the new open curve and the existing ones on both sides.

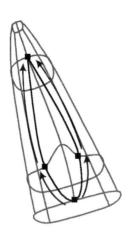

Fig. 1-34 Four of the indicated points are selected in order and connected with a closed curve. The two new points are pulled in to make a fin shape.

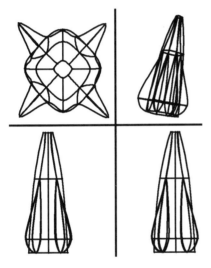

Fig. 1-35 Three more fins are added to the body.

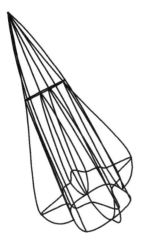

Fig. 1-36 The points at the top are selected and brought together with the scaling tool to make a sharp tip.

indicated in Figure 1-34, are selected and connected with a closed curve. The two new points that you inserted in the previous step are dragged toward the main body. You should now have a fin shape. All of the fin shape sections are three-sided. The shapes outside of the fin are four-sided.

Repeat the previous steps to create three more fins around the body (Figure 1-35). Perhaps by now, you have guessed that you are modeling a simple spaceship. Once you have completed all four fins, select all the points of the smallest oval at the top. Bring these together with your scaling tool so that the spaceship comes to a point.

Before surfacing the spline cage with polygons, you may decide to add more detail or refine the craft by moving specific points. Other features can be formed by using the previously-discussed techniques of adding points and making open or closed curves from them. Remember to make each section only three- or four-sided.

When you are satisfied with the shape of the object, surface it using the AutoPatcher plug-in or an equivalent software tool. Set the polygon level to a low subdivision like 1. The ship may look a little rough, but it is easier to make changes when you have fewer polygons to contend with. Use your polygon statistics to select only polygon surfaces. Separate the polygon object from the spline cage by either pasting it into another layer or moving it.

If you see dark areas, try merging points. If some polygons are flipped, they will appear as holes on the surface. You can select these individually and flip them, or use an "align polygons" command, or make the entire surface double-sided. Details can now be sculpted on the polygon surface using various tools. Minute areas are often easier to model on polygons by splitting them and moving their points. This was covered in a previ-

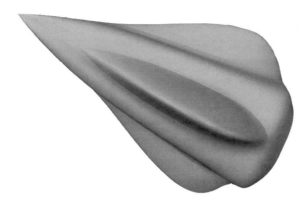

Fig. 1-37. A simple polygon ship with smoothing applied.

Fig. 1-38 Weights are painted on a NURBS surface. A weight of zero is on the bottom and indicated in black, while a weight of one is shown at the top in light gray.

ous exercise, which demonstrated how to create wrinkles or creases on a surface.

As a final step, apply a "smoothing" command to the polygon spaceship. Figure 1-37 shows the completed object.

NURBS Modeling

Non-uniform rational b-splines (NURBS) are composed of numerically stable algorithms. They are fast and can be altered with little effort. Curves bend easily with no kinks. NURBS models are also resolution-independent. They retain their smooth appearance no matter how close they are to the camera. This means that complex forms can be built with less data. NURBS can also be weighted. You can assign a percentage weight to each point to indicate how much each point should be affected by movement, rotation, or scaling of the cluster set. When the cluster of points is transformed, the points react according to the percentages specified.

To understand the effects of weights, Maya with Artisan was used to paint various weights on a NURBS plane (Figure 1-38). The grayscale indicates the different weights. The lightest area at the top

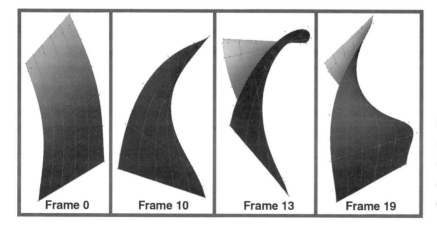

Frame 0   Frame 10   Frame 13   Frame 19

Fig. 1-39 The effects of weighted surfaces when the NURBS plane is rotated. Notice how the darkest areas at the bottom lag behind the lighter ones at the top.

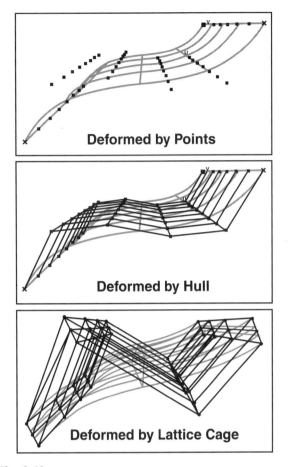

Fig. 1-40 A few methods for deforming a NURBS mesh.

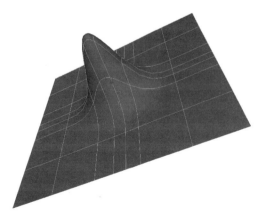

Fig. 1-41 Splines or isoparms are inserted to pull up a small section of the NURBS surface.

has a weight of 1, the middle, a weight of 0.5, and the bottom, a weight of 0. Once the weights were painted, the NURBS plane was rotated. Figure 1-39 shows the effects of weighting a surface. As the plane rotates, the bottom turns slower than the top. Cluster weights can be useful for cloth simulations, facial distortions, and so on.

NURBS surfaces can be deformed in a variety of ways. Some can be seen in Figure 1-40. Controlling the shape of a NURBS surface can occur in both modeling and animation. For example, a lattice cage, wire, cluster, and sculpt deformers can all be used to bend parts of a model.

A disadvantage of NURBS is that it is difficult to create shared surfaces. Unlike polygons, it takes more effort to join two NURBS surfaces with varying characteristics. Joining two objects like a sphere and a cone requires a blend between the two. The blend is sort of a skin that acts as a bridge between the two objects. Even though a blend updates by stretching, when one or both end objects are moved, it remains a separate mesh from the two. This becomes more obvious during animations when small fractures appear and disappear along the edges of seams as a kind of "popping."

Another disadvantage of NURBS is that it is difficult to isolate specific areas of detail. If one tries to insert extra splines or isoparms in a single section of the surface, the spline/isoparm is automatically inserted from the beginning of the mesh all the way to the end. Because NURBS surfaces are continuous, it is difficult to create smaller areas of detail.

Figure 1-41 illustrates this problem. Four splines/isoparms were inserted on a NURBS surface so that a small section could be pulled up. Rather than isolating the splines/isoparms to the pulled

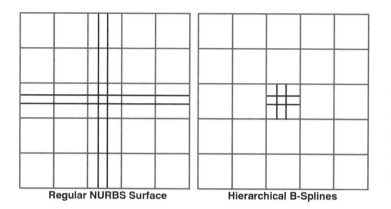

Regular NURBS Surface   Hierarchical B-Splines

Fig. 1-42 A top view of the surface from Figure 1-41 reveals the inserted splines/isoparms in black. A regular NURBS mesh will have continuous splines while the hierarchical b-spline surface on the right can have isolated patches of splines.

part alone, they run continuously from the beginning of the mesh to the end, beyond the necessary area of detail.

Figure 1-42 shows the regular NURBS surface from a top view. The illustration on the left depicts the inserted splines/isoparms in black. You can see how they extend beyond the middle area of detail. The illustration on the right in Figure 1-42 shows a different geometry, which makes it possible to isolate specific areas for detail. Developed by David R. Forsey, hierarchical b-splines are linearly independent multilevel b-splines that can control refinements locally. This means that patches containing more splines can be added only to parts of a model requiring extra detail.

Lofting/Skinning

Lofting or skinning, more commonly referred to as lofting, is a very useful method for creating a variety of shapes and forms. Many artists favor this as the tool of choice for creating organic characters such as humans. The following exercise should help you understand a few NURBS modeling basics. Some of the actions to be performed are lofting, isolating and duplicating a spline/isoparm, projecting it onto a surface, trimming, and blending.

Create a NURBS circle on the *y*-axis with a sweep angle of 360 degrees, a radius of 0.2 cubic degrees, and five sections. Duplicate the circle twice and move one above the other on the *y*-axis. Scale the top two circles so that all three look somewhat like those in Figure 1-43.

Select the three circles in order and loft them (Figure 1-44). If your software has a history option, you can alter the shape of the lofted model by transforming the original circles. If you have not tried this, now might be a good time.

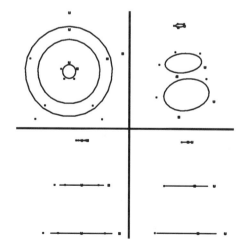

Fig. 1-43 A NURBS circle is created, duplicated twice, moved, and scaled.

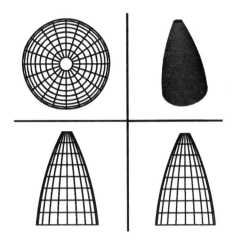

Fig. 1-44 The three circles are lofted.

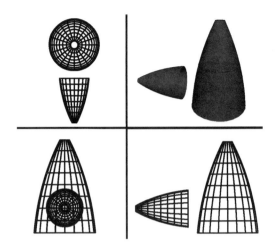

Fig. 1-45 The first object is duplicated, rotated, scaled, and moved.

Once you are satisfied with the cone-like shape, duplicate it and move it next to the original on the z-axis. Rotate it 90 degrees and scale it down. It should look somewhat like the shape in Figure 1-45.

Projecting a Curve on a Surface

Pick the smaller cone and select the option to choose individual splines/isoparms. Select the spline/isoparm at the large opening of the smaller cone (Figure 1-46). Duplicate the selected surface curve and make sure that it is not grouped with the original object. You should be able to move this duplicated curve away from the smaller cone.

While the duplicated curve is selected, pick the larger cone so that both the curve and the larger cone are active. With both objects selected, choose the option to project the curve onto the large cone. The circle should project onto the cone on the z-axis (Figure 1-47). If the circle projects on both sides of the larger cone, you can remove the circle on the opposite side. Select it in the side view and delete it or ignore it because it will not affect anything.

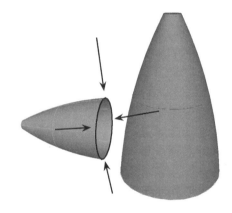

Fig. 1-46 At the large opening of the smaller cone (black arrows), the spline/isoparm is selected.

Fig. 1-47 The selected spline/isoparm is projected onto the larger cone.

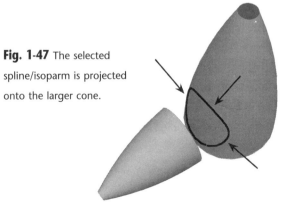

Trimming a Surface

Click on the large cone to make it active and select your trim tool. From your trim tool options, choose to discard the selected surface. Click in the center of your projected curve with the trim tool and activate the tool's function by pressing "Enter" or whatever command your software requires. You should now have a hole in the large cone the size of the projected curve (Figure 1-48).

Fillet/Blend Surfaces

Select the trim edge of the large cone and the spline/isoparm of the small cone's large opening (Figure 1-49). Both curves on each cone should now be selected.

Edit the surfaces by performing a freeform fillet to blend the two together. Figure 1-50 illustrates the blend between the two cones. View all three objects in the highest resolution. Try moving or scaling one of the cones. Notice how the fillet/blend stretches and changes to accommodate the transformation. Figure 1-51 shows the updated fillet/blend after the smaller cone has been moved and scaled.

Patch Modeling

This is a method of modeling in which several surfaces are stitched together in a pattern similar to a patchwork quilt. To avoid any breaks between adjoining surfaces, each one of them should have the same number of splines/isoparms. For example, if you want to patch together two NURBS planes on the *x*-axis, and one plane has four splines/isoparms running from left to right in the front view (U direction), then the plane next to it will also have to have four splines/isoparms in the U direction. Patch modeling is a difficult and time-consuming technique. Those who have the skill

Fig. 1-48 A trimming tool is used to make a hole in the large cone.

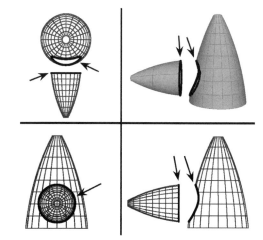

Fig. 1-49 Both the large cone's trim edge and the small cone's spline/isoparm are selected.

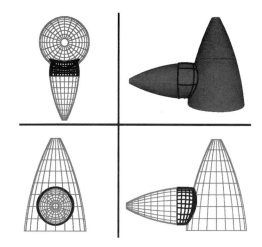

Fig. 1-50 A freeform fillet (shown in black) blends the two objects together.

Fig. 1-51 When the smaller cone is moved away from the larger one and enlarged, the fillet/blend automatically updates to conform to any changes.

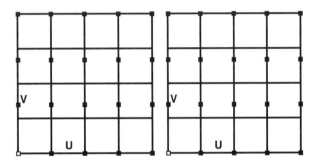

Fig. 1-52 Two NURBS planes with the same amount of points are placed next to each other.

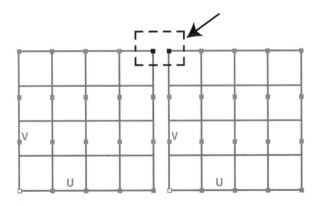

Fig. 1-53 The top two points are selected.

and patience to use it have created some very compelling humans, animals, aliens, and other figures. The following tutorial shows some of the basic principles of patch modeling using very simple surfaces.

Create a NURBS plane on the *z*-axis that has one U Patch and one V Patch. The surface degree should be 3 cubic degrees. Duplicate the plane and move the copy to the right in the front view. Select the two planes and look at them in the high resolution and component mode. You should be able to see the points on both of the planes (Figure 1-52). Most of the time you will want to have the same number of splines/isoparms for patching without exhibiting any cracks.

Draw a selection around the top two points that are next to each other (Figure 1-53). Edit the surfaces of the two selected points by using the stitch tool and choosing to stitch surface points. The normal option for the selected points is to assign them equal weights. Both points should now be merged together (Figure 1-54).

Continue selecting pairs of points and stitching them together until both planes share the same edge (Figure 1-55). Another approach for stitching two surfaces is to use a stitch edges tool. By selecting both edges with the tool, they should be joined automatically. If your software has a stitch edges tool, it might also have the option of sliding the edge of one of the planes up or down as seen in Figure 1-56.

If your software allows you to subdivide surfaces, select the part of the plane to the left in the front view and use your "subdivision surfaces" command to create a subdivision that replaces the original selected part. Figure 1-57 shows the effect of subdivision surfaces on part of the plane.

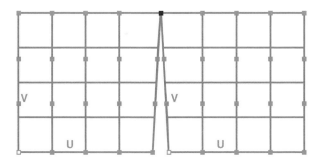

Fig. 1-54 The top points are stitched.

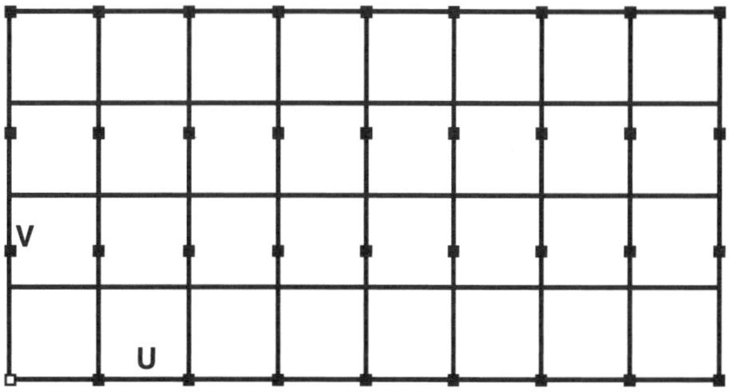

Fig. 1-55 Both planes after stitching the points.

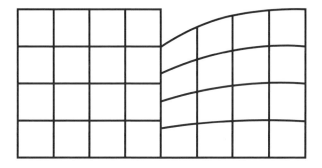

Fig. 1-56 Using a stitch edges tool allows one the flexibility to move one of the edges.

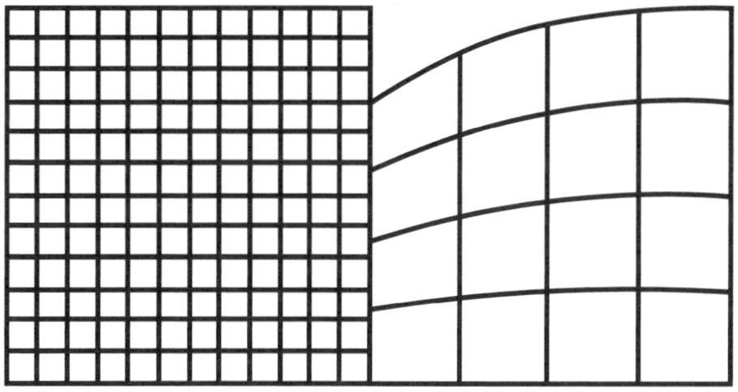

Fig. 1-57 Subdivision surfaces allow one the option to subdivide one part for finer detail while keeping the other part the same.

CHAPTER 2

Basic NURBS and Polygon Modeling

Polygon and NURBS modelers often employ similar tool sets, which include lofting/skinning, rail/birail extruding, lathing, and so on. Even though the various software packages may contain similar tools in certain respects, the techniques of modeling with the various packages are often very different. The following exercises demonstrate several approaches to NURBS and polygon modeling. The simple objects that are built are the same for each system. The manner in which the tasks are accomplished differs according to the contrasting surfaces of NURBS and polygons. All the models discussed in this chapter can be found in the Chptr2 folder on the CD-ROM.

Fig. 2-1 The goal of this exercise is to model a hand-held mirror like this.

Modeling a NURBS Hand-Held Mirror

This exercise takes you through the steps for creating a hand-held mirror (Figure 2-1). This is a fairly simple project that will teach you basic NURBS modeling techniques.

Create a NURBS circle with approximately fifteen sections. As part of a uniform approach, create the circle on the z-axis (Figure 2-2). Select the points at eleven o'clock and one o'clock. Use your scaling tool to move both points away from each other. Use your scaling tool whenever you move other points equal distances away from or toward each other. This applies mostly to horizontal moves. Use your move tool to move points on both sides up or down. You should end up with a shape like the one shown in Figure 2-3. This will form the inner part of the mirror frame.

Duplicate the shape just created and hide the original or template it so that you will not select it by mistake. Take the duplicate shape and enlarge it somewhat. You should now have two shapes like those shown in Figure 2-4. The larger shape will be

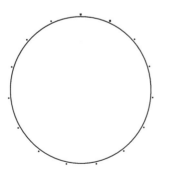

Fig. 2-2 A NURBS circle with about fifteen points marks the first step.

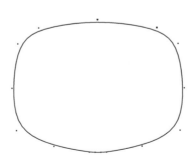

Fig. 2-3 Points are moved to make a mirror shape.

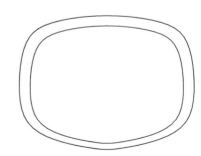

Fig. 2-4 The first shape is duplicated and enlarged.

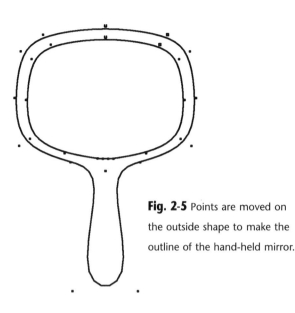

Fig. 2-5 Points are moved on the outside shape to make the outline of the hand-held mirror.

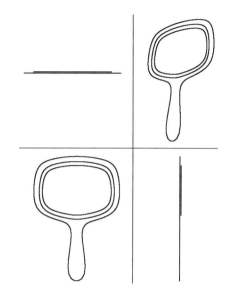

Fig. 2-6 The smaller inner shape is duplicated, reduced in size, and moved back a little on the *z*-axis.

made into the outline of the mirror frame and handle.

Select the two bottom points and move them straight down to make the handle of the mirror. Use the scale and move tools to make your adjustments until the shape looks somewhat like Figure 2-5.

The next step is to shape the mirror outline. Select the smaller inner shape and duplicate it. Scale it down somewhat and move it back a little on the *z*-axis. Your three shapes should now look like those in Figure 2-6. If possible, and for easier selection in the future, name this shape Mirror Outline.

Select the outside shape that forms the outline of the entire hand-held mirror. Duplicate it and move it back on the *z*-axis. This will serve as the outline of the back of the mirror. If possible, name it Back Outline. Figure 2-7 shows all four shapes.

Select the small inner shape that you named Mirror Outline, then select the surrounding shape, then the outline of the entire hand-held mirror, and finally, select the back mirror outline. Loft or

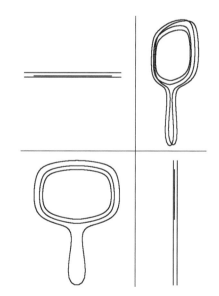

Fig. 2-7 The large outside shape is duplicated and moved back on the *z*-axis to form the back of the mirror.

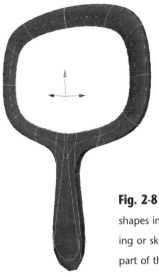

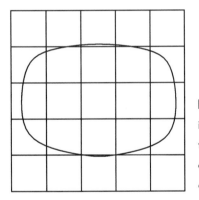

Fig. 2-8 Selecting the four outline shapes in the right order and lofting or skinning them will produce part of the mirror frame.

Fig. 2-9 After creating a NURBS plane, the smallest mirror outline is projected onto it.

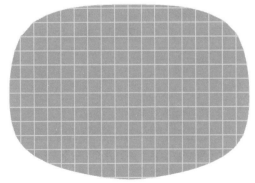

Fig. 2-10 Using a fillet or trim tool, the outside of the NURBS plane is cut away leaving a solid two-dimensional mirror object.

skin all of these selections. It is important that you select them in the right order. You now have most of the three-dimensional object done (Figure 2-8). The last part of this project involves forming the surface of the mirror and its back.

Hide everything except the smallest two-dimensional shape that you named Mirror Outline. Create a NURBS plane that is somewhat bigger than the Mirror Outline shape. The NURBS plane is made up of squares forming a grid that can be seen as a shaded surface. Move it back until both shapes occupy the same space on the z-axis. Select both shapes and project the Mirror Outline shape on the NURBS plane. The NURBS plane now has the outline as part of its mesh (Figure 2-9). Select the NURBS plane and use a fillet tool to trim away the outside so that you now have a solid shape like the one shown in Figure 2-10. This will be the reflective mirror surface. Display the three-dimensional outside frame of the mirror. Scale the trimmed mirror part so that it fits nicely inside the frame. The two objects should look somewhat like those in Figure 2-11.

Hide everything and display only the back of

Fig. 2-11 The size of the mirror part may have to be adjusted to fit inside the mirror frame.

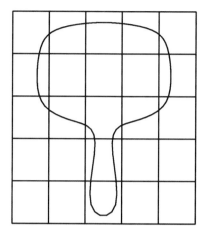

Fig. 2-12 Projecting the outline of the back against a NURBS plane.

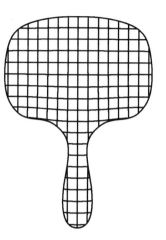

Fig. 2-13 A fillet/trim of the NURBS plane creates the solid two-dimensional shape of the mirror frame's back.

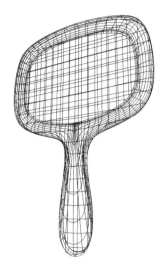

Fig. 2-14 The finished hand-held NURBS mirror.

the mirror outline that you named Back Outline. Create another NURBS plane that is somewhat bigger than the Back Outline shape (Figure 2-12). Move it back until both shapes occupy the same space on the *z*-axis. Select both shapes and project the Back Outline shape on the NURBS plane. The NURBS plane will now have the outline as part of its mesh. Select the NURBS plane and use a fillet tool to trim away the outside so that you now have a solid shape like the one shown in Figure 2-13. This will be the surface for the back of the mirror.

The hidden objects can now be made visible. Some of the parts may need some reshaping to fit together correctly. You can now assign surfaces and render the hand-held mirror (Figure 2-14).

Modeling a Polygon Hand-Held Mirror

When modeling with polygons, you can either use a spline cage in conjunction with polygons, or you can rely solely on polygon modeling.

Method 1: Using a Spline Cage

The following instructions show you how to create a hand-held mirror out of a spline cage that will subsequently be made into a polygon mesh. Splines used in conjunction with polygons offer the better of two worlds. You get the flexibility of

Fig. 2-15 Making points for one-half of the spline cage mirror.

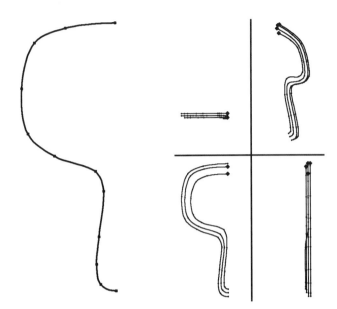

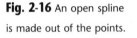

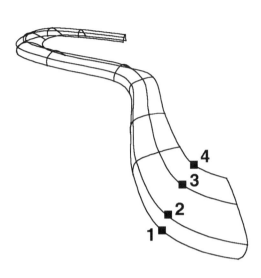

Fig. 2-16 An open spline is made out of the points.

Fig. 2-17 Duplicating the first spline and shaping the resulting ones create four splines for the frame of the mirror.

Fig. 2-18 Corresponding points are selected in the right order, starting from the back or the front (numbered points), and then connecting with open splines.

splines and NURBS coupled with the freedom of polygons.

Since most polygon modelers allow you to create half objects, mirror them, and then join the two halves, it is always quicker to model symmetrical objects in this manner. Figure 2-15 illustrates the first step, which is to create a series of points outlining half of the mirror and handle. The top and bottom points, which will be part of the middle, should be aligned to the middle of the *x*-axis using a set value of zero.

Select the points in order and connect them with an open spline (Figure 2-16). Duplicate this spline to make a total of four. Move the points on the duplicates to make the rest of the outlines for the mirror frame (Figure 2-17).

Now, select corresponding points in order and connect them as open splines. Figure 2-18 shows a set of these points with the numbers indicating the order in which they were selected. All points should be connected and all the splines should intersect at each point to form a four-sided shape.

Once all the points are connected, the resulting spline cage is patched with polygons. A higher subdivision level yields more polygons and finer detail. Most of the time, you can use a very low subdivision level and later, after editing some parts, subdivide the polygons even more. Separate the spline cage from the polygon mesh and delete it or save it as a separate object. From this point on, only polygons will be used to complete the mirror. You should be able to separate the spline cage using polygon statistics to select only curves.

Select the polygon mesh object, duplicate and mirror it so that the middle points of both objects fall exactly on top of each other. It should look like

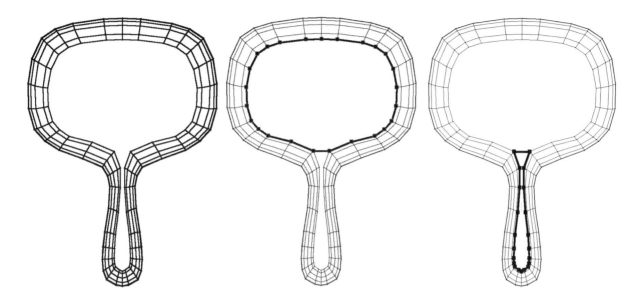

Fig. 2-19 After patching the spline cage with polygons and deleting all the splines, the poly mesh is duplicated and mirrored.

Fig. 2-20 The dark outline and larger points indicate which section is made into a polygon for the reflective mirror part.

Fig. 2-21 Points are selected and made into a polygon for the handle.

one whole object (Figure 2-19). Merge the points that overlap along the center axis. This will make both halves into one object.

Following either a clockwise or counterclockwise order, select each point that outlines the reflective mirror part and make a polygon out of it. Figure 2-20 shows this section and its points in heavier outline.

Select the points along the inner part of the handle and make a polygon from them. Figure 2-21 illustrates the polygon and points in heavy outline.

The back of the mirror must be made solid, so select the points that outline this part and make a polygon from them. Figure 2-22 shows this part in dark outline.

You can now select the various parts of the mirror and name them for texturing. If you want to

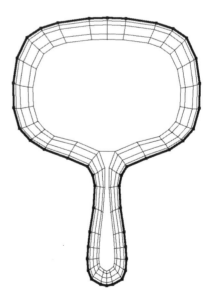

Fig. 2-22 The heavy outline indicates the polygon that was made for the back of the mirror.

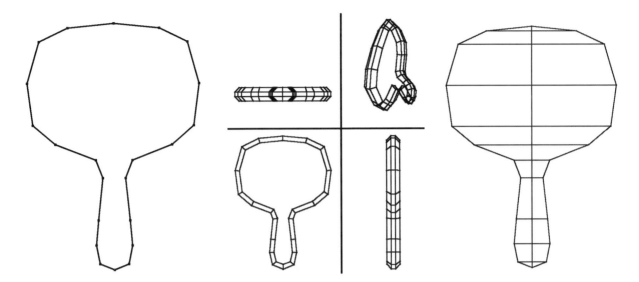

Fig. 2-23 A hand-held mirror modeled purely out of polygons can be started with a simple, twenty-two sided polygon.

Fig. 2-24 After beveling, extruding, and beveling again, you should have an object that looks somewhat like this.

Fig. 2-25 The large front and back polygons are split into four- and three-sided polys.

apply smoothing to the object by subdividing the polygons, then be sure to split the large polygons into four-sided shapes.

Method 2: Using Only Polygons

Working only with polygons, you can quickly model simple objects like the hand-held mirror. Figure 2-23 shows the basic outline that starts the process. You can either create a flat disk with twenty-two sides and shape it into this form, or create a set of twenty-two points and connect them to form the polygon. Either approach will work fine if you only model one half and then mirror and join the two halves together. The object should be facing forward in the front view.

It is always a good idea to model according to the actual physical scale of real-world objects. Therefore, size your polygon so that it measures 28 cm (about 11 inches) from top to bottom, by 20 cm (about 8 inches) from the widest points left and right.

Select the polygon and bevel it out (back on the z-axis) with an inset of about negative 1 cm, shift 1 cm, and inner edges. Select the polygon that you just beveled out. It will be the bigger one. Extrude it back on the z-axis about 1 cm. Now, select the extruded polygon and bevel it in toward the back (minus z-axis). The settings will be identical to the original bevel settings except that the edges (sides) are moved in, not out. The settings have an inset of about negative 1 cm, shift 1 cm, and outer edges. Figure 2-24 illustrates what the object should look like.

Make sure you have two large polygons: one for the front and one for the back. If you need to create these, select the points along the front edge and make a polygon out of them. Do the same with the back points. Delete any other large polygons. You should now have only two large polygons for the back and front surfaces and smaller ones for the sides. Be sure to align all the polygons so that they face outward, and merge points to get rid of any duplicates.

The large front and back polygons will now have to be split into smaller ones to make smoothing the entire mesh easier. Select the front polygon with twenty-two sides and split it into four- and three-sided objects. Do the same to the back polygon. Figure 2-25 shows how the two polygons are split up.

Figure 2-26 depicts the selected points that are now to be moved back on the *z*-plane. Drag the selected points back onto the *z*-axis approximately 1.5 cm. This will give the mirror surface somewhat of an inset.

Select the mirror surface polygons and name them so that you can apply a surface to them later. Name the polygons that define the frame of the hand-held mirror. The object is still in its rough form, so it needs to be made smoother by subdividing the polygons. Use your software's smoothing function to make the final hand-held mirror more refined. Figure 2-27 shows an example of the subdivided mirror.

Modeling a NURBS Stopwatch _____

Creating a stopwatch is a little more complicated than the last project. This exercise should help animators become more comfortable with three-dimensional modeling. A NURBS sphere created on the *y*-axis with eight sections and four spans should serve as the initial form.

Scale the sphere down on the *y*-axis so that it looks like the one shown in Figure 2-28. Select the spline/isoparm in the center. To edit the surface,

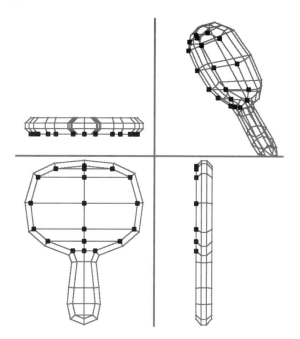

Fig. 2-26 Points that define the reflective mirror surface are selected.

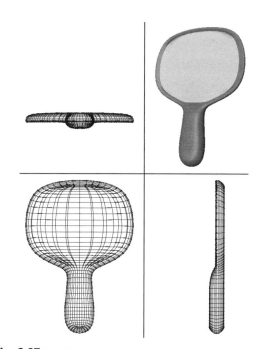

Fig. 2-27 The final hand-held polygon mirror after smoothing is applied to subdivide the polygons.

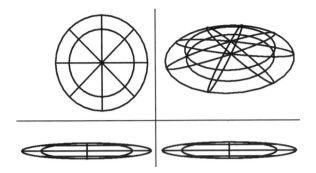

Fig. 2-28 A NURBS sphere is flattened somewhat to make the general shape of the watch.

Fig. 2-29 Selecting the middle spline/isoparm makes it possible to separate the two halves of the sphere.

Fig. 2-30 The two detached halves of the sphere are separated and moved apart.

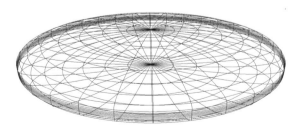

Fig. 2-31 A high-resolution display of the two halves and the fillet blended or lofted connecting section.

select "Detach Surfaces" (Figure 2-29). This will make two objects out of the original flattened sphere. Move the bottom half down somewhat so that your two objects look similar to those in Figure 2-30.

Select the bottom spline/isoparm of the top half of the detached sphere, and also select the top spline/isoparm of the bottom half sphere. With only the two isoparms selected, loft/skin them to make a connecting shape between the two halves.

Another option for making a connection between the two halves is to use a fillet blend tool. Deselect both surfaces and open the fillet blend tool. Click on the first surface spline/isoparm and press "Enter." Click on the second surface spline/ isoparm and press "Enter." You can now select all three objects and display them in high resolution to see how well they fit together (Figure 2-31).

To make the face of the watch, select the top spline/isoparm of the fillet or lofted connecting section and duplicate the curve. Scale this curve down to the smallest size you can (zero on the x-, y-, and z-axes). Once more, select the top spline/isoparm of the fillet or lofted connecting section and duplicate the curve. Loft/skin the two duplicate spline/curves. Figure 2-32 shows the lofted watch face.

At this time you may want to assign surface names and characteristics to the various parts. The

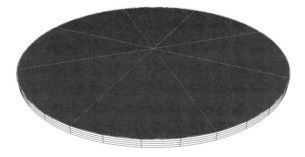

Fig. 2-32 The two duplicated splines/isoparms are lofted/skinned to make the watch face.

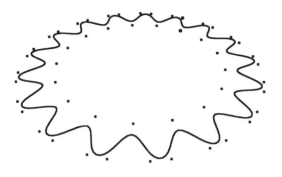

Fig. 2-33 After creating a NURBS circle and selecting every other two points on it, use the scaling tool to drag them in evenly.

Fig. 2-34 A duplicate is made from the first NURBS circle and scaled to zero. Both are lofted/skinned.

top half of the sphere is the semi-transparent glass part. The bottom half and the lofted, or fillet blended section, are the metal components. You will need to create an image map of the watch numbers to apply to the watch face object.

To make the wind-up knob of the stopwatch, create a NURBS circle on the y-axis with fifty-one sections. Make the control vertices appear and select every other two points (Figure 2-33). Use the scaling tool to drag these in. This will yield pairs of two vertices out and one vertex in.

Duplicate the circle and scale it down to zero on the x-, y-, and z-axes. Select the two circles and loft/skin them together (Figure 2-34). Choose the larger NURBS circle and extrude it down on the y-axis so that it looks somewhat like Figure 2-35.

Select the bottom spline/isoparm of the knob and duplicate it. Size the duplicate down to zero on the x- and z-axes. Select both of these splines/isoparms and loft/skin them. Create a NURBS cylinder on which to stick the knob. Add a torus to the knob and you should now have a wind-up knob to stick on top of the watch (Figure 2-36).

Fig. 2-35 The larger circle is extruded down.

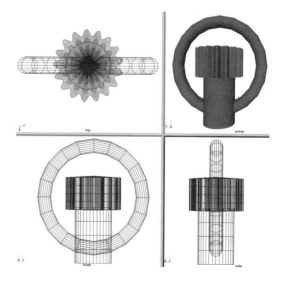

Fig. 2-36 The completed wind-up knob and ring of the watch.

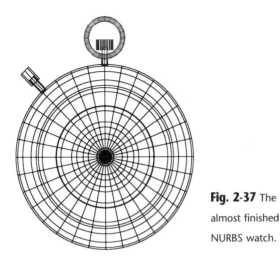

Fig. 2-37 The almost finished NURBS watch.

Fig. 2-38 (left) One side of the watch cursor is made by using a CV or edit point curve (spline).

Fig. 2-39 (right) After duplicating and mirroring the spline, the two halves are lofted/skinned.

The start and stop buttons can be made from two NURBS cylinders. Size and add the wind-up knob and start/stop buttons to the previously made parts of the watch. Group these components together. Figure 2-37 shows the stopwatch at this point in its assembly. All you have left to model is the timer hand.

Draw one side of the watch hand with a spline made from a CV or edit point curve (Figure 2-38). Duplicate and mirror this spline. Loft/skin the two together. You should now have the large watch cursor (Figure 2-39). Duplicate this cursor and scale it down for the smaller one. Rotate and move both watch hands into the right positions. Figure 2-40 shows the finished NURBS watch.

Modeling a Polygon Stopwatch

Modeling a polygon watch has many parallels to the previous methods used for the NURBS watch. Primitives and extruded objects are also utilized.

Sketch a spline with approximately eighteen points in the side view. This will form the top half

profile of the front and back of the watch. Figure 2-41 shows the spline. Notice the extra bump near the top. This will be used to form a decorative groove in the metal part of the watch. Move the spline so that its bottom two points fall at the zero center axis.

Use the lathe tool to lathe at the zero center (center of the universe) of the z-axis 360 degrees.

Fig. 2-40 The final rendered NURBS stop watch.

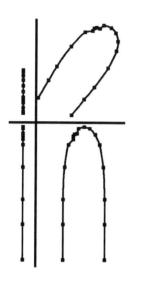

Fig. 2-41 A spline with about eighteen points is drawn in the side view.

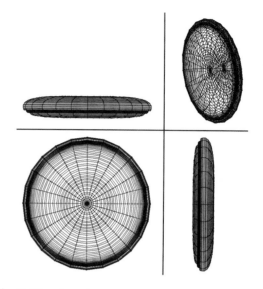

Fig. 2-42 Lathing the spline generates the main body of the watch.

If you want more detail, set the lathe tool to create a greater number of sides. When finished lathing the spline, you should end up with the front and back of the watch (Figure 2-42).

Select and name the various polygons that will define the metal and front glass parts of the watch. To make the face of the watch with numbers mapped onto it, pick the points somewhere along the center and make a polygon out of them. Another option is to draw a disk (circle). Size the face down a little and place it correctly inside the watch. Hide the glass part to see how the face conforms to the rest of the watch.

To make the wind-up knob of the watch, make a polygon in the top view with gear-like teeth (Figure 2-43). If your program can generate gear shapes, this would be the easiest way to do it. If you have to make your own, simply make a disk with sixty-four points and select every two points. Scale the selected points inward until you have a shape similar to the one shown in Figure 2-43.

Extrude the gear shape down on the *y*-axis (Figure 2-44). Finish the wind-up mechanism by

Fig. 2-43 A gear-like shape forms the beginning of the wind-up knob.

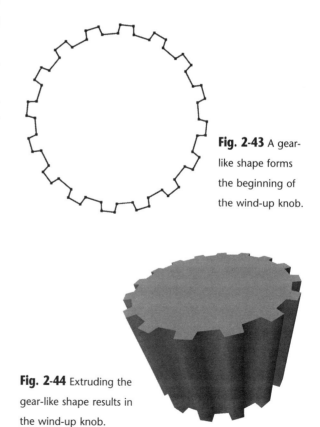

Fig. 2-44 Extruding the gear-like shape results in the wind-up knob.

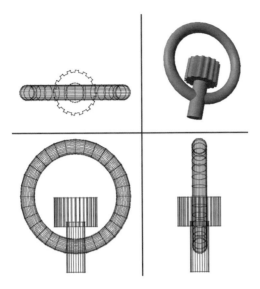

Fig. 2-45 Adding the torus and cylinder completes the wind-up part of the watch.

creating a cylinder for the shaft and a torus for the ring (Figure 2-45).

The watch hands can be made in the front view either by creating points which are connected to make the polygon and then reshaping a rectangle with about six segments on the *y*-axis, or by sketching a spline to lathe on the *y*-axis and then flattening it on the *z*-axis.

Figure 2-46 shows the final polygon watch after smoothing is applied to objects that are too faceted. The named watch face surface has an image map with numbers applied to it.

Modeling a NURBS Office Chair

Making an office chair is an excellent way of combining various modeling techniques. Some of the basic methods for creating three-dimensional surfaces are covered in the following tutorial. In a later chapter, the chair will be utilized in an animation.

The first part of the chair to be modeled is the back cushion. Create a NURBS sphere on the *z*-plane with eight sections and four spans. Using your scaling tool, shape the sphere into the approximate shape of a back cushion (Figure 2-47).

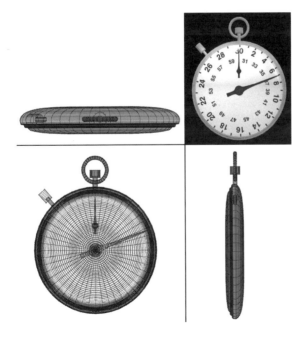

Fig. 2-46 The final polygon stopwatch after applying smoothing.

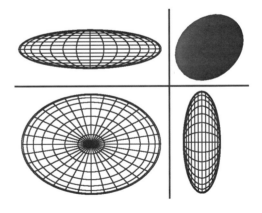

Fig. 2-47 The NURBS sphere is scaled into a rough, back cushion shape.

Deform the sphere by creating a lattice cage around it. Make the lattice cage with four divisions on the *x*- and *y*-axes and three divisions on the *z*-axis. Make the lattice cage selectable by its points. Pick points on the lattice cage and use the move and scaling tools to refine the shape of the back cushion (Figure 2-48). When you are satisfied with the appearance of the object, remove its lattice cage.

To make the seat cushion, create a NURBS cube with a ratio of one to one on the *x*- and *z*-axes and about one-third on the *y*-axis. The subdivision for the U and V patches should be two. Scale the shape and size roughly to the dimensions of the seat cushion. Using a lattice cage, hulls, or the points, sculpt the seat cushion until it looks somewhat like the one shown in Figure 2-49. If you select the points on the corners of the cube and drag them in a little using the scaling tool, it will give the cushion round corners.

The next step is to make the back brace that connects the back cushion to the seat. Create a NURBS square with a curve degree of two, and one span per side. Shape the square into a narrow triangle and bring in the corner points with the scaling tool. You are trying to create a cigar shape. If you prefer, you can do this by reshaping an oval. Figure 2-50 shows the shape in the top view plus the spline that you will now create for the path extrusion of this rectangle. Make your back and seat cushion visible. You can template these or make them into a reference object. The curve should extend from the inside middle part of the back cushion to the middle underside of the seat cushion. Starting with the rectangle, select it and the spline and then use "extrude" to make it into a tube-like shape. Your extrude options are at "profile" with a path direction. Figure 2-51 shows the results of extruding along the spline path.

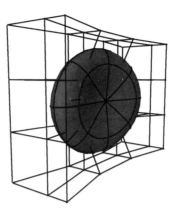

Fig. 2-48 A lattice cage is used to refine the shape of the back cushion.

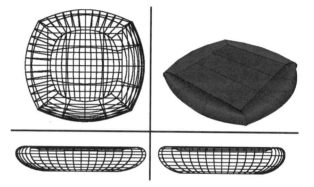

Fig. 2-49 A NURBS cube is shaped into the seat cushion.

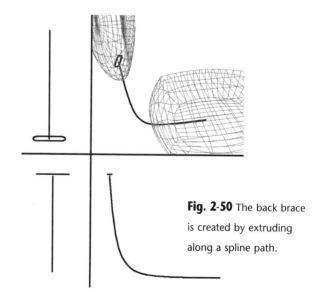

Fig. 2-50 The back brace is created by extruding along a spline path.

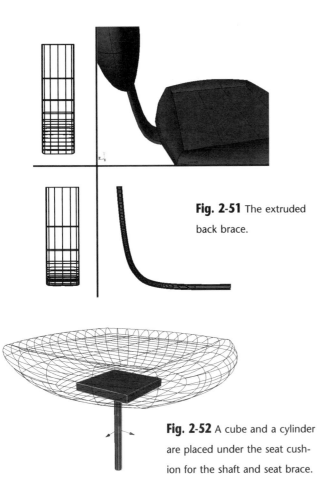

Fig. 2-51 The extruded back brace.

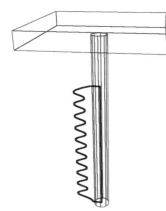

Fig. 2-52 A cube and a cylinder are placed under the seat cushion for the shaft and seat brace.

Make a flattened cube and place it under the seat cushion like the one shown in Figure 2-52. Create a NURBS cylinder and stick that underneath the cushion. These two objects are the seat support and chair shaft.

The spring cover that goes around the chair shaft can be made with a rectangle that has a zigzagging line on one side (Figure 2-53). When you create the square, make it on the z-axis with twenty spans per side. Select every other point on the left side of the square and drag them to the left. Use "grid snapping" if you have to. Lathe or revolve the deformed rectangle and you should now have a spring cover similar to the one shown in Figure 2-54. If your software has a "history" option, you can reshape the original spline/curve to change the shape of the revolved object. Figure 2-55 shows the partially completed chair.

One of the last things left to model is the feet. Set up five splines like those in Figure 2-56. You can create three of them for one side and then mirror them for the other side. The extra middle spline can be deleted or you can move the three dupli-

Fig. 2-53 The spring cover is made from a square whose alternating points on one side have been pulled to the left.

Fig. 2-54 The completed spring cover after revolving or lathing the rectangle.

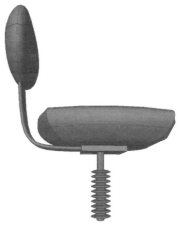

Fig. 2-55 A partially completed NURBS chair.

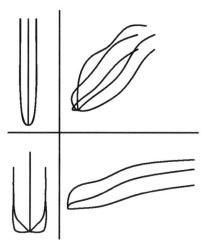

Fig. 2-56 A series of five splines are set up for one of the feet.

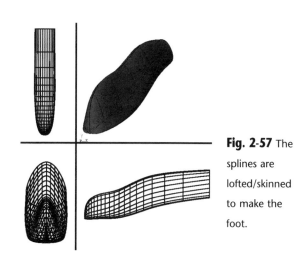

Fig. 2-57 The splines are lofted/skinned to make the foot.

cates a little apart from the other three and have six splines to loft/skin rather than five. Select the splines in order and loft them with the "closed" option on so that the loft connects completely around and ends with the first spline. Your completed foot might look somewhat like the one shown in Figure 2-57.

Create a cylinder for the stem of the wheel. Place it near the front and under the foot that you just modeled (Figure 2-58). The wheel is made from six ovals that will be lofted/skinned. You can make the two end ovals very small so that there will not be any holes in the sides. Three of the circles can be made for one side and then duplicated/mirrored for the other three. Select the six ovals in order and loft them. Figure 2-59 shows the completed wheel, stem, and foot.

The final step is to group the foot, stem, and wheel and duplicate them to make a total of five. All five will radiate around the bottom of the spring cover. Before duplicating the grouped set, be sure to move the rotation/pivot/insertion point to the end of the foot located at the center bottom section of the spring cover. This will make it easier

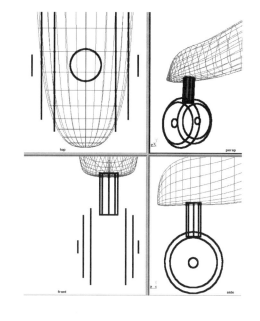

Fig. 2-58 Six NURBS circles are lofted to make the chair's wheel.

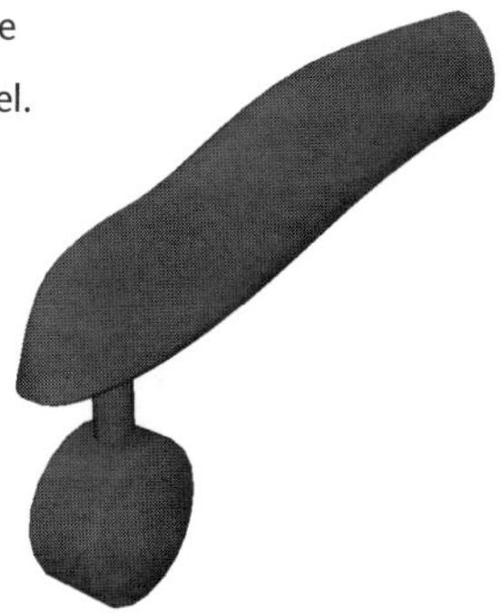

Fig. 2-59 The chair's foot, stem, and wheel.

Fig. 2-60 The foot is duplicated for a total of five and rotated 72 degrees.

Fig. 2-61 A NURBS chair.

to rotate the duplicated feet around the spring cover. Select all the foot components that you grouped and duplicate them with the following settings. Rotation is around the *y*-axis at 72 degrees. The number of copies is five. Figure 2-60 depicts the duplicated and rotated feet.

Figure 2-61 shows the final modeled NURBS chair. You may decide to add extra detail and improve parts of it that seem to be more generalized.

Modeling a Polygon Office Chair

The first part of the chair to be modeled is the back cushion. In this tutorial we will create four open splines arranged in the order shown in Figure 2-62. Each curve is a duplicate of the other so that each will have the same number of points on it. The splines form one half of the cushion's profile. Only half of the cushion is modeled because we will be

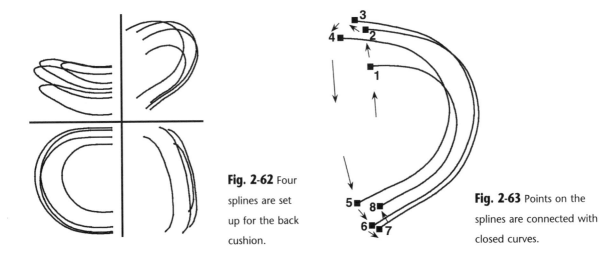

Fig. 2-62 Four splines are set up for the back cushion.

Fig. 2-63 Points on the splines are connected with closed curves.

duplicating and mirroring the other half later. The two halves will then be joined. If your software does not have splines or a method for creating a spline cage to convert to a polygon mesh, then reshape a primitive sphere into the back cushion.

Figure 2-63 shows the order in which the points are selected on the curves before connecting them as closed curves. Once you finish making the closed vertical connecting splines, insert an extra point along the middle of each vertical oval curve. Connect these middle points with an open spline to make the middle horizontal curve. Figure 2-64 shows the resulting spline cage. The front view depicts the middle connecting horizontal spline. Patch the spline cage with a polygon mesh. Separate the polygon mesh from the spline cage and paste it into its own layer.

Select the points that fall along the middle axis and align them so that when you mirror the half cushion, the duplicate points will fall right on top of the originals. Mirror the half cushion and merge the points of the two halves. Check for flipped polygons and align them with the rest.

The seat cushion is made from a box with three segments on the *x*-, *y*-, and *z*-axes (Figure 2-65). Apply smoothing to the box to round off the corners. Refine the shape and you might have a cushion that looks somewhat like the one shown in Figure 2-66. Place the back and seat cushion the right distance apart from each other.

Figure 2-67 shows the polygon shape for the back brace that will go inside the back cushion and under the seat. You can create a set of points to connect as a polygon or reshape an oval.

Extrude the polygon on the *x*-axis so that it looks somewhat like the one shown in Figure 2-68. Place the brace so that it extends from the inside middle part of the back cushion to the middle

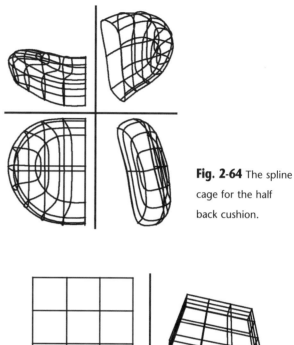

Fig. 2-64 The spline cage for the half back cushion.

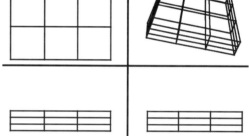

Fig. 2-65 A box with three subdivisions is used to make the seat.

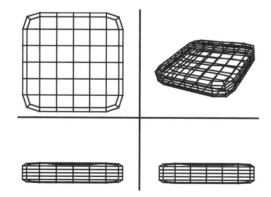

Fig. 2-66 Smoothing the box rounds out the corners and edges, thus completing the seat cushion.

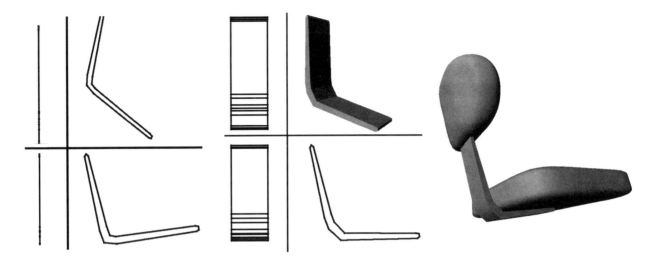

Fig. 2-67 The polygon for the back brace.   **Fig. 2-68** The extruded back brace.   **Fig. 2-69** The partially completed chair.

underside of the seat cushion. Your chair might now look like the one shown in Figure 2-69.

Make a flattened cube and place it under the seat cushion like the one shown in Figure 2-70. Create a NURBS cylinder and stick that underneath the cushion. These two objects are the seat support and chair shaft.

The spring cover that goes around the chair shaft can be made with a zigzagging spline (Figure 2-71). Lathe or revolve the spline along the *y*-axis. Place the spring cover over the chair shaft. Your chair might now look like the one shown in Figure 2-73.

The next step is to model the feet of the chair. If your software does not have splines or a method

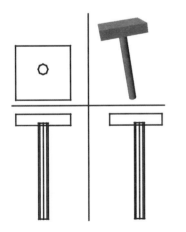

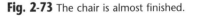

Fig. 2-70 A cube and cylinder are used to make the seat support and stem.

Fig. 2-71 A zigzagging spline will be lathed for the spring cover.

Fig. 2-72 The lathed spring cover.

Fig. 2-73 The chair is almost finished.

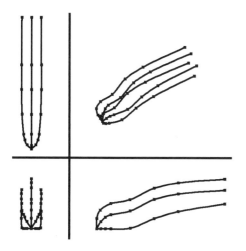

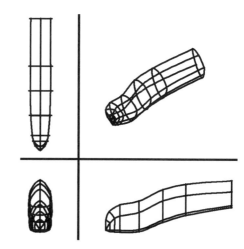

Fig. 2-74 The foot splines.

Fig. 2-75 The spline cage foot.

for surfacing them after they have been connected manually or through lofting/skinning, then skip the following instructions and shape a primitive like a cylinder or cube into a foot shaped like the one shown in Figure 2-75.

Set up five splines like those shown in Figure 2-74. You can create three of them for one side and then mirror them for the other. The extra middle spline can be deleted or you can move the three duplicates a little apart from the other three and have six splines to connect rather than five. Select the points on the splines in order and loft or connect them with closed splines so that they connect completely around and end with the first point. The bottoms of the connecting splines can have points added to them, and these, in turn, can also be connected. Your completed foot might look somewhat like the one shown in Figure 2-75. You can now surface the spline cage by patching it with polygons. Select the polygons and paste them into a separate layer. Make sure all polygons are aligned and fill any holes with additional polygons. If you want your leg to look rounder, you can apply smoothing to it.

The wheels are made by cutting a sphere or a ball in half and flattening it somewhat (Figure 2-76). The points along the cut are selected and made into a polygon. The polygon is then extruded a little. The smaller extruded section (Figure 2-76) is made by beveling the same polygon with a small numerical inset and zero shift. The beveled poly-

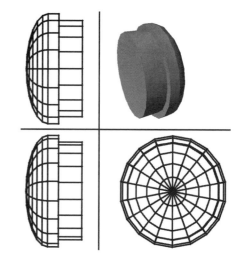

Fig. 2-76 One side of the wheel is made from one-half of a sphere that is partly extruded and beveled.

gon is scaled down and extruded. If this sounds too complicated, stick a cylinder against the half sphere. You should now have one-half of a wheel. Mirror the wheel and merge the points along the center seam. Stick a small cylinder on top and you will have a wheel that looks somewhat like the one shown in Figure 2-77.

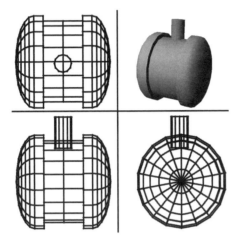

Fig. 2-77 The final wheel after mirroring and adding a cylinder for the stem.

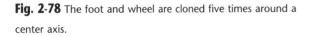

Fig. 2-78 The foot and wheel are cloned five times around a center axis.

The last part of building an office chair is to duplicate the leg. The wheel and stem should be stuck under the foot. Find the location of the spring cover's middle area. Once you get this information, write down the exact x, y, and z locations. You will now clone the leg and wheel around this axis. The settings for the clone tool follow. There should be five clones with a rotation of 72 degrees on the y-axis. The center of the rotation are the x, y, and z data that you recorded earlier. You should now have five feet radiating around the bottom center part of the spring cover (Figure 2-78).

The final chair can be seen in Figure 2-79. You may decide to add extra detail and improve parts of it that seem to be more generalized.

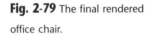

Fig. 2-79 The final rendered office chair.

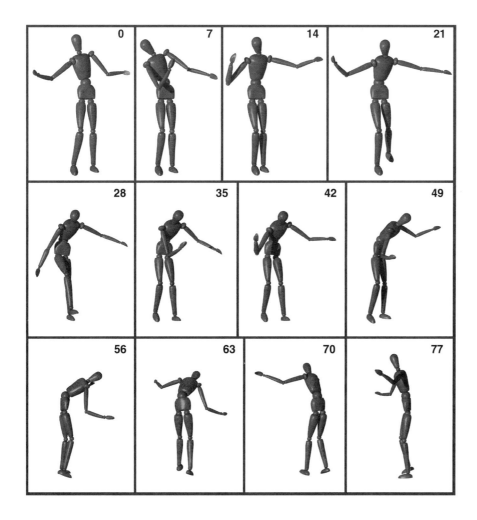

CHAPTER 3

Basic 3D
Animation

Animation is a process where the circumstances and aspects of a scene change over time. Events in 3D animation are created and controlled by key scenes. This is similar to traditional 2D cell animation where the animator designs the important frames and a junior animator draws the intervening frames that act as transitions between the key frames. This process is referred to as keyframe animation.

Most animation software has a visible timeline along which specific keyframes are set. If an object is placed in a specific location at frame 0 and then moved at frame 10 to another location, the animation shows it moving from point A to point B within the ten frames. Objects or events that are acted upon at a certain frame usually have to be keyframed in order to register the change. For example, in Maya, one of the ways in which keyframes are set is by pressing "s" for "Set Key." You can also select "Set Key" from the Animate menu. In LightWave 3D™, you set keyframes by pressing "Enter" on the keyboard or pressing the "Create Key" button and specifying the frame at which the motion key is set.

Not all events have to be keyframed to change. In a previous chapter, weights were painted on a surface. When the object was rotated, the difference in weights made the object twist. Although the object's rotational values were keyframed, the twisting motion occurred automatically due to the dynamic nature of weights. There are many other dynamics like wind, water, fire, gravity, smoke, and rain that simulate real-world physics without having to be keyframed. An animator simply specifies the characteristics and actions of the object, and the software figures out how to animate it.

This chapter focuses on creating very simple keyframe animations. The first part will have you move a spaceship around, and the second will show how to animate a simple mannequin.

Animating in a Straight Line

Using some of the techniques learned in previous chapters, model a simple NURBS or polygon spaceship and center it at zero on the x-, y-, and z-axes (Figure 3-1). This is the starting point from which the ship will fly.

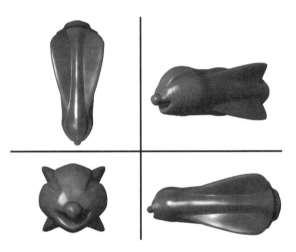

Fig. 3-1 A simple spaceship is created and placed in the center of all three axes.

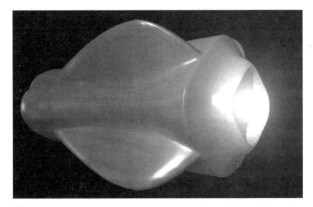

Fig. 3-2 Parenting a lens flare to the ship produces a quick and easy exhaust.

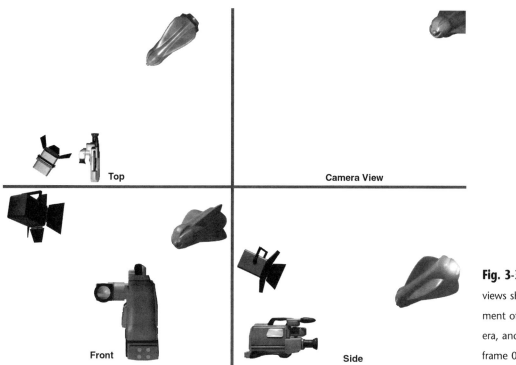

Fig. 3-3 These four views show the placement of the light, camera, and spaceship at frame 0.

If you are familiar with creating lens flares and parenting objects, then place one at the exhaust part of the spaceship and parent it to the ship (Figure 3-2). There are much better methods for simulating exhaust, but this is a fast and easy one.

Refer to Figure 3-3 to set up your camera, light, and object in similar positions. The ship is placed in the top right-hand corner of the camera view so that it is barely visible. The camera faces toward the back of the scene on the *z*-axis. For the light source, you can use a spotlight. For a basic animation like this, one light is enough. If you look through the light view while moving and rotating the spotlight, it will be easier to illuminate the entire ship.

Because there is no background for the ship to cast shadows on, you can turn off "trace shadows."

This will speed up rendering time. Another option is to use shadow maps instead of raytraced shadows. Shadow maps render quicker and have a softer look to them. Raytracing can often make a scene look harsh.

Keyframe the spaceship in the initial position at frame 0. Go to frame 30 and use your top and side views to move the spaceship across and down. It should be positioned similarly to the one in Figure 3-4. Keyframe the ship's new position at frame 30. You have just completed a one-second animation at 30 fps (30 frames per second). Preview the animation to check the speed and movement of the spaceship.

So far, the animation is pretty straightforward and not very interesting. Figure 3-5 shows a part of the animation that has the ship moving in a straight line across the camera's field of vision.

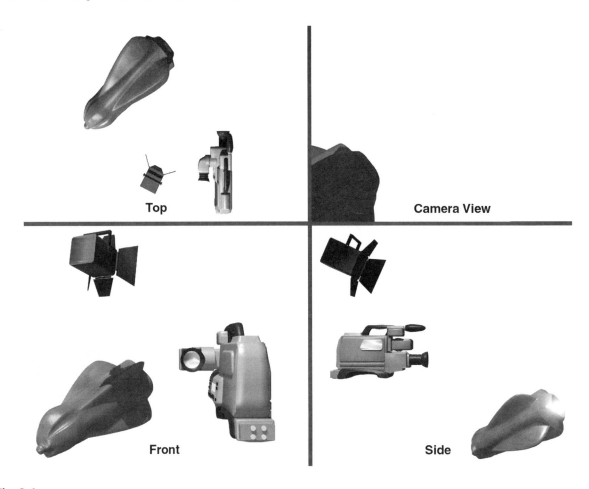

Fig. 3-4 Four views showing the position of the spaceship at frame 30.

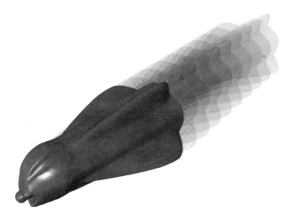

Fig. 3-5 A straight movement from frame 0 to 30.

Using a Graph Editor to Curve the Animation

Most mid- to high-end programs have a graph editor. Its function is to estimate the values between keyframes as motion graphs or animation curves. They provide a visual representation of your object's activity. Editing animation curves can be a powerful tool for altering your animation's behavior.

If you can, open the graph editor for your spaceship. The motion graph should be a straight line similar to the one shown in Figure 3-6. It is basically a line moving from point A (frame 0) to point B (frame 30).

You can save your animation before proceeding to the next step, which is to change the appearance of the animation curve. Advance to frame 15 and move the ship to a different location: up, down, closer, or farther away. You might also decide to change the direction in which the ship is flying. Keyframe the ship at Frame 15. Figure 3-7 shows the spaceship at frame 15 after being moved and redirected. Besides changing an object's direction and position, you can also change its size among other objects. These are all recorded in the graph editor.

Open the graph editor for the spaceship. Instead of a straight line, it should now have a curve in it. Figure 3-8 shows one kind of motion graph after adding the extra frame at frame 15. Preview your animation to see the changes. Now, open the graph editor for the ship and drag the point at frame 15 and, if possible, change its curve by manipulating the point's tangent handles or direction points. View the edited animation. This should give you some idea of how animation curves can be used to edit an object's behavior.

Most movements and forms in nature are curvilinear. Except for objects like crystals, the straight line and right angles are largely foreign to nature. You only need to observe plant life to see the irregularly curved forms. Forces in nature such as gravity tend to change all movement to circular patterns. Ball and hinge joints and spinal columns also contribute to rounded motions in humans and animals.

The curved motion graph will usually translate into more natural movements. When animating characters, it is important to be aware of this. Thus, you may want to correct any straight lines in your character's motion graphs.

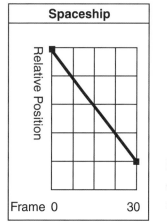

Fig. 3-6 The motion graph for the straight movement.

Fig. 3-7 At frame 15, the ship is moved to a different location: closer to the camera and down.

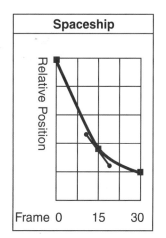

Fig. 3-8 The curved motion graph after adding a keyframe at 15.

Changing the Velocity of an Animation ___

So far, the spaceship is moving at a constant rate. Changing the tempo or pacing during an animation will usually result in a more dynamic presentation. In the next part of the exercise, we will have the ship begin to move slowly and gradually speed up. There are several ways you can do this, all of which depend on the capabilities of your software.

The first method is go to frame 15. With the spaceship selected, create a key at frame 25. This will place the ship in the same position at frame 25 as it is at frame 15. You can now delete frame 15.

Another way of changing the velocity is to go into the ship's motion graph and move or copy the settings from frame 15 to frame 25. You can also delete the point at frame 15 in the graph editor.

The motion curve may look somewhat like the one shown in Figure 3-9. Play the animation to see the difference from the previous one. It should be a little more interesting and dynamic.

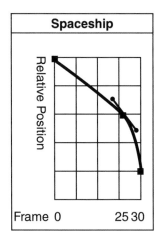

Fig. 3-9 Moving the settings from frame 15 to 25 makes the spaceship start slowly and accelerate at the end.

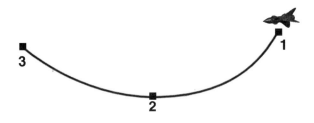

Fig. 3-10 A curved path with at least three points is made for the object to follow along.

Path Animation _____

By assigning an object or series of objects to a spline, you can create animations that follow a path similar to a train following railroad tracks. The path itself can be altered to change the course of the object's movement. The following instructions show how to animate a spaceship along a determined path.

After opening or modeling your spaceship, draw a curved spline. It should have at least three points for altering the arc (Figure 3-10). Set your playback end time (last frame) to 90. Make sure the ship's pivot is located in its nose cone.

Select your ship and while it is active, determine the path. Attach the ship to the path. For example, when working in Maya, you select "animate >path> attach to path." Test the animation by playing a preview of it. The object should follow the path. You might notice that the object does not turn to face the direction of the path. If that is the case, then you will need to edit the animation so that it always lines up with the point it is headed toward.

Some software packages let you align objects to a path by simply selecting the object and specifying that it follows or aligns to the path. If this is

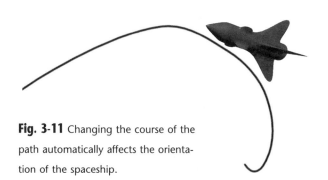

Fig. 3-11 Changing the course of the path automatically affects the orientation of the spaceship.

can be made to follow a path. The paths can be shaped to follow the contours of a landscape.

Segmented Character Animation

Characters can be animated in several ways. The two most common methods are segmented and skeletal. Segmented models are built from a number of separate parts that are hinged together at their joints like marionettes. The rotation of each segment is usually found at the joints. Their centers of rotation are named pivot points. Figure 3-12 shows a segmented character with its pivot points delineated as small stars.

not possible, then advance to the frame at which the object needs to be rotated to face in the right direction. Turn the spaceship so that it faces toward its goal and set a keyframe there. Repeat this process at any other points along the path that need correcting.

Try editing the path itself. Select one of its points and move it up or down. Play back the animation. The ship should align its course accordingly (Figure 3-11).

You might also try adjusting the tangents of the rocket's motion in your program's graph editor. Another option is to extend and alter the path. With an "add points" tool you can lengthen the spline and create more vertices for editing its shape. The line may change but the extent of the animation should remain the same. When you change the path, you will most likely have to correct any alignment problems along the way. The ship may no longer face the right direction at certain points.

If you have been able to follow these directions, you should have a fairly good idea of the usefulness of motion paths. Interaction among moving objects is simplified by creating separate paths for each one. Even more complicated objects like characters with repeating walking or running cycles

Skeletal structures are somewhat like real skeletons. They are placed inside seamless characters. Their bones are manipulated either directly with forward kinematics or indirectly with goal objects. This second system is called inverse kinematics. Skeletal structures are discussed in more detail in the next chapter. The rest of this chapter describes animating segmented models.

Fig. 3-12 The segmented character. Its pivot points are shown here as stars at the joints.

Before starting the next set of exercises, you will need a segmented model like a puppet, mannequin, dummy, or robot. If you lack modeling skills, you can place together a series of primitive forms like cylinders, spheres, and cubes.

The next step is to set each segment's pivot point. The mannequin in Figure 3-12 can be used as a guide for each point's placement. Every part

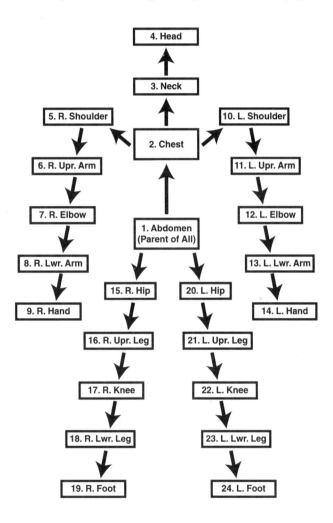

Fig. 3-13 The parenting order of each part. The abdomen is the parent of all. The chest is parented to the abdomen, the neck to the chest, the head to the neck, the shoulders to the chest, and so on.

must be hinged together in the right order. This is sometimes referred to as parenting: A child object is linked to a parent object.

Some software packages like the older Light-Wave 3D, which has a two-program format, require a little extra work for segmented character setup. The newer version of LightWave allows you to bring in segmented models as a single object. In the modeling program, each of the character's segments is saved as a separate file. These are opened one at a time in the animation program. When each section is brought in, it should be in the same spot as it was in the modeling program. The newer version of LightWave allows you to bring in segmented models as the single object.

Figure 3-13 shows the body's hierarchy in which each segment is linked to another. The arrows point in the direction of the child objects. The numbers correspond to the order in which each section is linked. For example, the right hip is parented to the abdomen, the right upper leg is parented to the hip, followed by the right knee, which is in turn parented to the right upper leg, and so on. Since the abdomen is the center of the body, it is designated as the parent to all. To translate all of the parts at the same time, you simply move the abdomen.

Once you have finished setting the pivot points and linked all the parts together, set up one light to illuminate the figure. Place the camera so that there is enough room for the character to move about without going out of the camera's viewing range. You should not have to move the camera or the light during the animation to keep the figure in viewing range and well lit.

Animating the figure can be accomplished in several ways. You can follow the poses in figure 3-14 to create a dancing sequence; follow the poses

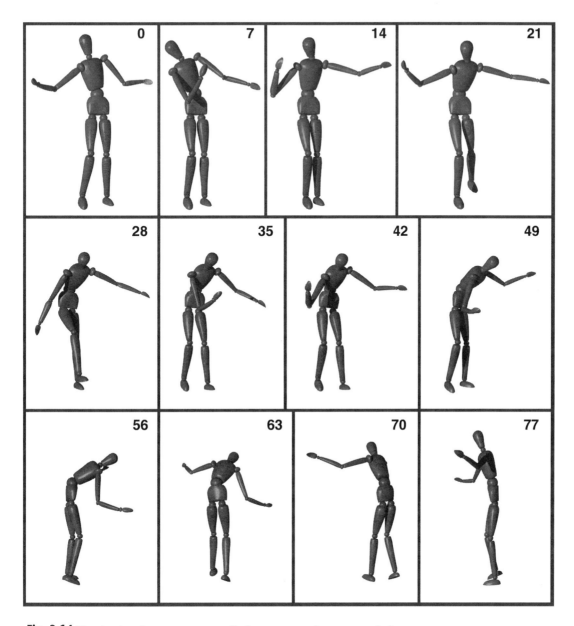

Fig. 3-14 The dancing dummy sequences. Keyframes occur at every seventh frame.

from a videotape; or use a book with illustrations showing movement. Another method is to act out or have someone else act out the movements for you. Each method is discussed in more detail in upcoming chapters.

If you decide to follow the poses in Figure 3-14, then set up the figure in the same pose as the one seen in frame 0 of the illustration. When you move each segment, set a keyframe for it. You can rotate each part and the linked sections should follow. The segments will also rotate around their set pivot points. Advance to frame 7 and pose your charac-

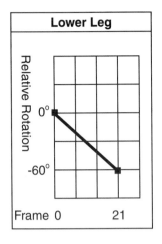

Fig. 3-15 A motion graph for a lower leg that was rotated at frame 21. This shows movement from 0 to 21.

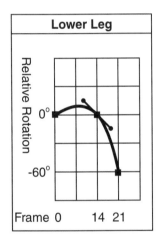

Fig. 3-16 To prevent motion between 0 to 14, an extra frame is inserted at 14 with the same values as the one at 0. The resulting curve between 0 and 14 means there will still be some extra movement between those two frames.

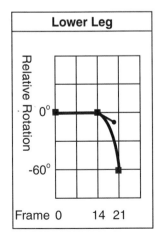

Fig. 3-17 The corrected motion graph after making it linear at frame 14. There will no longer be any movement between 0 and 14.

ter in a position similar to the one in frame 7 of Figure 3-14. Again, be sure to set a keyframe for each part after repositioning it.

Be sure to use the various view windows to make any corrections. Besides rotating parts, you may also have to move them back into their right spots. Sometimes, revolving segments will move them out of their proper places.

Go to frame 14 and position the various parts of the body similarly to those seen in frame 14 of Figure 3-14. Advance to frame 21 and follow the illustration for the right pose.

If you rotate a part, like a lower leg at frame 21, without having keyframed it at the previous frame 21, then that part will have movement starting at frame 0. To avoid this, keyframe it at frame 14 in the same position as it was at frame 0. Then when you change it at frame 21, it will only move between the two frames: 14 and 21. To avoid any inadvertent movements between frames 0 and 14, go into its graph editor and make it a linear spline at frame 14. This will make it a straight spline between frames 0 and 14.

Figure 3-15 shows the motion curve for a part like this. The graph is without correction and shows movement from frames 0 to 21. Figure 3-16 depicts what occurs when an extra keyframe is set at 14 that is identical to frame 0. The resulting curve between 0 and 14 means that the part will move a little between the two frames. Figure 3-17 illustrates the same motion graph after making the spline linear at 14. Now the part will stay motionless between frames 0 and 14. It will only move between frames 14 and 21.

You can take advantage of the natural curves that occur as a result of keyframing the same settings twice. Subsequent chapters discuss how you can use the curves for making objects appear to have more natural movement. Rather than having a part come to a dead stop, an extra keyframe placed at the end of the motion, with the same settings as the previous one, will make the part have a little bounce at the end.

Follow the rest of the poses in Figure 3-14 to finish the animation. The total number of frames is seventy-seven, a little over two seconds of animation. The keyframes in the illustration occur at every seventh frame, but you can insert extra ones here and there so that all of the parts do not always arrive at a keyframe at the same time. You might also want to skip certain frames for some of the segments (by drawing them out) to make the movements smoother.

When you are finished, render a test animation. If possible, turn on "data overlay" so that your software leaves a visible number on each frame of the animation. When you play it back, you will find it easier to correct any mistakes because you will be able to identify at which points they take place. The accompanying CD-ROM contains an animation of the mannequin. It is labeled CD3-14. As

with all the movies on the CD, it is better to copy it to your hard drive and play it back in real time.

Altering Animations with the Graph Editor

The animation exercises up to this point covered some basic movements and the rotation of objects. The next step is to learn how to use the graph editor to speed up, slow down, alter values, and create other changes in an animation. Graph editors contain a set of robust tools that animators should not ignore. Before using the graph editor, set up a short animation that matches the poses in Figure 3-18. Each pose occurs at every fifth frame for a total of twenty frames. The body should face toward the viewer in the front view (*z*-axis).

If you do not have a means of locking and unlocking feet to the ground, place a null object under your character's right foot (Figure 3-19). Null objects do not render and can be used as markers, goal objects, and points, which can have forces like voxels attached to them. Voxels are 3D volumes

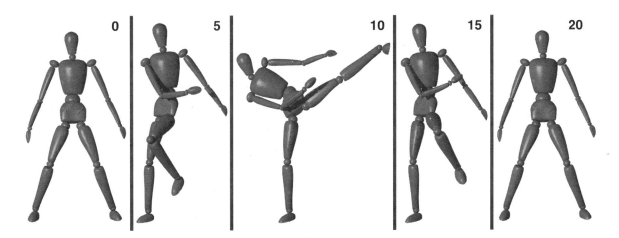

Fig. 3-18 Setting up a repeating animation. Note the first and last frames are identical. Keyframes in this example are set at every fifth frame.

without wire meshes that simulate surface effects such as smoke, fire, and so on. They are discussed in an upcoming chapter.

At frame 5, the body's center of gravity shifts to the right leg, which now supports all its weight. The abdomen is the parent of all the other segments, so it is moved on the *x*-axis toward the null. The body also turns clockwise in the top view at frame 5. To place the foot back on the null, rotate the right leg at frame 5 so that it is somewhat straight. You can do this by turning the right hip or upper leg. Move through frames 0 to 5 to check the movement. The foot should appear to remain

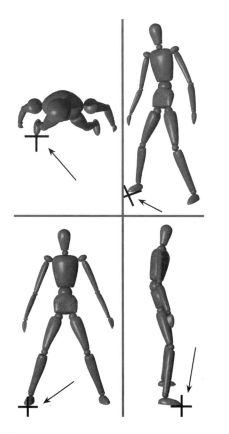

Fig. 3-19 Placing a null object at the right foot as a marker will keep track of where the foot should be placed in subsequent keyframes.

in the same spot throughout the weight shift. If you detect any extra motion, try straightening the abdomen's spline at frame 5 to make it linear. The foot may also have to be rotated at frame 5 so that it appears to remain flat on the ground.

When you advance to frame 10, straighten the right leg even more. Turn the body counterclockwise in the front view and adjust the body's position so that the right foot stays on the null. You will most likely have to fix the angle of the right leg.

The body's pose at frame 15 is very similar to the one at frame 5. This means that you can copy the settings from frame 5 for segments that were moved, and paste them into frame 15. One method of doing this is to go to frame 5 and select a section, say, the upper left shoulder, and keyframe its settings at frame 15. Some software programs such as LightWave 3D let you press "Enter" at frame 5 and type in number 15 to create a motion key. This applies the same settings to both frames: 5 and 15.

Another option is to go to the graph editor, select the point at frame 5, and copy it to frame 15 (Figure 3-20). The various software packages have different approaches for doing this. For example, in LightWave 3D, you would select the point at frame 5, press "Enter," and type in the new keyframe, which in this case is 15.

When all the segments have had the same values applied to frame 15, make a few adjustments so that the pose is not identical to the one at frame 5.

The position of the body at frame 20 is identical to the one at frame 0. Therefore, you can go back to frame 0 and keyframe any moving segments at frame 20 with the same settings. You should also be able to do this through the graph editor using the method shown in Figure 3-20. As you go through each part to make it the same at

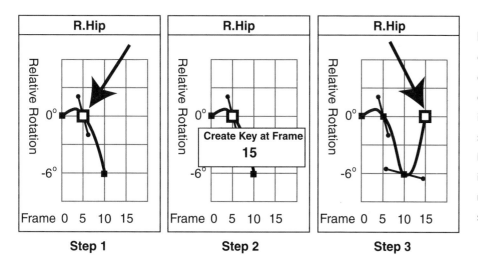

Fig. 3-20 Using the graph editor to make frame 15 a duplicate of frame 5. In this example, the point at frame 5 is selected in step 1. The next step shows how a "create a key" command for frame 15 is chosen. Step 3 depicts the new frame 15 with the same settings as frame 5.

frames 0 and 20, be sure to turn on the "repeat" command. This allows you to make the animation any length that you want. The character will repeat all the motions continually. The "repeat" command will not work correctly unless the first and last frames are identical. In this case, they are frames 0 and 20.

Render a test animation for 20 frames with "data overlay" on. Any corrections made at frames 0 and 20 will have to be the same. With "repeat" on, you can render a sixty-frame, eighty-frame, or longer animation. The accompanying CD-ROM has an eighty-frame repeating animation of the karate dummy. It is labeled CD3-18.

Save your animation because the next few steps will have you make some experimental alterations. Using the graph editor, keys will be shifted, scaled, and their values changed. The animations with the different settings can be saved as separate files.

Select whichever segment was rotated at frame 10 to move the leg up into the kick position. This might be the left hip or upper leg segment. Open its graph editor. Change the value of its rotation at frame 10 by dragging the point up, or scale its keys

by typing the following: *Low Frame 10, High Frame 10, Scale Frames by 1, Scale Values by 2.*

Setting the low and high frames at 10 will only affect that particular keyframe. Scaling the frame by 1 leaves it at its default normal rate. The final setting of scaling the value by 2 doubles its quantity, resulting in a higher kick. Figure 3-21 shows the two motion graphs before and after scaling the

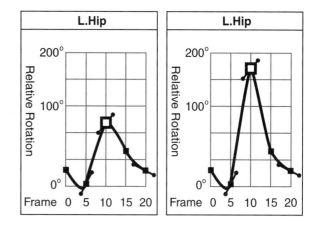

Fig. 3-21 Scaling the value of the left hip at frame 10 by twice the amount. The graph on the right shows the left hip's higher rotation degree after increasing its value.

Fig. 3-22 The mannequin's new pose after doubling the left hip's value at frame 10.

value at frame 10. Figure 3-22 depicts the body's new pose at frame 10. As you can see, the kick is much higher now. Save this file with a new name like "Value Scaled Karate."

Open the original twenty-frame karate animation. This time you will scale the frames to expand the duration of the kick. Before starting, turn off "repeat" for all the segments that have motion. Extending the length of a motion beyond frame 20 will disrupt the repeat command because frames 0 and 20 are no longer identical. You can save this as a separate file with a name like "No Repeat Karate."

Select a segment such as the left hip or upper leg that was rotated for the kick at frame 10. In your graph editor, scale the keys for this part with the following settings: *Low Frame 0, High Frame 40, Scale Frames by 2, Scale Values by 1.*

Low frame means that scaling will take place starting at frame 0. The high frame setting of 40 has the motion extend up to that point. Scaling the frames by 2 means that the rotation for the left hip has been expanded over the range of forty frames and the kick will take twice as long to complete (Figure 3-23). A scale value of 1 means that nothing was changed for this setting.

As you can see after playing back a test animation, scaling (expanding or contracting) frames is very useful for adjusting parts of animations that move either too fast or too slow. Scaling or changing the quantity of a motion can be set to start anywhere during the sequence by specifying a low frame value. In this case, it was set to start at the beginning (low frame 0).

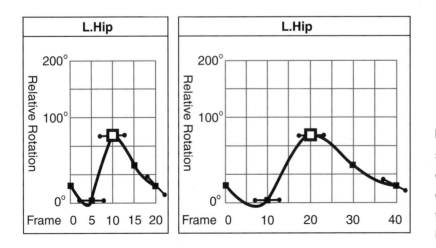

Fig. 3-23 Scaling frames can either shorten or lengthen the motion. In this case, the left hip rotation has been expanded by a factor of two, making the motion twice as long as evidenced in the graph on the right.

In this animation, scaling only the left hip to make the kick last longer made the motion out of sync with the rest of the body movements. If all the gestures appear to work together correctly, but the overall movement is too slow or too fast, then consider scaling the frames on a global level. This entails scaling all the keys in the entire scene, including camera, lights, and other object motions.

Some software packages have the option of splitting parts of an animation into separate channels. This makes it easier to control individual characters without having to worry about affecting other elements. Another method for singling out objects and characters is to save an animation as is. Delete all parts except for the objects you plan to change. Make alterations, such as scaling all the keys, and save this altered scene with a different name. Open the original scene and delete the objects that you just altered and saved before opening the original. Finally, select the "load from scene" option or import the second scene with the changes to the specific objects. Whenever possible, elect not to import the lights. If you end up with duplicates of anything, delete them.

Shifting keys allows you to control the beginning and ending of each movement. This can be set anywhere along the time track. For example, if an arm's motion extends from frame 0 to 20, then shifting the keys at frame 0 by 10 frames will expand its movement from frame 0 to 30. The motion will be now appear to be slower because it is drawn out over a longer period of time.

To get a better understanding of this, open the file that you might have named No Repeat Karate. This is the file without repeating motions. Select the left hip or upper leg segment that performs the kick. Open its graph editor and type the following settings for shifting keys: *Low Frame 10, High Frame 30, Shift Frames by 10, Scale Values by 0.*

Figure 3-24 shows what happens to the motion graph. The entire movement now lasts up to thirty frames instead of twenty. Starting at frame 10, the keyframes have all been moved by ten frames. This means that the motion that once extended from frames 5 to 10 now extends to frame 20. When you play back the animation, you can see that the kick is drawn out between frames 5 and 20, and then resumes its normal speed between frames 20 and 30. The kick also extends beyond the normal

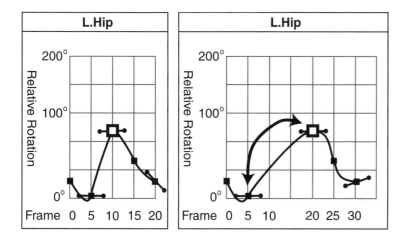

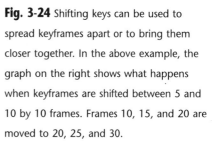

Fig. 3-24 Shifting keys can be used to spread keyframes apart or to bring them closer together. In the above example, the graph on the right shows what happens when keyframes are shifted between 5 and 10 by 10 frames. Frames 10, 15, and 20 are moved to 20, 25, and 30.

scope of the other segments: those movements that end at frame 20. The extended range in the middle of the motion makes the character appear to kick twice.

After running a test animation, close the scene without saving it and open the No Repeat Karate scene again. This time try shifting the frames for the kicking leg with these settings: *Low Frame 0, High Frame 40, Shift Frames by 20, Scale Values by 0.*

The motion graph should now be twice as long. Create an extra key at frame 20. Set the spline to be linear at frame 20. You should have a straight spline between frames 0 and 20 (Figure 3-25). Select any other segments of the kicking leg—like the knee, lower leg, ankle, or foot—that might have motions previously assigned to them. Go into each of their motion graphs and delete all their keyframes except for the first one at 0. Only the left hip or upper leg should have keyframes.

When you play a test rendering, you will see the kicking leg start its kick at frame 20 and end at frame 40. Frames 0 to 20 have the leg move only because other parts in the upper hierarchy are affecting it. In this case, the parent abdomen's movements affect the position of the leg.

To take this a step further, if you go into each segment's motion graph and type the same settings as you did for the left hip or leg, then you will find that the character will stand still for the first 20 frames and then begin its movements. Be sure to make the spline linear between frames 0 and 20, or you will get some motion due to the natural curve of the spline.

Another approach is to shift all the frames globally or for the entire scene. You will still have to go into each moving object's motion graph and add the extra keyframe at the same frame number as the amount that was shifted. In other words, if you shifted frames by twenty, then an extra keyframe will be set at 20. The spline between 0 and 20 will also have to be made linear.

This technique is useful when you want objects or characters to begin or end their motions at certain times to match the movements of other bodies or events. For example, let us say you want to create an animation of a character jumping from a building to avoid being burned by a fire. The burning building and the jumping man are animated separately. In the burning building animation, the fire doesn't reach the man until frame 50. In the

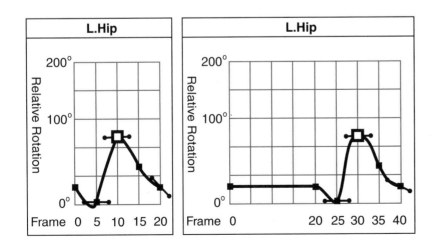

Fig. 3-25 The right graph shows the effects of shifting keyframes at the beginning of a motion by adding an extra frame at 20 and straightening the spline at frame 20 and making it linear. Frames 0 and 20 now have identical positions, which means the left hip does not begin its movement until frame 20.

jumping man animation, the subject starts jumping too soon at frame 0. You can shift all of his motions by fifty frames so that when you put the two together, the man begins his jump when the fire reaches him at frame 50.

Shifting values can increase or decrease the settings of an object's motions. It is similar to scaling values, except that it gives the animator a finer degree of control over the amount of movement. For example, if you key in 2 for the kicking leg's scale value, this action doubles the amount of the leg's rotation, making the kick much higher. If you key in 2 for its shift value, this action increases the rotation by only two meters or whatever unit of measure you are using. The leg's kick is only a little higher.

Having experimented with the graph editor, you should have a fairly good idea of its usefulness. A lot of manual labor can be saved by utilizing the graph editor. Be sure to use it whenever you need to make adjustments.

Place the object in the center of your universe. If you are using a NURBS cylinder, make the radius 0.1 and a ratio of height-to-radius of 10. Rebuild the cylinder's surfaces with four U and V spans.

To see the skeleton more clearly, set the cylinder's appearance in wireframe. Some may prefer to set the shading to points rather than NURBS or polygon surfaces. When setting joints or bones, it helps to have four different views available. This makes it easier to orient the bone/joint chain.

All animation software packages utilize different systems for creating skeletons. Rather than trying to write about every single one, the following exercises will concentrate on two of the more widely used 3D software packages: Maya and LightWave 3D. If you are using other software, you may still be able to apply these directions by utilizing your own software's commands and procedures.

Creating a Joint Chain or Bone Structure

In LightWave 3D, select the "add bones" option or draw a bone. When you add your first bone, rotate it so that the pointed end faces toward the right in the top view. Move the bone to the far left of the cylinder so that the wider end touches the left end of the cylinder. In the top view, use "rest length" to scale the bone so that it extends from the left end of the cylinder to its middle. Check the location of the bone in your various view windows. It should be inside the cylinder. Create or draw a child bone. It should extend in the top view to the far right end of the cylinder. The pointed end of the first bone faces toward the child bone. Activate the two bones so that they can begin to affect the cylinder.

In Maya, select the joint tool and set degrees of freedom for all three axes. Click on the left end of the cylinder in the front view. Move the cursor to

the middle of the cylinder and click again. Move to the right end of the cylinder in the front view and click once more. Complete the joint chain by pressing "Enter." The two bones are connected with the first one's pointed end facing toward the child bone. While all the joints are selected, shift-select the cylinder and choose to smooth bind the skin. This will activate the bone so that it will be able to deform the cylinder.

Figure 4-2 depicts two cylinders with a simple skeleton structure. The LightWave 3D cylinder is made of polygons and the Maya cylinder is NURBS-based.

Deforming the Cylinder with Forward Kinematics

Forward kinematics rotates each joint or bone individually. When one parent bone is rotated, all the other child bones down the joint chain also turn. Forward kinematics works well for detailed curving actions, but can take more time when animating large, complicated skeletons. When you move a foot forward, you normally do not think about how much the upper leg has to be rotated to bring the foot up and ahead.

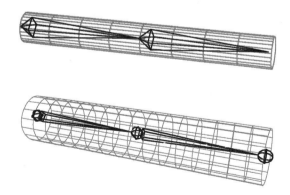

Fig. 4-2 The top cylinder shows the Lightwave 3D bone structure, and the bottom one depicts the Maya joint chain.

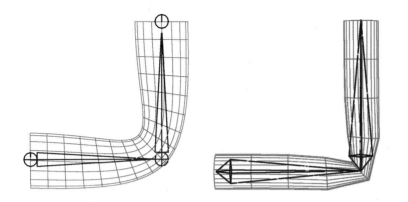

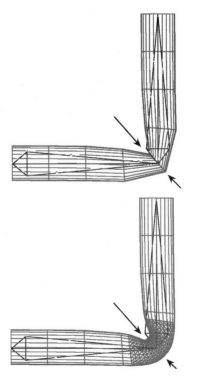

Fig. 4-3 Rotating the joint and bone bends the shape of the cylinder. The smoother NURBS cylinder on the left was deformed in Maya, while the polygon one on the right was distorted using LightWave 3D. Note the pinching in the cylinders' middle.

With the two bones activated in LightWave 3D, rotate the child bone so that it points straight up. In Maya, do the same thing by turning the second joint minus 90 degrees on the *z*-axis. Figure 4-3 shows how the bones change the shape of the cylinder. The centers of both cylinders are pinched and will have to be fixed.

Overcoming Pinching, Creasing, and Bunching Around Joints

Polygon models can crease when there are not enough small polygons at the joints. Figure 4-4 shows two cylinders with different polygon counts around the parts where they are bent. The cylinder on the top only has a few polygons at the joint, and thus shows abnormal pinching. The cylinder on the bottom has subdivided polygons and retains a fairly round shape around the joint. Whenever you create objects that will be deformed by a skeleton, be sure to subdivide the polygons around the joints or areas to be bent.

Even though the polygons were subdivided, the top part of the cylinder at the joint still does not look quite right. If you rotate your lower arm upward 90 degrees, you will find the skin at the joint comes together more than the cylinder's mesh does. A large part of this problem can be

remedied by changing the original orientation of the bones. Figure 4-5 shows that rotating the parent bone up, so that the pointed end faces the top part of the cylinder at the joint, fixes most of the problem. The bones had to be deactivated first and then rotated into their new positions. After activating them again, the child bone is rotated up.

Fig. 4-4 The top cylinder shows how faceted the cylinder appears at the joint, while the bottom one has subdivided polygons around the joint making the bent part look smoother.

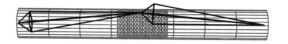

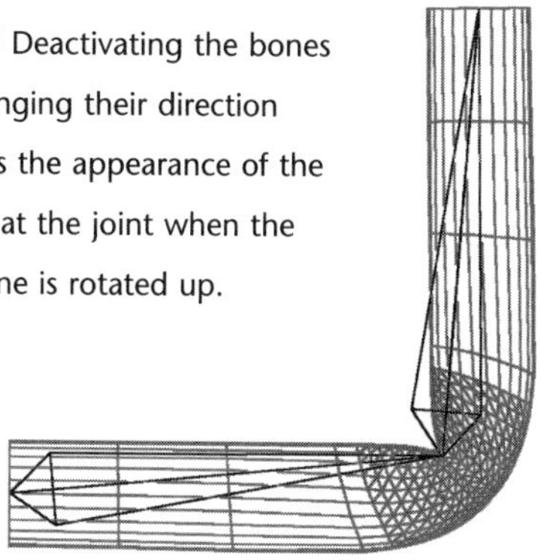

Fig. 4-5 Deactivating the bones and changing their direction improves the appearance of the cylinder at the joint when the child bone is rotated up.

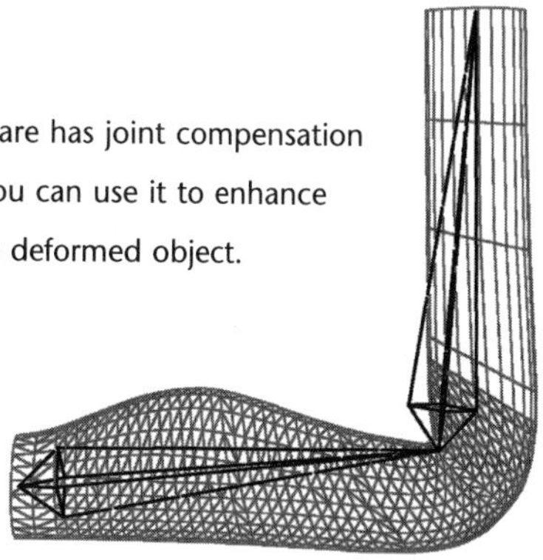

Fig. 4-6 If your software has joint compensation and muscle flexing, you can use it to enhance the appearance of the deformed object.

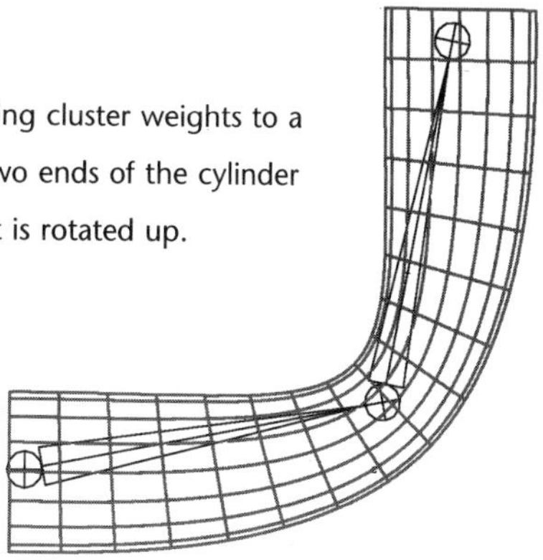

Fig. 4-7 Before adding cluster weights to a NURBS mesh. The two ends of the cylinder expand when a joint is rotated up.

This new placement also means the child bone will not have to be rotated up as much as before. When placing skeletons in your characters, consider using this type of configuration in key areas such as the armpits, elbows, knees, hips, and so on.

If your software allows you to turn on an option such as "joint compensation" and "joint compensation for parent," try setting these at 100%. In most situations, that should be enough. The affected points around the joints will retain their original volume.

Another useful option found in programs like LightWave 3D is "muscle flexing for parent." After selecting the child bone, you can turn on this option, thereby expanding the mesh around the middle of the parent bone (Figure 4-6). This is similar to flexing the arms' biceps.

Programs such as Maya allow the user to do a number of things for improving the appearance of a deformed NURBS mesh. One of these is the ability to paint weights on parts of the model. The weighted points react in a variety of ways to any deformation. All of this depends on the amount of weight

Fig. 4-8 Cluster weights are painted on the cylinder. The darker areas have a weight of 0 making them more resistant to deformation changes.

assigned to each. For example, a part of the model with points weighing zero will react slower to changes than other points with a weight value of 1.

Figure 4-7 shows the NURBS cylinder before painting weights on the points. The two ends expand when a joint is rotated upward. In Figure 4-8, weights have been painted with the lightest area in the middle having a weight of 1, while the

Fig. 4-9 When the joint is rotated, the varying cluster weights help the cylinder ends retain their original shapes.

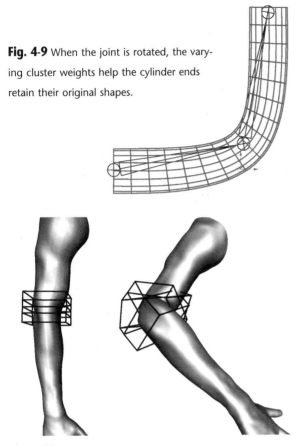

Fig. 4-10 A lattice flexor positioned at a joint gives deformed objects a more normal look.

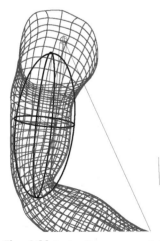

Fig. 4-11 Sculpt flexors are useful for creating dips and bulges when a joint is moved.

ends of the cylinder have a weight of 0. Figure 4-9 shows the result of weighted points when one of the joints is rotated upward. The ends of the cylinder are affected the least by the deformation, thereby retaining most of their original shape. Moving the cylinder's cluster handle can also be used to deform the mesh at different rates.

In Maya, one way to avoid pinching at a joint is to create a lattice flexor. This tool forms a cage around the joint that helps to smooth or wrinkle skin (Figure 4-10). Lattice flexors can also be used to show bulging muscles.

The skeleton should be in bind pose before applying a lattice flexor. This means that the joints should be reset to their original positions. Select the joint on which to create a joint flexor and then choose "skin" > "create flexor." Be sure to select "lattice" for flexor type. If you want more control over detail, then set higher S, T, and U divisions. Once you have the lattice flexor positioned correctly, rotate the joint to deform the object. Use the lattice flexor's attribute editor to correct any flaws. This can be done be setting "creasing," "rounding," "length in and out," "width left and right." If the lattice does not give you enough control, then change the division settings in the lattice history, also found in the attribute editor.

To help skin move naturally over a joint and to create swells and depressions, Maya uses sculpt flexors (Figure 4-11). Before selecting a sculpt flexor, be sure to put the skeleton in bind pose. When choosing "skin" > "create flexor," select "sculpt" from flexor type. The sculpt flexor can be edited in its attribute editor.

Another method for making skin move smoothly around joints in Maya is to use cluster flexors. The flexor type that you would select is called the "joint cluster." It creates a ring around

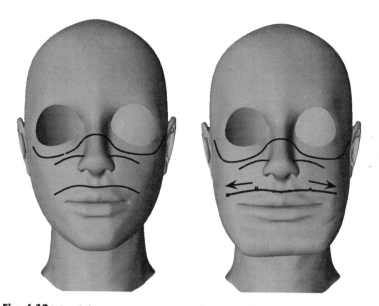

Fig. 4-12 Wire deformers use curves or splines to pull or push geometry. In this example, the two top curves are base wires to anchor the surface, while the bottom one pulls it apart.

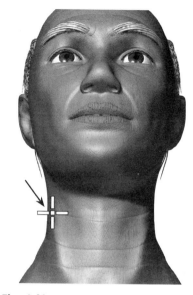

Fig. 4-13 A wrinkle tool can be useful for creating creases in the geometry.

the joint. The range and magnitude of smoothing are set by manipulators on each ring.

Other Deformation Tools

Several more deformation tools can be found in higher-end software. Wire deformers and wrinkle tools are part of Maya's impressive tool set. The following instructions provide a little information about them. They are not meant as a substitute for your software manuals. Obviously, software manuals provide much more detail about specific tools and their functions.

Wire deformers are curves/splines that can be manipulated to change the shape of an object's geometry. Curves are placed near the model and designated as influence or base wires (Figure 4-12). The influence wires, when moved, pull on the nearby geometry while the base wires anchor parts of it.

To create wire deformers in Maya, make some curves near the object to be deformed. Select "deform" > "wire tool." Click on the geometry with the tool, press "Enter," click "curve," and press "Enter" again. To make curves act as anchors, be sure to turn on the "holders" option in the wire tool settings.

Another deformation tool found in programs like Maya is one for creating wrinkles. It allows the user to specify the area in which the geometry will be changed (Figure 4-13). Once radial, tangential, or custom wrinkles are set, a cluster handle is manipulated to change the surface of the object.

After selecting the object to be changed, go to "deform" > "wrinkle tool." In the tool settings, you can specify the type of wrinkle and the effect that you want to achieve. Using the middle mouse button, click and drag on the geometry to create the area of influence. Once that is set, you can press "Enter." A letter *c* indicates the cluster handle,

Fig. 4-14 Morphing or shape blending changes an object's form into another. It is used most commonly for creating various facial expressions.

Morphing or Blending Shapes _____

One of the most common methods for deforming objects is morphing or shape blending. Of all the previously discussed techniques for deforming models, this one allows the user the most control. The original object is transformed into any number of target shapes. This can be accomplished by using deformation and/or modeling tools. After creating the various forms, a blend shape editor calculates the subtle changes among the target shapes (Figure 4-14).

Normally, there are a few rules you need to follow when setting up morph or blend shape targets. In some programs, the targets must have the exact same number of points as the original. Moving parts of the target model's geometry to other layers, mirroring them, or copying and pasting points or polygons will yield unpredictable results. It is usually acceptable to add, delete, or substitute separate parts of a model, such as hair, as long as the same thing is done to the original

and all of its targets. For example, if you want to reuse the morph targets of a character, but you want it to look like a different person, then you can eliminate the separate hair object on the original and all its targets. A new hair object could then be added to it and its morph targets. As long as the hair object is the same for all of them, morphing should work fine.

On the other hand, programs like Maya will accept morph targets with different CV counts. For this to work, "check topology" has to be turned off in the "blend shape" options window.

Morphing or shape blending is mostly used for facial animation. Setting up targets for facial expressions is discussed in a later chapter. Sometimes, artists will use morph targets for hand animation. Even though bones or joints will suffice much of the time, morphing is more precise.

If you are planning to use an envelope for setting up multiple morph targets, you should draw a simple diagram outlining the times between various targets. An envelope is a method of setting a specific value to change over time. Figure 4-15 illustrates a multiple target envelope for altering a facial expression over time.

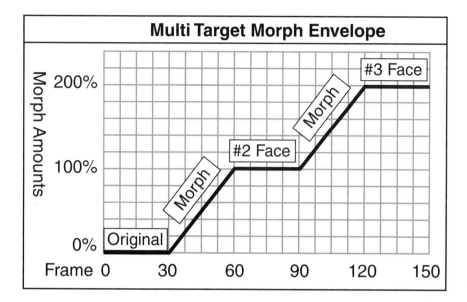

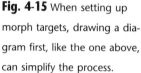

Fig. 4-15 When setting up morph targets, drawing a diagram first, like the one above, can simplify the process.

Animating with Inverse Kinematics

Kinematics is a branch of mechanics concerned with motion, without reference to force or mass. In 3D computer animation, kinematics usually deals with linked objects. If you followed the previous instructions to animate a segmented character, then you have already experienced forward kinematics. After setting up a series of linked forms, parents were rotated or moved in a chain, which subsequently affected the positions of their child objects. If the lowest part of a chain, like a hand, was rotated, it had no effect on any other items in the hierarchy.

Inverse kinematics (IK) is a system whereby a chain of bones, or other linked objects, can be moved or rotated by changing the position of the last object in a hierarchy (or the goal object connected to it). It is a reverse of forward kinematics. With IK, moving the hand affects all the other parts joined to it.

Software companies implement skeletons and

IK in a number of ways. Even if you are not using the software packages referred to in the following instructions, you may still find some of this information valuable. The procedures for implementing IK may differ, but the manner in which IK is used to accomplish certain objectives might be applicable to your software.

If you are using LightWave 3D, you can set up a simple IK chain by doing the following. Create a null object. Select "bones" and create a bone for the null object. Make several child bones linked to each other until you have six bones in total. In "objects" mode, create another null and move it to the end of the skeleton chain opposite the first null.

Select the first null and its bones. Find bone number 6 and open its "inverse kinematics" options. Set its goal object to be null number 2 and turn on full-time IK. Activate all the bones. Back in "object" mode, move null number 2. Notice how the rest of the bones follow, while null number 1 anchors the first bone (Figure 4-16). Null number

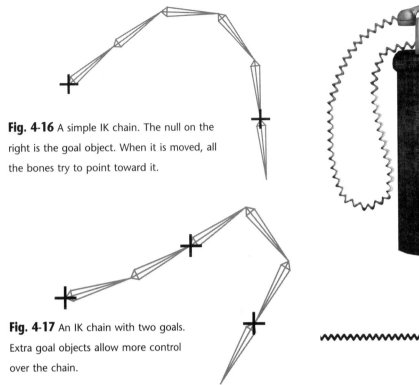

Fig. 4-16 A simple IK chain. The null on the right is the goal object. When it is moved, all the bones try to point toward it.

Fig. 4-17 An IK chain with two goals. Extra goal objects allow more control over the chain.

Fig. 4-18 The phone cord is bent with an IK chain.

Fig. 4-19 Modeling the cord in a straight line is simpler than trying to bend it as well.

2 acts as the goal object, at which the bones will always try to point.

An IK chain can have several goal objects. This is useful when you want to have more control over the object being deformed. Create a third null and move it near bone number 3. Select the first null's bone number 3. In its inverse kinematics options, set its goal object to be null number 3 and turn on full-time IK. Now move null numbers 2 and 3. Notice how both goal objects control the IK chain. One goal moves the bones while the other is useful for making small adjustments.

A practical application of multiple goal objects can be seen in Figures 4-18, 4-19, and 4-20. Figure 4-18 shows a phone cord that has been deformed by a skeleton. Originally, the phone cord was mod-

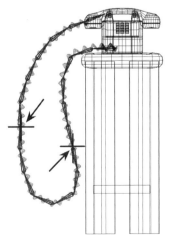

Fig. 4-20 After placing the skeleton in a straight line, the two goal objects, indicated by the arrows, are moved to bend the cord.

eled in a straight line (Figure 4-19). This made it simpler to make the spring-like loops in the cord using "sweep." The bones were then placed in a straight line inside the cord. Two goal objects were added to the IK chain. The goal objects were positioned so that the cord would bend down in the middle (Figure 4-20). When used in an animation with a character picking up the phone receiver, the nulls acting as goal objects can be moved to straighten or bend the cord as needed.

Inverse Kinematics is used mostly for character animation. Because the skeletal hierarchy in animals, humans, and other entities can often be very complicated, IK with its goal objects simplifies the process of locomotion. Figure 4-21 shows a female with three nulls as goal objects in one of her legs. To lift the leg, the knee null is moved forward. The ankle null is parented to the toe null. This is useful for walking cycles in which the foot rolls from the heel to the toe as the body moves forward. The toe null acts as an anchor securing the toes to the ground so that they are the last part of the foot to lift up. In Figure 4-21, the toe null is moved up and the ankle null follows. Minor adjustments are made by moving the ankle null.

Figure 4-22 illustrates the bone chain inside one of the legs. The small bone at the very top, seen in the front view, is the hipbone. It is set to be unaffected by IK of descendants. This means that moving any of the goal objects in the lower hierarchy, such as the knee, ankle, and toe nulls, will not affect this bone. The hipbone acts as a sort of anchor to the IK hierarchy. There is an extra knee bone inserted as a child bone to the upper leg bone. The knee null is set as the goal object to this knee bone. At the end of the toe bone, an extra child bone is created to which the toe null is attached as its goal object. The knee and toe-tip

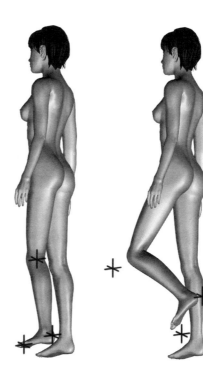

Fig. 4-21
Three nulls are used as goal objects to move the lower leg.

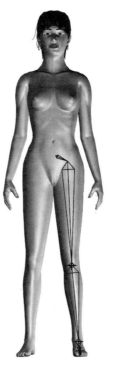

Fig. 4-22
The front and side views show the partial IK setup for the left leg bones and goal objects.

bones with their goal objects add a little more control to the IK chain. Finally, an ankle null is attached to the back of the foot bone.

Some software programs allow the user to set limits on bones. Before doing this, you should be familiar with the degrees of rotation of your character's joints. For example, in humans, the ball joint allows a great degree of freedom. Located at the hips and shoulders, it gives legs and arms free reign to rotate in any direction.

Goal objects have different names according to their specific software. Maya names goal objects IK handles. The IK handle runs through the entire joint chain like a wire. Using an IK handle tool, the user clicks on the first joint, which is named the start joint. This defines the root of the chain. The joint that is to be connected to the root joint is the end joint, also known as the end effector. The end joint is defined by clicking on another joint with the IK handle tool. The following exercise shows how to set up a simple IK chain in Maya. If you are not a Maya user, you may find it interesting to see how IK works in Maya. There is always something to be gained by learning about other software packages.

In Maya, select "skeleton" > "joint tool" and go into the tool settings. Turn on the "create IK handle" option. For a current solver, select ikSCsolver. This is the single chain (SC) solver and is a straightforward mechanism for posing and animating an IK chain. The other option is the rotate plane solver (ikRPsolver), which provides more options for manipulating the chain such as twisting.

Using the joint tool, click once to create the first joint. Move the cursor to another area and click again for the second joint. Finally, click once more in another spot to create a third joint. Press "Enter" to complete the IK chain. Figure 4-23 shows the three joints and the IK handle at the end.

Select the IK handle and move it around to see how the joints respond. The joints move as if they were strung together with a rubber band. Think of the joints as an arm. The first joint is the upper arm and the last joint is the hand. Notice how the arm rotates well at the shoulder and elbow, but is hard to control at the wrist. You can add another IK handle at the wrist to control the rotation of the hand.

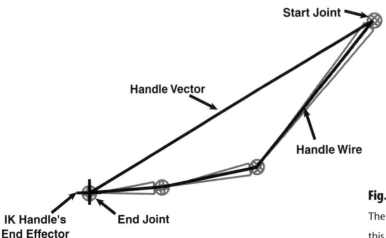

Start Joint

Handle Vector

Handle Wire

IK Handle's End Effector

End Joint

Fig. 4-23 An IK chain with a single chain solver. The end effector is the only IK handle used in this configuration.

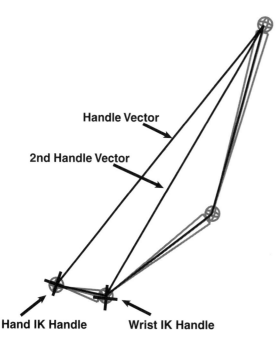

Handle Vector

2nd Handle Vector

Hand IK Handle   **Wrist IK Handle**

Fig. 4-24 Adding an extra IK handle at the wrist improves control over the entire IK chain.

Start with a new scene and go into the joint tool settings. Turn off "create IK handle." Using the joint tool, click three times on different parts of your front view to create a series of connected joints. Press "Enter" to make the joint chain. Select "skeleton" > "IK spline handle tool" and in the tool settings, click the "reset" button. With the IK spline handle tool, click the start joint (root) and then the end joint. A handle wire, handle vector, and an IK handle are now a part of the chain. Undo the spline handle so that your joint chain is back to what it was before using the tool.

Now it is time to create your own spline with cluster handles for better control. This method works well for curving motions like tails, necks, whips, snakes, and so on. The curve or spline can be created either before or after making the joints. In the following example, the curve/spline is made after the joints.

Go to "skeleton" > "IK handle tool" and in the tool settings, set the current solver to "ikSCsolver." Click on the start joint of your skeleton and then click on the wrist joint just before the end joint (Figure 4-24). Now, move the IK chain by selecting and dragging each of the IK handles. Notice that with two handles, it is easier to fine-tune the position of the joints. Both handles act similarly to the two goal objects that were placed in the phone cord or the female's leg. Each can be used to move the skeleton and make minor adjustments.

Another method for manipulating an IK chain is to create IK spline handles. A curve (spline) is created with handles that can be moved to pose the skeleton. It is similar to moving points on a spline, except that when the spline is bent, the joints respond.

Using the CV or EP curve tool, make a spline that follows along the joint chain. Try to use a minimum number of points to do this (Figure 4-25). Before pressing "Enter" to complete the curve, click the "insert" key and move the points so that the curve aligns fairly well with the joints. After

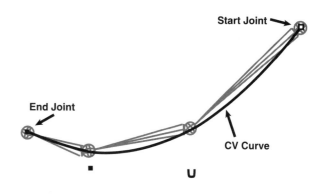

Start Joint

End Joint

CV Curve

U

Fig. 4-25 Creating a spline for controlling the IK chain.

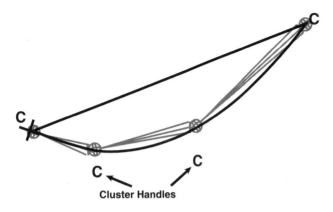

Cluster Handles

Fig. 4-26 The control vertices are changed into cluster handles for easier manipulation of the IK chain.

clicking the insert key again, press "Enter" to complete the curve.

Select "skeleton" > "IK spline handle tool" and in the tool settings, turn off "auto create curve" and turn on "snap curve to root." With the IK spline handle tool, click the start joint (root), then click the end joint, and finally, click the curve. This completes the spline IK.

Select the spline and go into component mode (F8). Pick the CVs along the spline and move them randomly. You should see the skeleton react accordingly. Undo a number of times until the skeleton is back in its neutral pose. Go into the cluster options box ("deform" > "create cluster"). Turn on the "relative mode" option. While keeping the cluster options box open, select the first CV near the root joint. Click the "create" button in the cluster options. This makes a cluster handle which is indicated by a C. Select the curve again and click the next CV and then click the "create" button in the cluster options. Continue selecting the curve and the remaining CVs and the "create" button.

You should now have approximately four cluster handles to control the curve of the skeleton (Figure 4-26). These handles can also be viewed in the outliner. Open the outliner if you have not done so ("window" > "outliner"). Rename the first cluster handle by double-clicking it, typing the name "shoulder," and pressing "Enter." Name the next one "elbow," then "wrist," and finally "hand." Now, select the different cluster handles in the outliner and move them around. You can see that you can have a great amount of control over the skeleton by using spline handles.

One last step involves parenting all the cluster handles under the root joint. Shift-select each of the cluster handles and finally the root joint. Press p on the keyboard to parent them under the root. When you select the individual cluster handles and move them, the other ones follow.

The final exercise involves applying the previously discussed techniques to an object like an arm, leg, or snake. The following examples use a female arm. Joints will be created for it, as well as flexors, and a CV curve with cluster handles. To simplify the process, no finger joints will be created.

Starting with a new scene, import a model of an arm. The CD-ROM has a model of a basic arm without any detail that you can use for this. It can be found in the chapter 4 folder. Another option is to make a cylinder that acts as an arm. Using the CV curve tool, draw a curve/spline that goes through the arm, starting at the shoulder. It should have only four CVs: one at the shoulder, the second at the elbow, the third at the wrist, and the fourth at the end of the fingers (Figure 4-27).

Select the joint tool (skeleton creation tool) and in its option box, turn off "create IK handle." Using the spline as a guide, click once at the shoul-

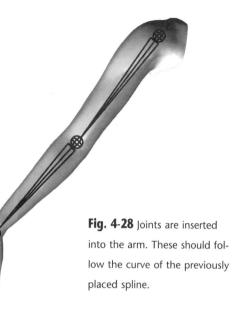

Fig. 4-27 After importing an arm, a curve/spline is drawn through it with four points.

Fig. 4-28 Joints are inserted into the arm. These should follow the curve of the previously placed spline.

der, next at the elbow, then the wrist, and finally at the end of the fingers. It helps to have four views up for this. Press the "insert" key and using your up and down arrow keys, select each joint and adjust its position with the move tool. Once you are done adjusting the joints, press "insert" again to finish modifying them and press "Enter" to create the skeleton (Figure 4-28).

Now it is time to add spline IK to the skeleton. To make this process easier, hide all the meshes (the arm) in the various view windows. This will simplify the process of selecting the spline CVs and the joints. Go to "skeletons" > "IK spline handle tool" > options box. Turn off "auto create curve" and turn on "snap curve to root." With the IK spline handle tool, select the root joint at the shoulder and then click the end joint at the fingertips. Finally, click the spline. This will create the spline IK. You can test it by selecting the curve/spline, going into component mode (F8), and then moving one of the CVs. When you are

done, be sure to undo any changes to the joint positions so that the skeleton is back to its original place inside the arm. Return to "select" by object type (F8).

The next step is to bind the skeleton to the arm. To do this you will need to make meshes (the arm) visible in at least one of the windows. Select the root joint at the shoulder. This will select the entire skeleton. While it is active, shift-select the arm mesh. Go to "skin" > "bind skin" > "smooth bind" > "options box." Select "bind" to complete the skeleton and click the "bind" button. You can move the arm by manipulating the CVs on the curve/spline, but it is better to create clusters.

Select the curve/spline that is controlling the skeleton. Go into component mode (F8) so that you can see the CVs on the curve. Open the cluster options box ("deform" > "create cluster"). Turn on the "relative mode" option. While keeping the cluster options box open, select the first CV near the root joint. Click the "create" button in the clus-

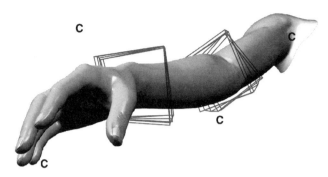

Fig. 4-29 Flexors are added to control joint deformations. Cluster handles are indicated by the letter *c*.

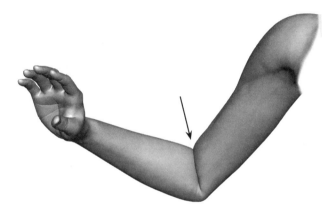

Fig. 4-30 When the arm and hand are bent, the flexors control the shape of the deformation.

ter options. This makes a cluster handle indicated by a C. Select the curve again, click the next CV, and then click the "create" button in the cluster options. Continue selecting the curve and the remaining CVs and the "create" button.

You should now have approximately four cluster handles to control the curve of the skeleton. These handles can be viewed in the outliner. Open the outliner if you have not done so already ("window" > "outliner"). Rename the first cluster handle by double-clicking it, typing the name "shoulder,"

and pressing "Enter." Name the next one "elbow," then "wrist," and finally "hand." Go into "object select" mode (F8). Select the different cluster handles in the outliner or in the view windows. Another option for easier selection is to turn on only "deformers" from the show menu for one of the views. You can then use that view window to select the cluster handles. Move them around to see the effects on the arm. Shift-select each of the cluster handles and finally the root joint. Press p on the keyboard to parent them under the root.

The last step involves placing flexors at the elbow and wrist joints (Figure 4-29). The skeleton should be in bind pose before applying a lattice flexor. This means the joints should be reset to their original positions. Select the elbow joint and then choose "skin" > "create flexor." Be sure to select "lattice" for flexor type. If you want more control over detail, then set higher S, T, and U divisions. Repeat the previous steps to create another flexor for the wrist. Once you have the lattice flexors positioned correctly, rotate the joints by moving the cluster handles. This should deform the arm. Use the lattice flexor's attribute editor to correct any flaws. Use the sliding buttons to set creasing, rounding, length in and out, and width left and right. If the lattice does not give you enough control, change the division settings in the lattice history, which is also found in the attribute editor. Figure 4-30 shows how the flexors control deformations when the lower arm and hand are bent.

Creating a Skeleton for a Two-Legged Character

When building an entire skeletal structure for the first time, you should take a moment to do a little planning. Before starting, consider the limitations

Top View

Angled View

Front View

Side View

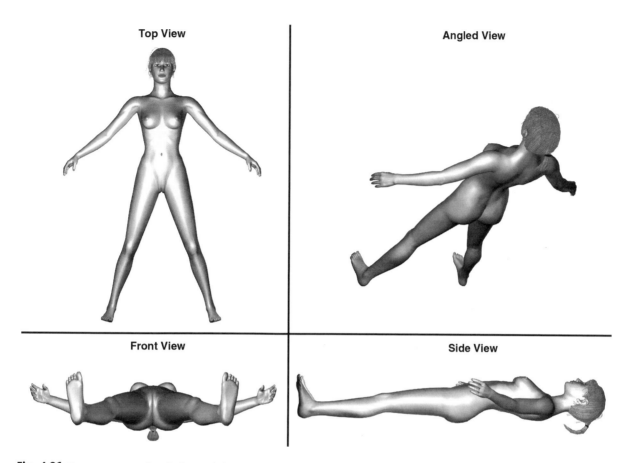

Fig. 4-31 The proper pose for placing a skeleton in some software packages that have limited bone rotations resulting in gimbal lock problems. Placing a skeleton in a character lying down requires minimal rotation of bones because they are generally oriented in the right direction from the start.

of your software. Find out if it has gimbal-lock problems. This means that when a bone is rotated more than 90 degrees on one axis, it begins to overlap onto another axis. The bone then becomes difficult to control because you can no longer tell on which axis to rotate it. Once it goes past the 90-degree limit, it has to be rotated on two axes at the same time.

If your software has gimbal-lock problems, find out in which direction a bone lines up when it is first created. If it faces toward the back on the *z*-axis (+*z*), then it makes sense to have the character lie in the same direction before placing any bones. Figure 4-31 shows the right orientation for a female character in a software package that creates bones facing on the +*z*-axis. Due to the model's orientation, the individual bones require very little rotation when they are placed inside her. The female figure in the illustration has been centered on all three axes so that when the bone is created in the center of the universe, it will require minimal movement.

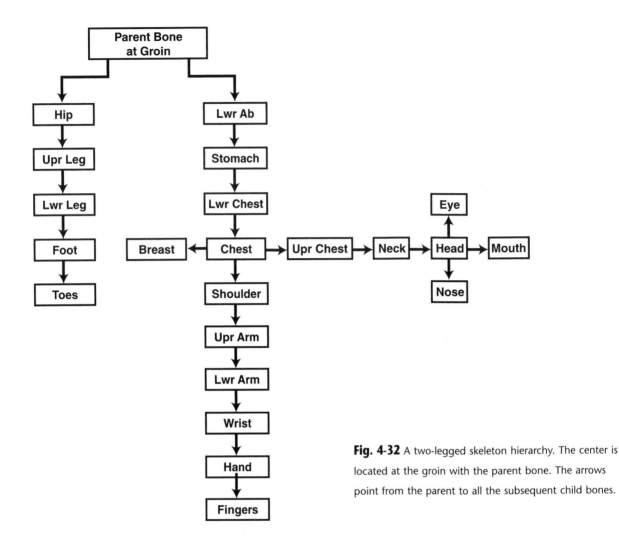

Fig. 4-32 A two-legged skeleton hierarchy. The center is located at the groin with the parent bone. The arrows point from the parent to all the subsequent child bones.

Another problem that some software packages have is that once you place bones, you cannot reorient the direction of their hierarchy. This means that bones cannot be detached from one parent and attached to another, nor can the ordered grouping of parent and child bones be turned. If that is the case with your software, then it helps to plan out the hierarchy of bones in advance. Figure 4-32 shows a typical two-legged skeletal structure that should work for most soft-ware packages. The center of the skeleton is at the groin, which has the parent or first bone of the entire hierarchy. All the remaining ones are linked to it through others in the structure.

Figure 4-33 illustrates the bones and their placement inside the figure. The numbers correspond to the order in which the bones were created. If your software does not allow you to mirror bones or sets of them, then you may want to create all the lower body bones first, followed by the spinal column and

they, in turn, change the orientation of these extra stabilizing bones.

If you plan to use an inverse kinematics skeleton, you can refer to the previous chapter's described methods for setting up IK chains, solvers, and handles. Some software allows you to use a mix of inverse and forward kinematics. Figure 4-37 shows a setup in which IK is applied only to the legs leaving the arms and upper body in forward kinematics mode. Cycling movements like walking can have the arms use repeating motions while the lower half with IK can have goal objects that anchor the feet. To get the rolling motion of the feet as the body's weight shifts from the heel to the toes, you can parent the heel null (object handle) to the toe null. When the IK handle or null at the toe is moved forward, the heel null will follow. Since the heel null is not responsible for the main actions of the foot, it can be used to make minor adjustments to the foot's orientation. Figure 4-37 shows a few extra bones at the knee, heel, and tip of toe. The nulls or IK handles are attached to

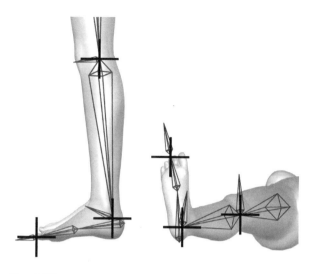

Fig. 4-37 Inverse Kinematics uses goal object handles or nulls (black + signs) to control the movement and orientation of the legs. The heel null is parented to the toe null to control the rolling motion of the feet.

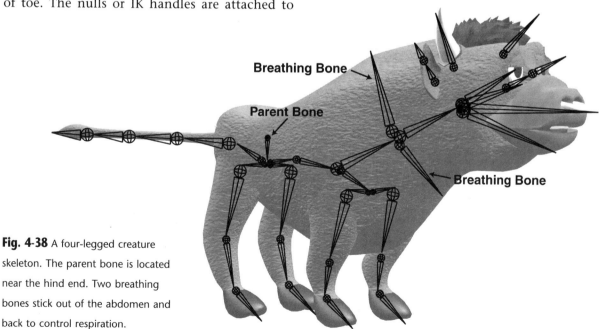

Fig. 4-38 A four-legged creature skeleton. The parent bone is located near the hind end. Two breathing bones stick out of the abdomen and back to control respiration.

Breathing Bone

Parent Bone

Breathing Bone

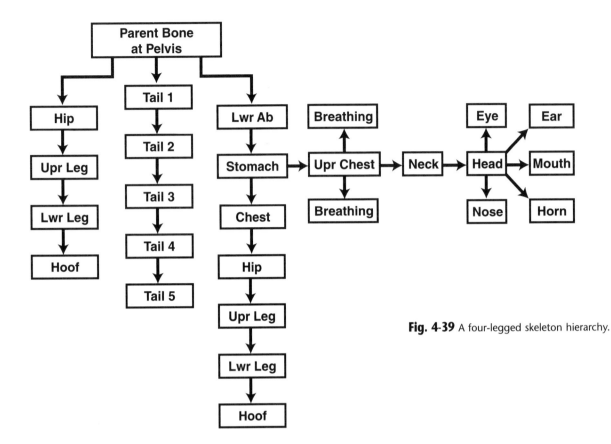

Fig. 4-39 A four-legged skeleton hierarchy.

these. These extra bones make it easier to identify the location of goal objects.

Creating a Skeleton for a Four-Legged Character

Figure 4-38 shows the skeleton for a four-legged character. In some ways, it is similar to a two-legged character skeleton, except now you have a tail and another set of feet instead of hands. The parent bone is located near the rear and has tail, hip, and lower abdomen bones joined to it in a lower hierarchical order. Depending on how much you want to bend the tail, you can add more bones for extra flexibility.

The hierarchical arrangement of a four-legged

skeleton can be seen in Figure 4-39. Each arrow points to a lower order of child bone. Special bones are added in the face for software that does not allow the assigning of vertices to specific bones. Their function is to stabilize and keep other bones from distorting parts of the head.

Once you have become familiar with the way your software creates skeletons, you can experiment with some of the techniques in this chapter. You can model your own human or two-legged character following the directions in chapters 6, 7, and 8, or use the sample models for those chapters found in the CD-ROM. Most of these models are generic and lack the necessary detail found in humans. They are meant to be used as templates for your own creations.

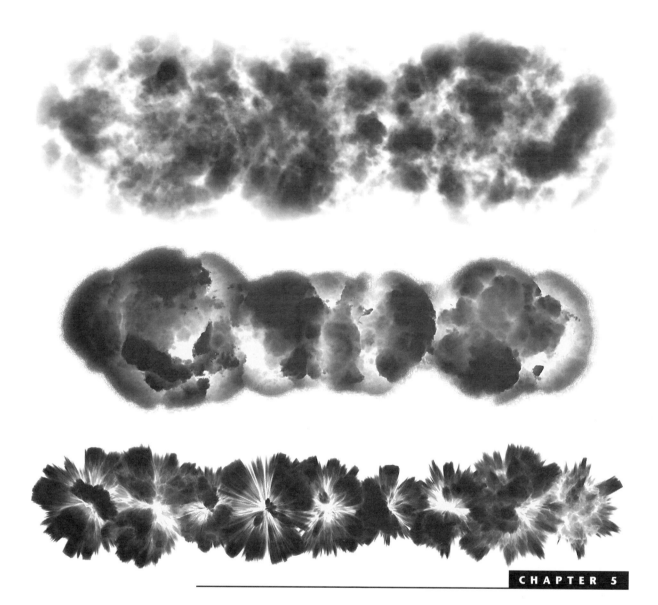

CHAPTER 5

Special Effects

Special effects often add a touch of brilliance and grandeur to an otherwise ordinary animation. This is a branch of computer graphics that is both enjoyable and full of meaning. There is no doubt that this multifaceted field could have an entire book devoted to it.

Many artists use visual effects to enhance their animations. These can range from corporate identity projects all the way to action sequences. Special effects may just involve the use of particles to simulate ordinary sparks from a grindstone, or they might be used to show a dazzling cataclysmic explosion.

This chapter covers some of the more common effects used in animation, which include explosions, liquids, atmospherics such as steam, smoke and clouds, fire, and electricity.

Explosions

Some of the most frequently used visual effects are explosions. There is nothing like a violent burst of energy to get someone's attention. Unfortunately, due to their overuse, they have lost some of their excitement. There are many ways to create a computer-animated explosion, and artists are constantly trying out new methods for making more dazzling detonations.

The variety of explosions that you can create depends largely on your software's capabilities. Most mid- to high-end packages utilize particles in one form or another. Others use 3D volumes like voxels. A few have dynamics that simulate real-world physical forces.

The following examples range from simple explosions using objects and shading techniques through the more sophisticated voxels.

Making a Simple Explosion from Spheres

This low-tech method involves the use of balls or spheres clumped together, shaded a special way, and then scaled during the animation. It is very simple to do and most animation packages can handle it. It does not yield the most realistic explosions, but it might do the job if your software does not have advanced particle effects or voxels. The most difficult part of this technique is getting the right shading on the balls.

In the modeling part of your software, create a number of spheres and lump them together like the ones shown in Figure 5-1. Name its surface "explosion" and save it as Explosion. Rename the object's surface "smoke" and save it as Smoke.

The next step involves surfacing and animating the two clumps. Load the explosion and smoke objects into the animation part of your program or select the animation mode in your software. Move the pivot points of each object into their centers.

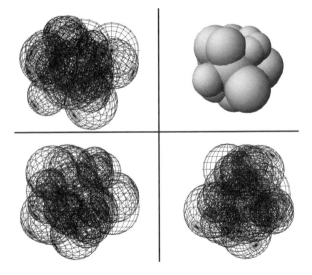

Fig. 5-1 A simple explosion object is made by clumping a number of balls together.

Select a pale yellow color for the Explosion object surface. Apply a second surface color that is bright red and runs through the surface as fractal noise. Make the red fractal texture surface about ¼ (.25) size on the *x*-, *y*-, and *z*-axes. In order to give the texture movement during the animation, set texture velocity to about 1 meter on the *x*-, *y*-, and *z*-axes. The amount of velocity may vary according to the size of your object.

Set the transparency to about 10%. Under the transparency settings, apply another fractal noise texture with a value of 100%. This will give it an overall transparency. Make the transparency fractal noise size about .75 on the *x*-, *y*-, and *z*-axes. Now the transparency part is larger than the color areas. Set the contrast size of the transparency fractal noise to .75 to get a fading effect.

The other texture settings for the explosion part should be set to the following: *Luminosity 50%, Diffuse Level 100%, Specular Level 0%, Reflectivity 10%, Edge Transparency 100%.*

The Smoke object has the same surface settings as the Explosion object. You only have to change the colors. If your software allows you to save the explosion surface, then you can apply it to the smoke surface. Change the smoke color to a light gray and change the second color from red to dark gray.

Make some test renderings of your explosion and smoke objects. The surfaces of both should have transparent edges while the centers show thicker billowing colors and grays (Figure 5-2).

Animating the explosion involves correct pacing. At first there is the expanding explosion, followed by the billowing smoke. The explosion then contracts while the smoke continues to expand and dissipate. You can use the following instructions as a rough guide for the timing. Depending

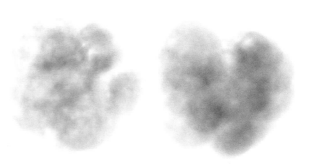

Fig. 5-2 The cloud on the left is the explosion clump of objects after surfacing and the one on the right is the smoke object. Both have 50% dissolve applied to them.

on the effect that you are trying to achieve, you may need to alter the rates of the explosion and smoke dissipation.

Place both clumps together. You may decide to rotate one of them so that they appear a little different. To make it easier to move and rotate both at the same time, you may want to parent them to a null object.

Set up your camera and lighting. At frame 0 keyframe the null or both objects. Go to frame 10 and keyframe the null or both objects again. Move to frame 30 and rotate the null about 120 degrees clockwise in the top view and about 80 degrees clockwise in the front view. Keyframe the null at frame 30. If you did not parent the objects to a null, then rotate and keyframe them according to the previously stated settings.

Go back to frame 0 and scale both the explosion and smoke objects down to 0% so that they cannot be seen. Create a keyframe for both at 0. Select the explosion object and go to frame 10 and scale it up to 100%. Advance to frame 20 and size it down to 20%. Move to frame 30 and scale it back down to 0%.

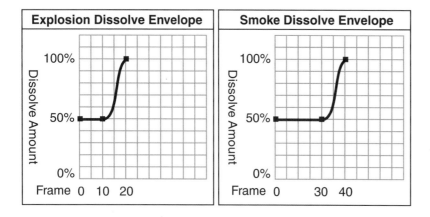

Fig. 5-3 A dissolve envelope is made for both the explosion object and the smoke object.

For the smoke object, move to frame 20 and scale it up 100%. At frame 30, enlarge it to 200%. The last step involves setting dissolve envelopes for both objects.

Figure 5-3 shows the dissolve envelopes for the explosion and smoke objects. The explosion object starts out at frame 0 with a 50% dissolve. This adds to the overall transparency of the object. Another 50% dissolve is set at frame 10 and a 100% dissolve is set at frame 20. This means the explosion disappears totally at frame 20.

The smoke object also starts with a 50% dissolve at frame 0. Another 50% dissolve is applied at frame 30. The smoke object disappears with a 100% dissolve at frame 40.

Create a 40-frame test animation of your explosion. The fiery explosion should quickly increase in size between frames 0 and 10. Its size decreases between frames 10 and 30. The dissolve envelope makes it disappear at frame 20. The smoke object increases in size between frames 0 and 30 and the dissolve envelope makes it disappear at frame 40. Both objects rotate during the animation and the fractal texture moves throughout the sequence. A sample animation of the ball explosion can be found on the CD-ROM as CD5-4. Figure 5-4 illustrates one frame from the animation.

There are many ways to enhance this simple explosion. You can add particles, have objects break up, and introduce lens flares. These are discussed in the next part.

Particle Explosions

A particle is a point in 3D space that can be animated and assigned specified properties. Particles can have color gradients, velocity, collision detection, age, goal following, and so on. They can be influenced by dynamic forces such as gravity, wind, drag and other particles and objects. All of this depends on the software that you are using.

Particles can be created by using a particle tool or deleting surfaces from polygons, leaving only points to act as particles. Emitters are also used to

Fig. 5-4 A frame from the ball explosion.

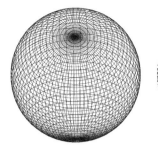

Fig. 5-5 A polygon sphere is used to make particles.

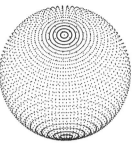

Fig. 5-6 The polygons are eliminated, leaving only the points.

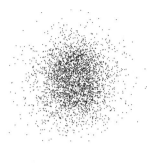

Fig. 5-7 The points are converted to polygons and jittered randomly.

Fig. 5-8 A gradient texture is created for the particles.

generate particles. When you set up an emitter, you can usually specify the degree of the particle spread, the birth rate in particles per second, the speed at which they pour out, the size and shape of the emitter, and so on.

The following exercises show how particles can be created using several methods. The first one, another low-tech method like the ball explosion, is fairly direct and simple. It does not use emitters, but is made from a polygon object. The polygon surfaces are eliminated, leaving only the points. These are jittered randomly and converted to one-point polygons. A surface color is assigned to them and they are then animated by scaling the particles during the animation. The second method uses an emitter to generate the particles. Dynamic forces are applied to the particles for realistic motion. The emitter particles are not keyframed with traditional animation methods.

Some software programs that utilize polygons let the user eliminate the surfaces, leaving only their points. If you can do this, then you might want to try the following.

If your software does not have a particle cloud tool, then create a polygon sphere or ball with eighty sides and forty segments (Figure 5-5). This should yield enough points for the particle explosion. Remove the polygons so that only the points remain (Figure 5-6). Convert the points to polygons so they can be seen in your shaded view. This will make them show up when they are rendered. Jitter the points so that they form a randomly scattered particle cloud (Figure 5-7). You can then name the surface of the points and save the file as an object.

Using a paint program, create a gradient to use as texture for the particle cloud (Figure 5-8). The gradient can be radial or angled. It can have a spectrum of colors or it might just have several like yellow to red. It depends on the type of effect you are trying to achieve. In the animation part of your program, apply the gradient texture to the particles. You can use planar mapping on the z-axis at 100% size setting.

Set up your camera and lights. At frame 0 scale the particle down to size 0. Advance to frame 30 and enlarge it eight times normal size (8.0) on the x-, y-, and z-axes. Go to frame 45 and enlarge it a little more, to about size 10 (10 times larger than normal).

Turn on "motion blur" and "particle blur" and make the blur length at least 100%. This will make

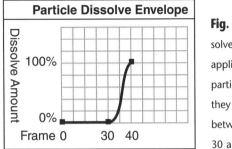

Fig. 5-9 A dissolve envelope is applied to the particles so that they disappear between frames 30 and 40.

the particles look like they have streaks as they fly toward the camera. Set a dissolve envelope for the particles. Figure 5-9 shows the settings for the envelope. The dissolve amount is 0% between frames 0 and 30. This means the particles are visible for the first 30 frames. At frame 40, they dissolve completely (100%). Be sure to make the spline linear at frame 30.

Preview the 45-frame animation and render a few test frames. The particles should enlarge quickly between frames 0 and 30 making them look like a burst of energy (Figure 5-10). After frame 30 they slow down and gradually die out. You can also parent the particles to a null. In the future, this will make it easier to position the particles when you decide to combine them with other effects. Save your file and render an animation between frames 0 and 45. The particle cloud animation can be found on the CD-ROM as CD5-10.

A closely packed particle animation made up of blobs can be made out of this particle cloud. All you need to do is increase the size of the individual particles. Use the largest particle size possible. To add to the blotchy effect, apply the previously described ball explosion texture. The transparency settings of this texture should enhance the look of the explosion (Figure 5-11). A sample animation of the blobby particles can be seen on the CD-ROM as CD5-11.

Other options might include applying a displacement map, which will randomly scatter the particles and/or rotate the entire particle cloud during the animation. The displacement map can have an envelope controlling the intensity of the displacement during the explosion. A glow effect could also be put onto the particles. Figure 5-12 shows the particles with a displacement map and

Fig. 5-10 A particle explosion with the gradient texture.

Fig. 5-11 An explosion composed of large particles with transparency maps.

Fig. 5-12 These particles have a displacement map to scatter them randomly. A glow effect was also applied.

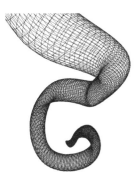

Fig. 5-13 A spiral shape is modeled.

Fig. 5-14 The polygons are deleted and the remaining points are jittered.

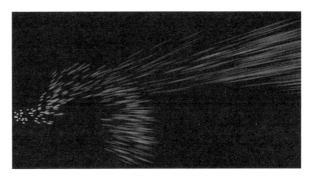

Fig. 5-15 Scaling the spiral particles during the animation produces another type of explosion.

glow effect applied to them. The displaced and glowing particle explosion can be viewed on the CD-ROM as CD5-12.

You can come up with all kinds of variations for this low-tech approach to making particles. One more option is to model a shape into a cone or spiral (Figure 5-13). The polygons are deleted and the points converted to one-point polygons and jittered slightly (Figure 5-14). Before animating the particles, the pivot point is moved to the narrow end where the object begins to enlarge. The same scaling parameters and texture mapping that were used for the previous particle explosion are utilized again. The texture center is set to 0 for all three axes. This places the beginning of the texture at its pivot point. The camera should be moved to a spot where the overall particle shape can be seen enlarging during the animation. Figure 5-15 shows a frame from this type of particle animation. The spiral particles can be viewed on the CD-ROM as CD5-15.

Dynamic forces can alter high-end particle effects. Since these vary a great deal among software packages, the following information describes how particles are produced with some of the more common dynamic forces.

When creating particles that stream out of emitters, it helps to position the camera at an angle or to the side of the emitter. This makes it easier to see the particles as they shoot out.

Figure 5-16 depicts particles streaming from an emitter. Particle collision was turned on so that particles colliding with a NURBS or polygon surface ricochet off. You may want to experiment with the emitter settings. Changing the spread, velocity, birth rate, and so on can yield some interesting

Fig. 5-16 Particles with collision detection bounce off a surface. A particle emitter creates the particles.

Fig. 5-17 Applying gravity to the particles enhances their physical presence.

results. A pipe, gun, or a face with an open mouth are a few of the objects in which the emitter can be placed. Bounciness or elasticity of the collision object can usually be adjusted. Friction or the roughness of the surface will also affect the manner in which particles bounce off the object. For example, a smoother surface will make the particles have more bounce. The CD-ROM contains an animation labeled CD5-16 showing a particle collision.

Gravity is another important dynamic quality that can usually be assigned to particles. It can be useful for water sprinklers, fountains, sparklers, and so on. Figure 5-17 shows the same emitter and collision objects as the ones in Figure 5-16, except this time, gravity was applied to the particles. An animation showing how gravity affects the particles can be viewed on the CD-ROM as CD5-17.

Many other dynamic forces can be applied to particles. Some of these are force, drag, wind, and death. Particles can even be set to follow or match goal objects. The CD-ROM contains an animation labeled CD5-17b in which particles follow a null object as their goal.

Particles usually do not work that well on their own for explosions. Therefore, they are often used in conjunction with other forces to simulate detonations. One of these 3D effects that works very well with particles are voxels.

Using Voxels to Simulate Explosions

Voxels are 3D volumes that exist on the *x*-, *y*-, and *z*-axes. Imagine a series of cubes spaced on a 3D grid. Each cube can have several attributes. The most common ones are density, temperature, and velocity. Voxels are similar to pixels except that, unlike pixels, they are not limited to 2D space. Otherwise, a pixel and a voxel are identical because each represents a value at a position in space. Voxels have mostly been used in computational fluid dynamics and medical visualization. Now that animators have added them to their digital tools, we are starting to see some truly stunning effects.

When it comes to explosions, voxels are hard to beat. Since voxels are capable of showing much greater detail than polygons and can be blended into each other, they are perfect for billowing volumetric effects. Voxels can have envelopes to control their color gradient, size, luminosity, opacity, density, thickness, and so on. Different filters, textures, and blending modes can also be applied to voxels. Figure 5-18 illustrates various voxel-type of explosions. A color image of the voxels can be viewed on the CD-ROM as CD5-18. The voxels are attached to a row of nulls to give them their horizontal shape.

The most significant disadvantage of using voxels is the amount of memory required to store them. This problem should cease to be a concern as computers continue to become more powerful.

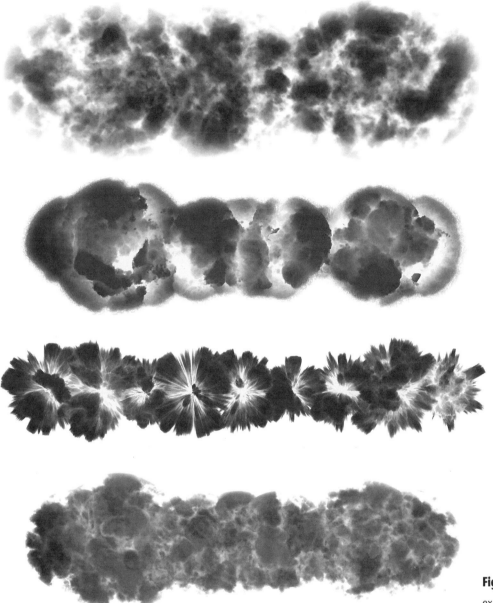

Fig. 5-18 Various voxel explosion clouds.

Figure 5-19 shows a frame from an explosion using voxels. One null was used as the goal object. The null was enlarged during the animation, thus creating the blast. The voxel fireball animation can be viewed on the CD-ROM as CD5-19. The CD also contains a voxel gradient explosion illustrating how voxels can have a gradient envelope applied to them that changes over time. It is labeled CD5-19b.

Besides atmospheric effects, voxels can be used to render various surfaces. Some of these are liq-

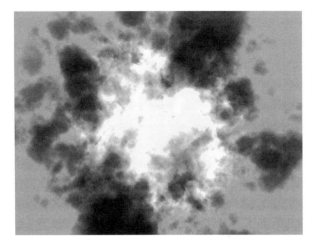

Fig. 5-19 A voxel type of explosion. In this case, the voxels were attached to one null that was enlarged during the animation.

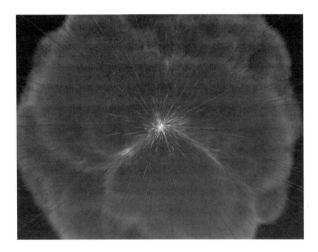

Fig. 5-20 Particles and voxels combined add to the fullness of an explosion.

uids that will be discussed later. If your software implements voxels, you may be able to experiment by applying some of the previously discussed envelopes, filters, textures, and blending modes. If you attach voxels to objects, you can size, move, or rotate the object over time. Combining voxels with some of the previously discussed particle effects can produce some dazzling animations. Figure 5-20 depicts a scene from a combination voxel/particle explosion. Two particle and voxel explosions can be viewed on the CD-ROM as CD5-20a and CD5-20b.

Polygon or NURBS Object Fragmentation

Although polygon or NURBS objects do not produce a good explosion by themselves, they nevertheless form an important part of a total detonation. If you can show fragments of the damaged object(s) flying by the camera or through space, you will get a much more interesting explosion.

The following exercise uses a bottle, but any object can be broken into pieces. For example, you can show a spaceship breaking up. Figure 5-21 shows the bottle object after lathing a spline outline.

Place the finished bottle on the spot where it will blow up and save the model. Make a duplicate of the bottle and hide the original. Try not to move the duplicate. We want it to occupy the same space as the original bottle. Cut the duplicate up into fragments (Figure 5-22). A polygon object works better for this because you can use stenciling, slicing, and Boolean operations to cut across the polygons.

One method that works well for slicing objects apart is to make a 2D polygon shape with jagged edges in another layer. The shape can then be extruded to extend beyond the thickness of the bottle that you plan to cut up. A drilling operation is used to stencil the jagged object onto the bottle. If you named the stencil surface, it will be easier to select the fragment later. Continue creating jagged polygon pieces to stencil onto the rest of the bottle. Vary the size of the fragments. Approximately seven pieces should be enough. To give the pieces some thickness, extrude each of them a little. Even

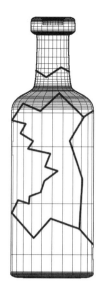

Fig. 5-21 (left) The bottle before slicing it up.

Fig. 5-22 (center) The jagged lines show where the bottle was cut apart.

Fig. 5-23 (right) A view of the separate bottle pieces.

though Figure 5-23 shows the separate pieces, you should keep them in their original location. During the animation, they will be moved apart.

The next step is to create a smoky and burnt-looking texture (Figure 5-24), which is then applied to the fragments' surfaces. The original bottle should have a clean look to it.

Some dissolve envelopes are now prepared for all of the fragments and the original whole bottle. In this particular animation, the bottle sits for

thirty frames and then begins to break apart starting at frame 31. Figure 5-25 shows the dissolve envelope for the fragments. Between frames 0 and 30, the fragments remain invisible (100% dissolve). At frame 31, they suddenly show up (0% dissolve).

The undivided original bottle has the opposite dissolve envelope applied to it (Figure 5-26). It is visible for the first thirty frames (0% dissolve) and then disappears suddenly at frame 31 (100% dissolve). Frame 31 has the whole bottle disappear, while at

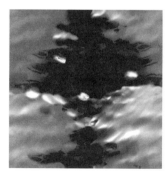

Fig. 5-24 The bottle fragments have a texture that makes them look burnt and smoky.

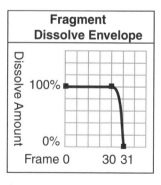

Fig. 5-25 A dissolve envelope makes the fragments invisible until frame 31.

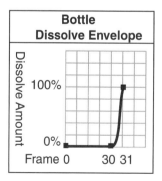

Fig. 5-26 The bottle remains visible for the first 30 frames and dissolves completely at frame 31.

the same time, the fragments appear and begin to move apart. One-thirtieth of a second is too fast for the human eye to notice the switch. It is another example of digital sleight-of-hand. This technique can be used for switching characters on the fly or for any other object that you wish to change.

Now it is time to create keyframes for the bottle and fragments. If you plan to apply this method to a moving object like a rocket, you should parent the fragments and the whole object to a null. You then move the null that, in turn, propels all the objects at once without having pieces come apart before their time.

Select one of the bottle pieces and keyframe it at frames 0 and 31. These two frames are identical so be sure to set the spline control to linear at frame 31. Do the exact same thing to the other fragments. Pick the first fragment again and advance to frame 41. Move and rotate the piece a little past the camera view so that it looks like it is hurtling away from the explosion. Once it is moved out of camera range, keyframe it at frame 41. Use your own judgment as to how fast you want the piece to fly. To make the fragment fly faster, place it further out of camera range or move it at an earlier frame than 41, perhaps at 36. Make a preview to see how fast the piece flies.

Advance to frame 44 and select the next fragment to move and rotate out of camera range.

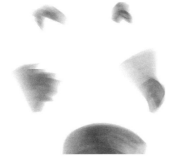

Fig. 5-27 Bottle fragments flying away from the explosion at frame 37.

Keyframe it at 44. You may decide to move it at an earlier or later frame depending on how fast you want it to travel. Continue moving and rotating the rest of the fragments out of camera range and keyframe them anywhere between frames 40 and 46. They should fly apart in different directions. Figure 5-27 shows some fragments at frame 37. "Motion blur" is turned on.

Adding Lens Flares

Lens flares bring a nice touch to explosions. They will look like bright lights that flare up quickly and die out. Aside from the lights that you are using to illuminate the scene, create three new lights for the lens flares. Make each of them a point light with an intensity of 50%. You may decide to give all of them a different color. Set your flares to have a central glow and a red outer glow. They can also have random streaks. A flare intensity envelope will have to be set for all three lens flares. Each one will vary by a few frames. Figure 5-28 shows the flare intensity envelope for the three lens flares. Lens flare number two had its frames shifted forward by two frames starting at 30. Number three lens flare had its frames shifted forward by four frames starting at 30. The first lens flare reaches its apex at frame 42 with an intensity of 150%, while the second arrives at frame 44, and the third achieves its brightest point at frame 46. Figure 5-29 illustrates the lens flares combined with the flying fragments at frame 39. The CD-ROM contains a short animation labeled CD5-33 showing only lens flares combined with particles.

Combining Particles with the Fragments and Lens Flares

Particles form an important part of the explosion. Their fast movement and haphazard distribution

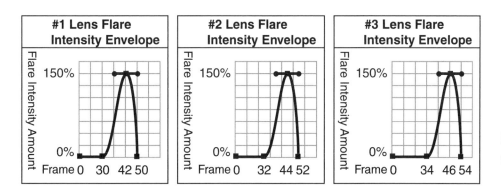

Fig. 5-28 The three lens-flare intensity envelopes.

in all directions contribute to the chaotic effect you are trying to achieve. As discussed previously, you can create particles with an emitter or from a point cloud. If you use an emitter, it should eject particles in all directions.

For this explosion, a point cloud is used that is scaled over time. To make the particles appear more random, a morphing or shape-shifting target is used. Two identical sets of particle clouds are created. Both have the same number of points. The second cluster is jittered and then used as the morph target. During the animation, the particle cloud will not only expand, but also scatter randomly in all directions as its shape shifts into the second particle cluster. Figure 5-30 shows the particle cloud morph envelope in which the first group morphs into the second between frames 42 and 60.

A gradient texture is applied to the particles. At frames 0 and 30, the original particle cloud is reduced in size to a value of 0 on the x-, y-, and z-axes. Frame 30 has a linear spline control to keep the zero size constant between frames zero and 30. At frame 60 the particle cloud is enlarged 200%. This may vary according to the size of your object and the distance of your camera from the explosion. If you want the particle cloud to expand

Fig. 5-29 Three lens flares are combined with the fragments at frame 39.

quickly and then slow down, you can insert an extra keyframe somewhere between frames 30 and 60. The in-between frame shows a higher percentage of growth than the ending one at 60 (Figure 5-31).

One final envelope needs to be set for the particle cloud. This is a dissolve envelope (Figure

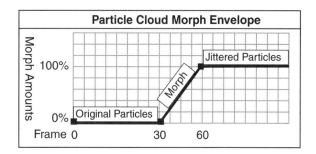

Fig. 5-30 Two particle clouds are made with the same number of points. The second group is jittered and becomes the morph target at frame 60.

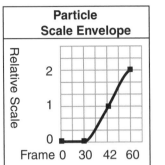

Fig. 5-31 The particle cloud is enlarged between frames 30 and 60.

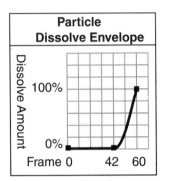

Fig. 5-32 A dissolve envelope is set to make the particles gradually disappear between frames 42 and 60.

5-32). Frames 0 and 42 have a 0% dissolve, which means that the particles remain opaque. Frame 42 has a linear spline control to keep the appearance of the particles constant up to that point. Between frames 42 and 60, the particles become transparent and disappear.

Render a few test frames to see how the particle cloud works with the previously set objects and lens flares. Figure 5-33 depicts frame 38 from the particle, fragment, and lens flare parts of the explosion. The final step involves setting up a smoke and fire cloud.

Mixing in Fire and Smoke to Complete the Explosion
Two separate volumes or objects are added for the fire and smoke parts of the explosion. If your software implements voxels, then you should be able to create very realistic fire and smoke. Particles can

also serve as smoke and fire objects. Another option is to use NURBS or polygon spheres clumped together. This method was discussed at the beginning of this chapter. The first part of this tutorial uses voxels for fire and smoke. The second utilizes the previously discussed cluster of spheres.

In the same scene that has the bottle, fragments, particles, and lens flares, create two nulls. Name one Fire Null and the other Smoke Null. Assign your fire and smoke voxels to the appropriate nulls. Experiment with some of the voxel settings until you are satisfied with the appearance of the fire and smoke. The two nulls now have to be scaled over time. The fire will appear before the smoke, quickly grow, and then shrink to nothing. The smoke will show up more gradually and retain its size, but will dissipate at the end.

Figure 5-34 shows the fire and smoke envelopes that control the scale of each over the course of 60 frames. Since the volumes are attached to the two nulls, the nulls carry the envelopes. The fire voxel null is scaled back to size 0 at frames 0 and 30. Frame 30 has a linear spline control to keep the

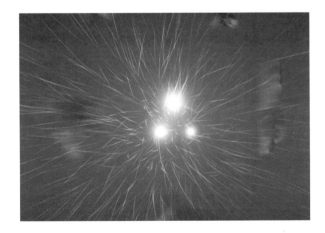

Fig. 5-33 Particles are mixed in with the lens flares and fragments. This shot was taken at frame 38.

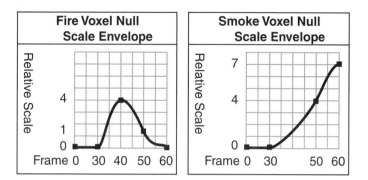

Fig. 5-34 After attaching the fire and smoke voxels to two separate nulls, each null is enlarged at a different rate between frames 30 and 60.

size constant for the first thirty frames. At frame 40, the fire voxel null is enlarged four times. This may vary according to the location of your camera. Frame 50 shows the fire voxel null reduced dramatically to size 1 and finally it is set to size 0 at frame 60. Placing the extra keyframe at frame 50 makes the reduction ease out. Instead of the fire gradually becoming smaller over twenty frames, it begins to shrink quickly for the first ten frames (40 to 50) and slows for the last ten frames (50 to 60).

The scale envelope for the smoke voxel null in Figure 5-34 depicts the same 0 setting for the first thirty frames, after which it enlarges dramatically until frame 60. As mentioned before, the size of your fire and smoke will vary according to the placement of your camera.

Figure 5-35 illustrates the dissolve envelope for the fire voxel null. It is set to make the volume disappear between frames 40 and 50. This is usually adjusted in the voxel's settings. The smoke voxel's dissolve envelope, seen in Figure 5-36, controls the appearance and disappearance of the smoke. It is also important to set some kind of deformation to the fire and smoke voxels. This turbulence or billowing effect agitates the fire and smoke so that it does not just sit there fixed in place. Test animations should determine the right effect speed.

If your software does not implement voxels or

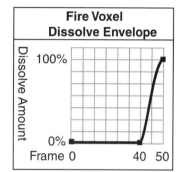

Fig. 5-35 To make the fire disappear between frames 40 and 50, a dissolve envelope is set for the voxels.

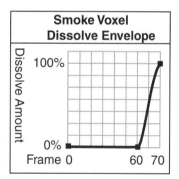

Fig. 5-36 The smoke voxels have a dissolve envelope. The smoke should clear between frames 60 and 70.

your particles do not have settings to give them the appearance of fire and smoke, then you can use the low-tech method of sphere clusters seen in Figures 5-1 through 5-4.

If you are considering using the sphere cluster method and have already set them up before the final explosions, then shifting frames and importing the scene into the bottle explosion scene will save you time.

NURBS or Polygon Fire & Smoke Object Envelopes

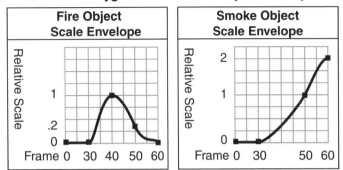

Fig. 5-37 The fire and smoke objects are enlarged at different rates between frames 30 and 60.

NURBS or Polygon Fire & Smoke Object Null Motion Graph

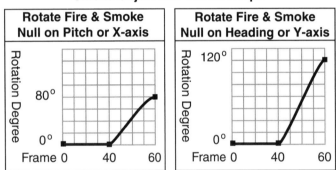

Fig. 5-38 The null, which has the fire and smoke objects parented to it, is rotated 80 degrees on the *x*-axis (pitch) and 120 degrees on the *y*-axis (heading) at frame 60.

NURBS or Polygon Fire & Smoke Objects Dissolve Envelopes

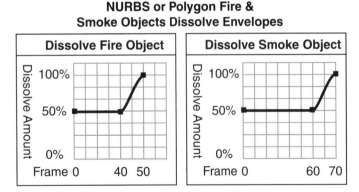

Fig. 5-39 A dissolve envelope is set for the fire and smoke objects. Both have a 50% dissolve in the beginning. The fire object disappears totally at frame 50, while the smoke object clears at frame 70.

After creating the spheres and naming each cluster surface "fire" and "smoke," texture them according to the instructions at the beginning of the chapter. Refer to Figure 5-37 to set size envelopes to both objects. As depicted in the illustration, each is scaled at a different rate and amount.

Parent the two sphere clusters to one null. The null should be rotated using the settings shown in Figure 5-38.

Dissolve envelopes are set for the fire and smoke spheres (Figure 5-40). Both start with a 50% dissolve to make them semi-transparent.

Figure 5-40 shows a few frames from the final bottle explosion. The animation can be viewed on the CD-ROM as CD5-40. Voxels were used for the fire and smoke parts of the explosion. Once you create an explosion of this type, it can be saved for future projects. The scene can have its keys shifted or scaled according to the animation in which you plan to use it. After adjusting the keys globally, you can import it into your other animation.

Liquids

3D animation of fluids can mean any number of things: a water drop, waterfall, sludge, syrup, lava, and so on. Since there are so many variables when depicting liquids, it is necessary to limit the scope of this section to a few common ones like a water drop, running water, and thicker fluids like sludge or syrup.

Particle effects are used quite often

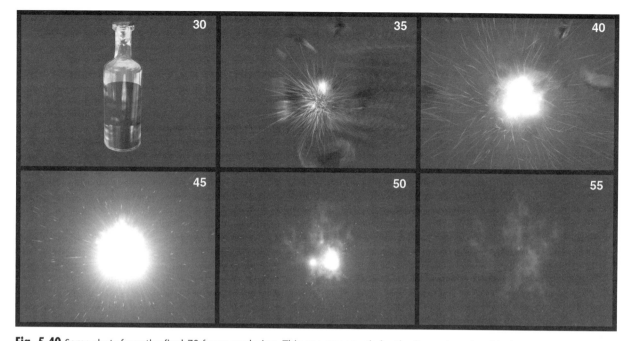

Fig. 5-40 Some shots from the final 70-frame explosion. This one uses voxels for the fire and smoke objects.

when portraying running water. Combined with voxels, a realistic enactment of water becomes even more attainable. Emitters do not always have to be used with particle effects. A particle cloud can be created that morphs into another shape. Attaching voxels to the morphing particles produces some interesting effects. The first liquid, a water drop, makes use of this technique.

Animating a Water Drop

If your software allows you to create particle points from objects as well as morph and attach voxels to them, then you can try the following technique. If you do not have voxels or cannot make points out of objects, then try this method with some creative texturing. Follow the steps but use simple NURBS or polygon forms instead of particles. Shape-shift the objects into each other and texture them similar to the surfaces described for the voxels.

Model a sphere with the poles pointing up and down on the *y*-axis. Use a taper tool in the top view to make the upper portion of the sphere narrow. It should resemble a teardrop. Delete the polygons and convert the remaining points to one-point polygons (Figure 5-41). Place it in the center of the modeling universe. This is our primary particle cloud. Save it as WaterDrop.

Figure 5-41 shows the other particle cloud shapes that will now be modeled from the original. These will be the morph targets. For the first

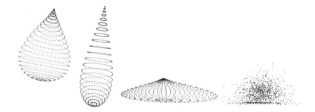

Fig. 5-41 A cluster of points in the shape of a water drop. The other three are the morph targets.

morph target, make the particle cloud long and narrow, the second flat, and the third with its points jittered. When the original drop begins to fall, it shape-shifts into a longer form, then flattens when it hits the bottom surface, and finally splashes (jittered points). Save each target with a separate name. Unless your software can handle morph targets or shape blends with different quantities of points, make sure each particle cluster has the same amount.

Model a water faucet, pump, hose, or any kind of spout. Place the original particle cloud named WaterDrop in the tip of the spout. Keyframe it at frame zero. Go to frame 7 and move the water drop down to where it would hit a surface before splashing and keyframe it at 7. Advance to frame 10 and move the water drop particle cluster up a little to give the droplets some bounce.

Now it is time to set up the morph targets. Use the diagram in Figure 5-42 as a guide to arrange the three particle cloud targets. Each morph lasts about one frame. By the time you reach frame 7, the particles will have changed to the third target of jittered points. Be sure to indicate in your software that this is a multiple-target, single envelope.

The final step is to attach the voxels to the WaterDrop particles. The water surface for the voxels will most likely have a high transparency with medium refraction and specular setting. It should also have Fresnel effect turned on, which will make the surface appear more reflective when viewed edgewise and more transparent when seen straight on. A particle size envelope is set so that the particles appear to separate into drops after hitting the surface. The size is relative, but so that you can get an idea of the differences, the original size of the voxels is set at three between frames 0 and 8. At frame 11, the voxels are reduced to 0.5. As the par-

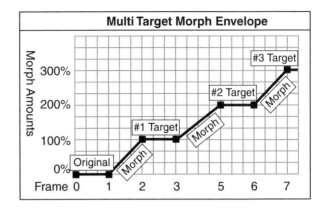

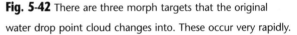

Fig. 5-42 There are three morph targets that the original water drop point cloud changes into. These occur very rapidly.

ticles change into smaller ones between frames 8 and 11, they separate into droplets. This occurs right after they hit the surface and bounce up.

Figure 5-43 shows a few frames from the water droplet animation that can be viewed on the CD-ROM as CD5-43.

Running Water

Creating fairly realistic running water effects usually requires software with particles and particle emitters. The particles emanating from a source

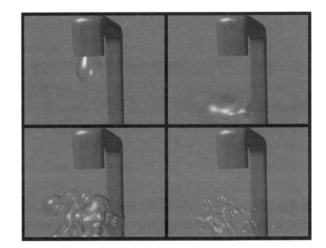

Fig. 5-43 Some rendered frames from the water drop animation.

(emitter) form the foundation upon which voxels or other dynamic attributes are placed. This is a form of dynamic animation in which motions are calculated from one frame to the next. There is no keyframing involved. To make changes, you have to adjust dynamic forces like gravity, particle size, collision amount, and so on. The following instructions may serve as a guideline for creating running water. As usual, there will be some variables, depending on the software used and the effect that you are trying to achieve.

Create particles and an emitter. If you plan to apply voxels to the particles, use the smallest number of particles possible. It will cut down on the rendering time. About 200 particles should be enough. The emitter only needs to create about one hundred particles per second. Of course, if you are not using voxels, you will want a higher amount of particles per second.

The spread from the emitter should be fairly small, or about 15 degrees. This may vary according to the size of the spout from which the water pours. The speed of the particles should be fast. If the water runs from a faucet, then rotate the emitter down 90 degrees on the *z*-axis or pitch. Apply gravity to the particles.

Collision detection adds a nice touch to running water. The collision object should not have too much bounce. If you rotate the collision object down slightly, you can get interesting water runoff after the water hits the surface. Figure 5-44 shows the particles as they stream down, collide, and run down the surface.

Once the flow of the particles has been set up, you can apply attributes and behaviors. This will vary a great deal according to the software. If you have voxels, apply them to the particle stream.

Some voxel parameters for running water might be the metaball blending mode, a luminosity of 0%, diffuse level of 100%, specular level of 50%, low to medium glossiness, 100% transparency, low to medium refraction, Fresnel effect, and small reflectivity. Figure 5-45 shows a section of the water stream with voxels applied to the particles.

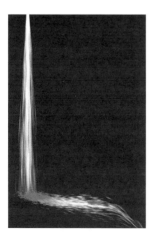  

Fig. 5-44 A stream of particles constitutes the groundwork for the running water animation.

Fig. 5-45 A close-up view of the water after applying voxels to the particle stream.

Fig. 5-46 A few scenes from the running water animation. Voxels were applied to the particles.

Fig. 5-47 The particles that will be used for the sludge.

Fig. 5-48 An image from the sludge animation. Voxels were applied to the particles.

Fig. 5-49 These particles will have the steam attributes placed on them.

To make the animation more interesting, create some objects for the water to flow from and collide with. Figure 5-46 shows a few images from the running water animation that can be viewed on the CD-ROM as CD5-46.

Sludge

Thick, messy substances like sludge, syrup, slime, and muck can be made in a fashion similar to running water effects. It just takes a few extra ingredients such as lumps, color, textures, and other surface effects to turn them into sluggish masses.

The particles and emitter are made in a similar way to those for running water. Dynamic forces like gravity, collision, wind, and so on can be assembled according to the context of the animation. Since this will simulate physical forces, there is no need for keyframing.

Figure 5-47 shows how particles and an emitter are placed inside a pipe. Gravity and collision detection are turned on. The speed of the particles is set fairly slow because the substance should appear to be sluggish. Figure 5-48 shows an image from the sludge animation, which can be viewed in several variations on the CD-ROM as CD5-48a, CD5-48b, and CD5-48c. Voxels are applied to the particles. A metaballs blending mode and texture are added to give the substance a lumpy look.

Atmospherics

Gases, steam, smoke, clouds, and other atmospheric conditions are usually created in a similar fashion to the previously discussed explosion, and fire clouds and particles often form their basis. Particles are set to have blobby surfaces like those found in metaball blending mode. The amount of mixture among blobs can be increased or decreased by the size of the particles or voxels. A steam or spray quality usually requires fast moving particles pouring out of an emitter.

Steam

Figure 5-49 shows particles with about a 45-degree spread flowing out of a spray can nozzle. The amount of particles used can be fairly low with a medium to fast speed. In this case, the particles were parented to the nozzle and set to stream forth after depressing the nozzle button.

Adding a light to the particle stream often improves the look of steam. A light is placed behind the particles and points in the direction of their flow. Color also plays an important role in determining the outcome. This can be adjusted through the light's color or through the volume surface. The particles should have a lifespan set so that the spray appears to dissipate after a certain distance. Transparency and glow settings should be adjusted for this type of effect. Figure 5-50 illustrates one frame from the steam animation found on the CD-ROM as CD5-50.

Clouds

Since smoke was described earlier under the explosion descriptions, the final atmospheric effect, clouds, is discussed briefly. A number of different software packages have the ability to render skies with clouds either with plug-ins or with a built-in renderer. This does not mean the clouds are actual volumes, but appear to be so in the distance.

To make clouds appear volumetric, you will most likely have to use particles. Setting the blobbiness or metaball factor on them will determine the magnitude and thickness of the clouds. If you can use voxels, then you should get an even higher degree of realism. The following instructions show

Fig. 5-50 One of the frames from the steam animation.

how to make a layer of clouds from a series of particles in a rectangular pattern.

Depending on your software, you can make a 2D polygon rectangle with twenty segments on the *x*- and *z*-axes. The polygons are then deleted and the points converted to one-point polys. These points serve as the particles to which voxels are attached (Figure 5-51). Another approach is to use a particle tool and apply attributes to the particles to give them blobby surfaces with self-shadowing.

The context in which you want to show your clouds will vary greatly among users. In Figure 5-52, a mountain range was created and overlapped with particles. This makes it look as if the clouds actually surround the mountains (Figure 5-53). You can add several sets of rectangular particle groups to show various strata of clouds. Some can be jit-

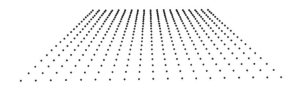

Fig. 5-51 A series of particles in a grid formation is created for the layer of clouds.

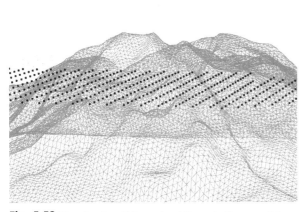

Fig. 5-52 The cloud particles extend through the mountain range.

Fig. 5-53 The final rendered cloud scene. Fog was turned on to make the clouds appear hazy in the distance.

tered or agitated to make the clouds appear more random. Be sure to turn on fog so that the clouds appear to be hazy in the distance.

The last step involves setting voxels to the particle points. Metaball blending mode is used with a light gray and white coloring. Luminosity is set at 40%, opacity at 10%, and density at 100%. A 100% size variation was chosen for the voxels. A short cloud animation can be seen on the CD-ROM as CD5-53.

Fire

Fire is an effect that can be created in a number of different ways by using displacement mapping on objects, volumetric properties, particles, and dynamic forces like wind, drag, gravity, collision, and so on. Particles acting as sparks and smoke add another degree of realism to the animation. Particles can also be placed inside the fire and set to explode at different times. The resulting sparks bounce off the ground before disappearing. The following instructions show how you can use sev-

eral different techniques to create a campfire, smoke, and sparks. Once you have your fire, you can take parts of it and alter them later for other effects such as a burning matchstick, torch, candle, and so on.

Modeling and Texturing Logs

You can model some logs out of cylinders. Jittering or displacing the points randomly should make them appear less perfect. A wood or bark texture applied as a planar image map on the *z*-axis works nicely (Figure 5-54). The finished pile of logs can be viewed in Figure 5-55.

Creating the Fire Objects

As usual, there are several methods you can use for making the fire. One of these is with volumetric effects such as voxels. Another approach is to use particles that have blobby surfaces similar to cloud or smoke objects except that the texture is different and contains more velocity and turbulence. A low-tech approach to fire can be attained by modeling a flame-like object that has an amorphous

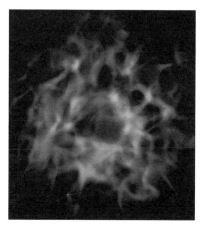

Fig. 5-54 The log texture.

Fig. 5-55 The logs after stacking and surfacing them.

Fig. 5-56 The fire voxel.

shape. Applying creative texturing and displacement mapping transforms it into a fairly good fire. The following directions explain how to make a high-tech voxel fire and a low-tech polygon or NURBS object fire.

Using Voxels to Make a Fire

Each voxel flame is attached to a single item such as a null or point. You will most likely need approximately three nulls or points for all the flames. Place these around the logs and scale them so that they almost touch one another. This makes the flames overlap.

Settings for the voxels should include a blending mode with metaballs and a small- to medium-size variation and scale. Opacity is set low, at about 10%, and density fairly high, at approximately 100%. Orange and yellow are the dominant colors with yellow set at 100% ambient. One frequency with a 200% scale and 100% amplitude is applied to the flame. A turbulence effect with a low speed of 1 will deform the flames through dynamic animation. This makes the flames flicker without hav-

ing to create any keyframes. It will take some experimenting with test animations to get the right settings for your specific project. Figure 5-56 shows a rendered image of the voxel fire. A few enhancements, such as lens flares and particles for sparks, will improve the fire later on.

Using Polygon or NURBS Objects to Make a Fire

With some creative texturing and a displacement envelope, you can create a decent low-tech fire object. Start by modeling a cube with ten segments on the *x*-, *y*-, and *z*-axes, a scale of two feet on the *x*- and *z*-axes, and three feet on the *y*-axis. Apply a radial jitter of one foot to the cube's points (Figure 5-57). Subdivide the surfaces to smooth all the edges. You may have to do this several times and triple the polys if you are working with a polygon cube. Figure 5-57 shows the three steps to creating the fire object. Name this surface OutsideFire, color it yellow, and make it two-sided if you are using polygons. Duplicate the fire object and scale it down a little on the *x*- and *z*-axes. Scale it up somewhat on the *y*-axis and place it inside the first fire

Fig. 5-57 The three steps for creating a flame object. A subdivided cube is jittered after which smoothing is applied by further subdividing it.

object so that it now looks like the image in Figure 5-58. Name this part of the fire InsideFire and color it orange with two-sided polygons. Both the inside and outside of the fire should fit on the logs; therefore, scale the logs to fit the flames. If your software consists of two modules, one for animation and the other for modeling, then save the inside and outside parts of the fire as two separate objects.

Now it is time to texture the two fire objects. The luminosity and diffuse levels for the OutsideFire object are 100%, specular and reflectivity are 0, and transparency is 100%. For the texture's transparency setting, assign a fractal noise for its texture type. The texture opacity is 100%, its texture value 0%, 1 frequency, and a contrast of 1 with a small power of .5. The texture size can be 30 cm on the x- and z-axes and 3.6 m on the y-axis. The texture amplitude falloff is 6.6% on the x- and z-axes and 20% on the y-axis. The transparency texture pattern should have a texture velocity of 45 cm set on the y-axis and 0 on the x- and z-axes.

The orange InsideFire object has the same texture settings as the outside object except that the transparency fractal noise texture size is 15 cm on the x- and z-axes and 60 cm on the y-axis. The texture amplitude falloff is 12% on the x- and z-axes and 16% on the y-axis. The texture velocity is 12.5 cm on the y-axis and 0 on the x- and z-axes.

An edge transparency with an edge threshold of 1 or 100% should complete both of the flame textures. When you test render the flame object, it should be semi-opaque and glowing yellow with orange streaks running up and through it. The last step involves deforming the flame object with a repeating displacement envelope. This will make the flames appear to flicker.

Apply a displacement map to the OutsideFire object. For texture type, use "Ripples" with 100% opacity. The displacement map's texture size is 1.2

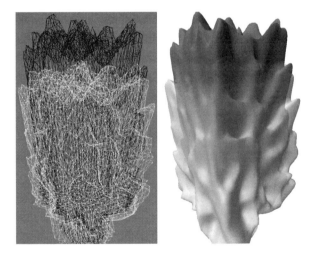

Fig. 5-58 The flame object is duplicated. The inside part of the flame is scaled smaller on the x- and z-axes and longer on the y-axis.

m on all three axes. The texture center is set to 2.25 m on the *x*-axis and 0 on the *y*- and *z*-axes. The texture amplitude is set to .15 with one wave source, 1.2 wavelength, and .06 wave speed.

The InsideFire part also has a "Ripples" displacement map applied to it. Its texture size is 2.5 m on all three axes. The texture center is 50 cm on the *x*- and *y*-axes and 0 on the *z*-axis. The texture amplitude is .25, wave source is 1, wavelength is 2.5, and wave speed is .125. The displaced flame shapes and textures can be seen in Figure 5-59.

Fig. 5-59 The inside and outside flame objects after texturing and displacing their points.

Adding Lens Flares

Lens flares that flicker make the fire appear to glow. They are an important ingredient, whether you are using voxels, particles, or modeled objects.

Create four or more yellow lens flares and place them within the flames. Make sure that they are set to fade behind objects so that they do not appear in front of the logs. You only need to turn on a central glow. For flare intensity, create an envelope like the one shown in Figure 5-60. This causes the brightness to vary throughout the animation. As depicted in the illustration, the envelope graph has a closely spaced up and down curve. The intensity amount usually stays within 43% to 50%. Be sure to set the envelope for repeat with the first and last frames having identical values. Figure 5-61 shows the inside and outside flame objects after adding lens flares.

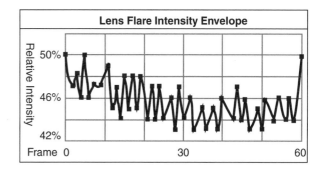

Fig. 5-60 A lens flare intensity envelope controls the brightness of the lights placed within the flame objects.

Making Particles for the Sparks

Particles acting like sparks enhance the look of the fire. To make lazy looking, spiraling sparks that slowly drift up and disappear, use an emitter or create particles from points.

If you use an emitter, set the particle speed to slow. Place the emitter under the fire, pointing up,

Fig. 5-61 Lens flares are placed within the flame objects.

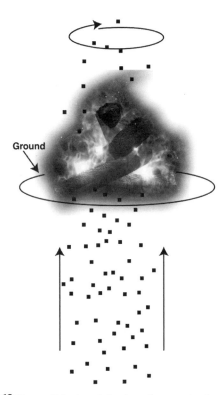

Fig. 5-62 The particles travel slowly up from under the ground and through the fire, all the while turning around the *y*-axis.

(Figure 5-63). This makes them appear hot at one point and then die out as they drift up. The texture should be placed on world coordinates on the *z*-axis. This will position the gradient according to camera placement. Thus, when the sparks drift near the top of the camera's view, they will turn black and disappear.

Sometimes tiny bursts of sparks occur inside a fire. You can create these with an emitter that has a 360-degree spread. You only need to use about twenty particles with a birth rate of approximately 3,000 particles per second. The initial speed should be set very high. They are made to die out, be affected by gravity, and have collision detection. The times when the particles begin to burst should vary. For example, one cluster can be made to explode between frames 10 and 33, while another between 60 and 83. Use however many you want and space them out accordingly. Place these little time bombs around different parts of the fire. Be

and make its size about the circumference of the fire. Only a few particles need to be emitted. Give the particles a death rate so that they disappear after drifting upward. Color them white or yellow.

Another method for creating drifting sparks is to make a cylinder and delete the surfaces, leaving only the points. Agitate the points by jittering them so that they appear to be randomly placed but still conform to the overall cylinder shape. Convert the points to polygons and assign them a name for texturing. Figure 5-62 shows how to place the particle cloud under the fire and keyframe the particles so that they slowly move up and revolve. Assign a gradient texture to the particles: the bottom, yellow; the middle, white; and the top, black

Fig. 5-63 A gradient texture is applied to the particles to make them appear brighter at first and then die out as they drift above the fire.

Fig. 5-64 A few exploding sparks are added to the fire.

sure to turn on particle and motion blur (Figure 5-64).

Creating Smoke

Smoke is an integral part of a fire and should not be neglected. In a similar manner to fire, the smoke object can be made from voxels, particles, or a NURBS/polygon object. The following directions are for creating the smoke part of the fire using voxels or a modeled object.

When preparing voxel smoke, attach the voxel to a null or a particle. You can use several nulls or particles, but usually one is plenty if the smoke particle size is set large enough. For billowing smoke, this should be about 1.2 or 120%. The size variation can be 30% while the size variation scale might be about 40. If possible, turn on a metaballs blending mode. The color should be a gradient that can be made of grays, blues, and yellows. The luminosity is 100%, opacity is 50%, and density is 100%. Be sure to specify a fractal noise. There are no frequencies, and the scale and amplitude are set at 100%. Finally, a low turbulence effect with a speed of only 0.2 will make the smoke change in a slow and lazy way.

This completes a voxel fire composed of logs, voxel flames, lens flares, drifting particles, exploding particles, and voxel smoke. As with most voxel scenes, when you render your animation, be prepared to wait a long time. Figure 5-65 shows a few frames from the final voxel fire animation, which can be viewed on the accompanying CD-ROM as CD5-65.

Creating smoke from a NURBS or polygon object is another low-tech approach similar to the fire above except that smoke form and textures differ. It may not have the realism and drama of voxels, but the advantage is that it renders much quicker.

Create a cylinder with a circumference that is about the same as the fire. Its length should run up and down on the *y*-axis and measure approximately four times as high as the fire (Figure 5-66). Place the cylinder behind the fire with most of its length below the logs. It can overlap into the fire, but should not appear in front of the logs. The top of the smoke cylinder should be out of camera view. If you model a polygon cylinder, make sure it is double-sided.

The surface of the smoke cylinder is similar to the one on the fire objects. Assign a medium to light gray shade to the cylinder and set its luminosity to 40%, diffuse level 100%, specular 0, reflectivity 0 and transparency 95%. For its texture type, use fractal noise with three frequencies, a contrast of one, and a black texture color.

Under transparency, use another fractal noise for its texture type, with a texture value of about 40%, three frequencies, and a high contrast of three. Assign a texture velocity to the fractal noise. This is only on the *y*-axis with a very slow speed, perhaps two centimeters. Assign an edge transparency with an edge threshold of 1 or 100%.

Make test renderings to check its appearance. It should be a semi-opaque, dingy gray with dark gray streaks running upward.

During the animation, the smoke cylinder should be moved up gradually on the *y*-axis. To make a billowing effect, rotate the cylinder about 3 degrees on the bank or *z*-axis at frame 30. Move to frame 60 and rotate it minus 3 degrees on the bank or *z*-axis. Continue doing this every 30 frames. Add force and drag to the cylinder object so that it appears to swirl lazily upward. In a program like LightWave 3D, this means assigning the Inertia or Lazy Points plug-in to displace the cylinder's points.

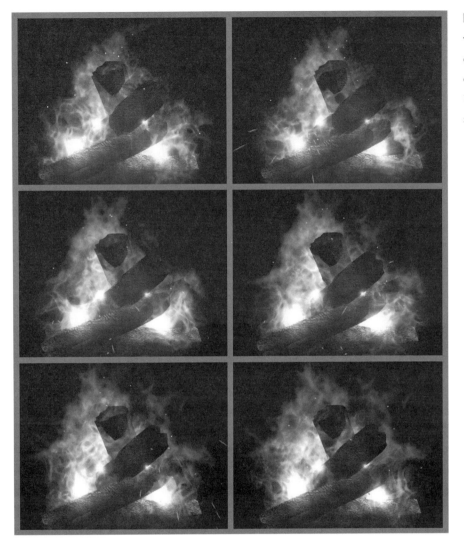

Fig. 5-65 Images from the final voxel fire animation composed of logs, voxel flames, lens flares, drifting particle sparks, exploding particle sparks, and voxel smoke.

Fig. 5-66 A cylinder serves as the smoke object.

When you test the animation, the cylinder should appear to slowly undulate up like a snake. Figure 5-67 illustrates one frame from the object fire animation with logs, flame-shaped objects, lens flares, drifting particles, and the cylinder smoke object. It can be found with the voxel fire on the CD-ROM as CD5-67. A large color image from the animation can also be viewed. It is labeled CD5-67b.

Electrical Effects

Creating electrical effects, like lightning bolts or electrical arcs, is a much easier process than one would think. The electricity object requires minimal modeling skills and the animation is simple and straightforward. Granted, there are plug-ins and other methods for creating electrical effects. The following directions should work for most software packages.

Fig. 5-67 A scene from the final object fire.

Modeling the Electric Object

Create a spline with 100 points. This line has to be surfaced and have the quality of showing up in a rendering. One way to achieve this is to make a single point, convert it to a polygon, and extrude it with a numerical setting of one hundred segments. The result of this will be a line with one hundred points on it (Figure 5-68).

Give the surface a name such as Bolt and assign it a blue or yellow color. The next step is to animate the bolt.

Using Displacement Mapping

Assign a displacement map to the one hundred-point line so that it deforms in a haphazard manner during the animation. For the displacement map, select a fractal bump texture. Set texture size to 10 mm on the x-, y-, and z-axes. The texture amplitude is .05 with three frequencies. A texture velocity of 1 millimeter on the x- and y-axes and

10 millimeters on the z-axis should also be set. Position your camera so that you can see the side of the electrical bolt. Scroll through the animation and you should see the lightning bolt change its shape. It will most likely resemble a random jagged line like the one in Figure 5-69.

Surfacing the Lightning Bolt Object

The quality of the electrical object should be flat and glowing. Therefore, give it 100% luminosity. Diffuse, specular, reflectivity, and transparency levels should be 0%. Finally, apply a 100% glow to the bolt. Figure 5-70 shows a rendering of the surfaced electrical energy.

Adding a Skeleton

Aside from the displacement map, bones deform the bolt shape and also bring about a higher degree of control during the animation. You can add,

Fig. 5-68 A lightning bolt is made from a single line with about one hundred points on it.

Fig. 5-69 After applying a displacement map to the line, it starts to resemble the haphazard appearance of lightning.

Fig. 5-70 The lightning bolt after surfacing and applying glow. The image was rendered with "motion blur" on.

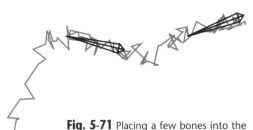

Fig. 5-71 Placing a few bones into the bolt adds an extra degree of control for deforming the lightning.

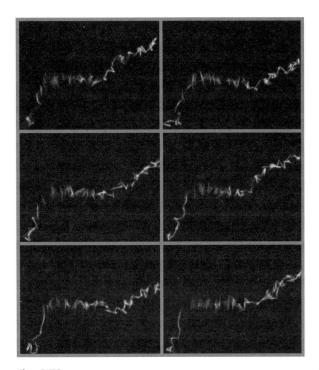

Fig. 5-72 Rendered frames from the final electricity animation.

however, as many bones as you want to the lightning object, but usually three is enough. Two placed at both ends and one in the middle should complete the skeleton. Rather than making child bones from one parent, create each bone independent from the others. After activating the skeleton, rotate and move the bones so that they resemble the ones in Figure 5-71.

Animating the Lightning

You can keyframe the bones in various positions and gyrations to make an energetic effect. After setting a number of keyframes, you may decide to turn on repeat behavior for each bone. When you render the animation, be sure to turn on "anti-aliasing," "motion blur," and "dithered motion blur." This will give the bolt a gauzy look (Figure 5-72).

To enhance the animation, you may want to try adding particles for sparks, create some clouds, plasma bursts, and so on. Another option is to make a few other bolts and combine all of them in one animation. A few electrical animations can be viewed on the CD-ROM as CD5-72a and CD5-72b.

PART II

Advanced 3D Modeling

rebuild type. Be sure to specify approximately thirty points for the number of spans.

It is usually a good idea to loft the curves as you continue to draw or duplicate and move them (Figure 6-5). This will give you a general idea of how it will turn out and thus avoid unpleasant surprises. If your software has a "history" option like Maya, Softimage, or Rhinoceros, you can move the second curve's points to deform the mesh surface until you are satisfied with the results. If you are using a three-dimensional head to model from, try templating it and using the "X-ray Shade" option for the lofted/skinned section. This will let you see the relationship of the loft to the template as you deform the original curve. Another useful tool in Maya is the "Layer Editor." You can use it to keep the curves and the three-dimensional head in separate layers, which in turn, can be hidden or templated. When you are finished refining the curves, you can delete the temporary, lofted/skinned section, leaving only the splines.

Resume drawing, copying, and moving points on the newly duplicated curves. Beginning with the third or fourth curve, you will most likely have to shape the wings around the nostrils. Many 3D artists consider this part to be one of the most difficult sections of the face. This is especially true when trying to form the hollow at the corner of the wings. Some artists prefer to model that section separately, and then use a fillet blend to join it to the rest of the nose. If you prefer to keep the entire nose as a part of the overall mesh, then shape the hollow at the wings by keeping two of the adjoining curves close together at this point. Remember to loft/skin parts of the curves and make corrections accordingly.

As you continue drawing, duplicating, and moving curves, check the spans in the U and V

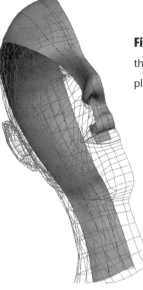

Fig. 6-5 Editing the curves on the partial loft against a templated three-dimensional head.

surface direction. The connecting spans can be seen after lofting/skinning sections. They should flow smoothly without any severe angles. You can usually spot areas that will cause you problems later on. These are the ones where the curves lack a gentle turn. Figure 6-6 illustrates the head when almost all of the curves, except the ones for the jaw, have been drawn.

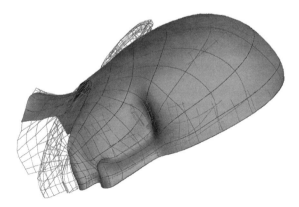

Fig. 6-6 Edit the points so that the curves in both the U and V directions flow smoothly.

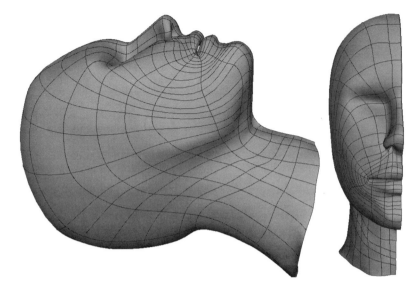

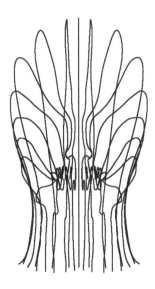

Fig. 6-7 The finished half face. Note the directions of the U and V curves. The placement of points on each curve determine the success of your connecting lines.

Fig. 6-8 Curves are duplicated and mirrored for the other half.

When you start to shape the curves of the cheeks, the number of points that you needed for facial detail start to accumulate in a smaller area. This often increases the likelihood that the surface becomes bumpier. The side of the face leading to the undersurface of the jaw can be one of the more difficult areas to form. The process for creating curves and correcting surfaces is one of the more tedious aspects of modeling a head. The extra time that you spend on this will save you a great amount of labor after the final loft. Figure 6-7 shows all of the curves for half the head.

Once you finish making all the curves for half of the face, loft/skin the entire set. At this point, it would be a good idea to tweak the original curves with "history" on to smooth out any bumps on the mesh.

Duplicating and Mirroring the Curves

When you are satisfied with the curves and the placement of their points, select all of them, except

for the middle ones, and duplicate them. While the copied curves are still selected, mirror them so that they are located on the other side of the face (Figure 6-8). Starting with the top middle curve, select each of them in a clockwise or counterclockwise direction. Loft/skin all of them with the "close" option on.

At this point, you may want to fix any trouble spots by manipulating the original curves or by working directly with the mesh, using either control vertices or the hull. Shaping the mesh with the points on the hull allows you to see if any hull points and lines are out of position from the norm. If you are working with Maya, you can use Artisan to smooth parts of the mesh. Although this may work for some, others have found this method difficult to control because points can become severely displaced. Since you are working with two sides of the face, you will have to select corresponding points on both right and left surfaces. Most of the time, you can use the "move" tool, but sometimes, when two points need to be brought closer together or farther apart, the "scale" tool will have to be used.

Creating the Eye Area

Some 3D artists prefer to model the eye out of the same face mesh. The method described here, which uses curves that originate inside the mouth, makes it difficult to do. The curves around the eye are turned almost 90 degrees, making it just about impossible to form the eyelids. A more sensible approach is to cut holes for the eye sockets, model the eyelids separately from the mesh, and then blend them to the face. The advantage to making the eye area separate from the face is that you have the freedom to apply extensive detail without worrying about making the rest of the face too complicated. Another bonus to separating eyelids is that the round forms follow the contour of the *Orbicularis Oculi*, the circular muscle circumscribing the eye. The face remains easier to animate because it does not have the extra isoparms/splines that would have made it necessary to form eyelids.

One warning about using trim blends. When you fillet blend a surface, it continually updates because it uses construction history. As the character is animated, a slight popping or flicker can occur in the blends, which is seen when rendered. It is most visible if direct lighting and a smooth texture are applied. Blends can also slow down your computer's response time. The directions given here try to limit the use of blends to areas of the face that do not deform too much during the animation process.

The first step to making eyelids is to cut holes for the eye sockets. Create an oval with approximately fifteen points. Place the oval above and in front of the eye socket region (Figure 6-9).

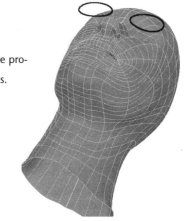

Fig. 6-9 Two ovals are projected for the eyeholes.

Duplicate and mirror the oval for the other side of the face. Select the first oval and the head, and then project the curve on it. Do the same with the other oval. The head should now have two ovals projected on it in the eye socket orbits. If there are any on the back of the head, delete them. Use a trim tool to delete the projected ovals. The head should now have two holes cut into it for eye sockets (Figure 6-10).

Select the original oval that you projected on the head. Duplicate and shape it into an eyehole

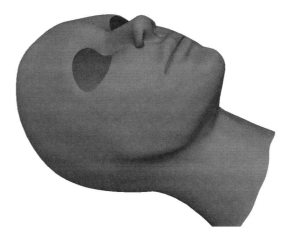

Fig. 6-10 Use the projected curves to trim holes for the eyes.

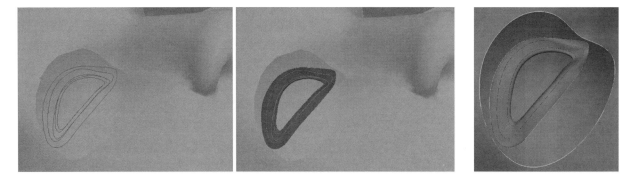

Fig. 6-11 The eyelid curves are lofted/skinned.

Fig. 6-12 Preparing to fillet blend the eyelids to the eye socket.

that defines the outline of the eyelids. Continue duplicating and shaping the ovals so that they look somewhat like Figure 6-11. Select and loft the eyelid ovals.

Once you have the eyelid portion of the face, duplicate it and mirror it for the other eye socket. Fillet blend the edge of the eyehole to the edge of the lofted/skinned eyelid part (Figure 6-12). Do the same to the other eye socket. The eyelids should now blend in with the rest of the face (Figure 6-13). The next step is to model the ear.

Modeling an Ear

The ear is one of the most complicated objects to model. Its convoluted cartilage and its varying elevations and concavities present quite a challenge.

It is best to think of the ear as a flower. The initial curves project outward from the inner part to curve around the outer rim and end at the head (Figures 6-14 to 6-16). Each curve should have approximately eleven points. You can duplicate curves or draw them individually and then rebuild them with six spans and a degree of five. This should give you the right amount of points for most of the detail (Figure 6-17). You can also use

the ear templates on the enclosed CD for reference.

Loft all of the curves. If you have a "history" option, adjust the curves until you are satisfied with the shape of the ear (Figure 6-18). The isoparm/spline or curve that connects the ends of the original curves is the one that is projected onto

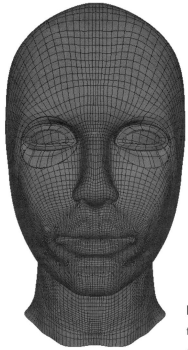

Fig. 6-13 The fillet/blend eyelid curves.

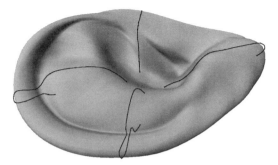

Fig. 6-14 The first four curves for the ear against a shaded template.

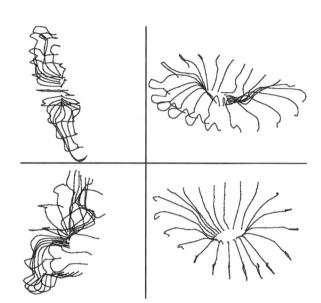

Fig. 6-17 Four views of all the ear curves.

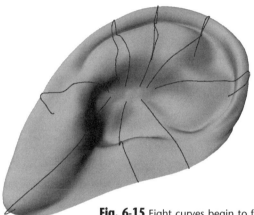

Fig. 6-15 Eight curves begin to form the inner and outer bowl of the ear.

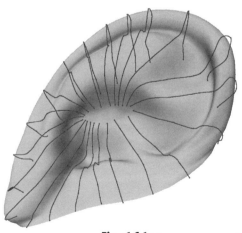

Fig. 6-16 More curves are added for extra detail.

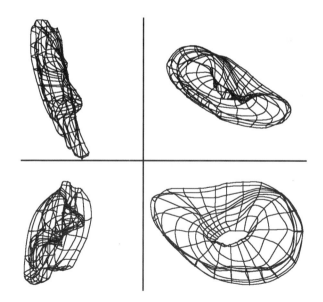

Fig. 6-18 After lofting/skinning the curves and keeping history on, adjust them to shape the ear.

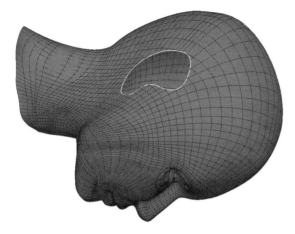

Fig. 6-19 Trim a hole for the ear blend.

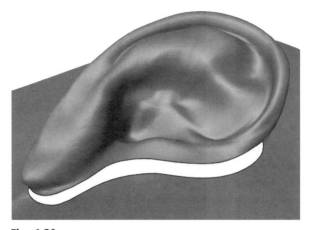

Fig. 6-20 Select the isoparms/splines to blend between.

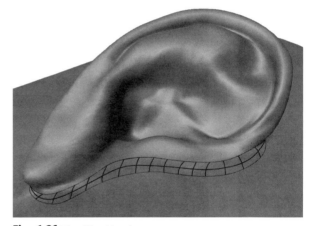

Fig. 6-21 The fillet blend.

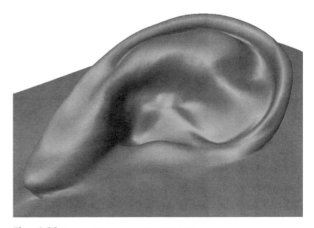

Fig. 6-22 The finished ear after fillet/blend.

the head in the next step. It should only be altered by manipulating the curve with "history" on.

There are two options available after modeling the ear. Some prefer to stick it against the head to avoid using fillet blends. As mentioned before, the reason they refrain from using blends is that fillet blends take extra time to update during the rendering process and there is noticeable flashing that occurs with blends. Because the area around the ears does not really become deformed during facial animation, it should not matter if you use blends to attach the ears. If you decide to use fillet blends, follow the next step.

Place the ear slightly away but close to the head. Select a connecting isoparm/spline or curve on the outermost area of the ear closest to the head. Duplicate it and enlarge it somewhat. Hide everything except the head and the curve to be projected. Select this enlarged duplicated curve and the head itself. Project the curve on the head and trim away the projected portion to make a hole in the head where the ear will be attached (Figure 6-19).

Make the ear visible and select the first isoparm/spline that is closest to the head. To make the blend between this isoparm/spline and the head, you now need to select the outline of the hole that you trimmed in the head (Figure 6-20). Create the fillet blend (Figures 6-21 and 6-22).

Adding Eyes

Primitive spheres can be used for the eyeballs. Rather than trying to map a texture with an iris and pupil to the sphere, you may decide to make a separate iris for the texture map. The iris model can be made by selecting a horizontal isoparm/ spline from the primitive and then detaching the surface. The iris pattern can be scanned or created in an image manipulation program through the skillful use of filters (Figures 6-23 and 6-24). For a more realistic eye, see Figures 6-40 and 6-41.

Modeling the Teeth and Gums

You can model the teeth with just a few ovals. Once these are lofted/skinned, close up the ends that can be seen. The other ends that are to be embedded in the gums can be left open because they will not be visible. You can get away with modeling only one tooth and then reshaping it into the five or six other types. Half of the upper and lower teeth are shaped, duplicated, and mirrored for the other side of the mouth (Figure 6-25).

The gums are very simple. A NURBS sphere is flattened and made concave for the mouth cavity. This sphere is placed at the root of the teeth so that it encloses all of them. Once it is placed against the teeth, it may need to be adjusted somewhat.

Another Method for Modeling a NURBS Head

A different way of modeling a NURBS head is to start the curves at the top of the head. The first

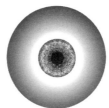

Fig. 6-23 The iris is relatively small compared to the eyeball.

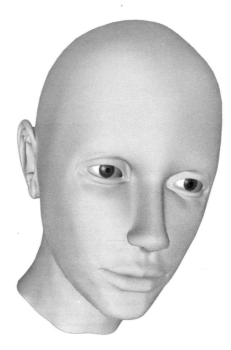

Fig. 6-24 After texturing the eye, duplicate it and move it into the other eye socket.

Fig. 6-25 The upper teeth and gums and the entire set of teeth and gums.

Fig. 6-26 The curves start at the top of the head.

curve defines the profile. It begins at the crown of the skull and curves down around the forehead, nose, lips, chin, and neck. The curve could continue down to the torso's waist or even to the feet. If you try to model the head and torso or the entire body at the same time, then be prepared spend a lot of time tweaking points all over the place. Some prefer to concentrate on one part at a time; therefore, they model the head, torso, legs, arms, feet, and hands separately.

Figure 6-26 illustrates the rest of the vertical curves. This method works well for shaping eyelids, but for the most part, the curves are not facing in the general direction of the head muscles. You also find extra isoparms/splines around the corners of the mouth, which can result in creasing. The jawbone is more difficult to model because the curves are not naturally aligned with the direction of the mandibula.

Once all of the curves for either the right or left side of the head are formed, then they can be duplicated, mirrored, and lofted/skinned. Another approach is to loft half the head. The "loft" option remains open instead of going all the way around and closing the half head. The lofted/skinned head

is then duplicated and mirrored. The two halves of the head are aligned or attached to each other. Figure 6-27 shows a head with the two halves aligned. Extra isoparms/splines may show up where the two halves are joined. Connecting two halves will also work for the first NURBS modeling technique.

The next part discusses modeling a head with polygons. As mentioned above, the main disadvantage to polygons is that if they are not split into many smaller ones, they will not deform or render as smoothly as NURBS. On the other hand, many artists prefer to work with polygons when creating models that have a great amount of detail. This is especially true when modeling faces, hands, feet, and so on. The ability to split polygons anywhere and to weld points together easily gives polygons a distinct advantage over NURBS.

Modeling a Polygon Head

Although polygons have some disadvantages, they also have some compelling advantages. One of the main ones is that extra polys can be inserted into areas that require more detail. NURBS and splines,

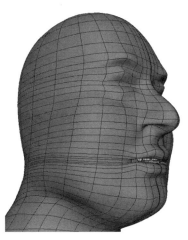

Fig. 6-27 A lofted/skinned head with vertical curves.

on the other hand, run throughout the mesh. When you insert extra isoparms/splines, they appear from the beginning to the end of the mesh. In other words, if an isoparm/spline is inserted at the eyelid, this extra curve will flow all the way down to the base of the neck. If your software is capable of modeling with hierarchical b-splines (h-splines), this should not be a problem. As mentioned in an earlier chapter, h-splines allow you to have one mesh with varying levels of detail.

Another plus for polygons is that isolated areas can be selected and worked on while hiding all the rest. This is usually not possible with spline or NURBS meshes because they are one connected unit.

Some people may find it easier to texture polygon surfaces. Rather than trying to work with complex parametric mapping, they can simply select specific polygons and assign a name and texture to them.

Welding points to connect polygon surfaces can yield seamless models that do not have to update like NURBS models with fillet blends.

Although there are many techniques for polygon modeling, one of the best and a favorite method for this author is to use the same approach discussed previously for modeling a NURBS head. Vertical curves are used that begin on the inside of the mouth and radiate outward to follow the contours of the features and finally end at the base of the neck (Figure 6-28). The lines again follow the direction of the muscles. If you wish to model the entire figure out of a spline cage, refer to the last part of chapter 8. It tells how to complete the body from the finished spline cage head.

The Spline Cage Method

To start, you may want to load several image files of the front and side of the head. An image of the

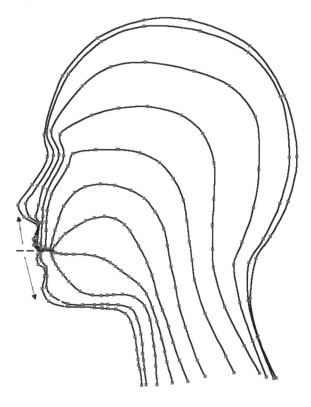

Fig. 6-28 All the splines originate on the inside of the mouth and radiate outward to end at the base of the neck. The dashed line indicates the beginning of each spline.

top of the head is also useful but not as important. You might also decide to use an existing model of a head and then shape the curves around it. Some head templates and models of heads can be found on the accompanying CD.

Beginning with the first curve, start drawing from the inside of the mouth, curve it over the top lip, around the nose, forehead and skull, and end at the base of the neck (Figure 6-29). This curve is located in the middle of the head and forms the outline of the head's profile. The side view is used most often for this outline. Once you are finished with this curve, you can either delete extra points

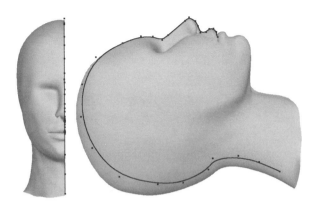

Fig. 6-29 The first curve defines the profile and middle of the head. It starts on the inside of the mouth and ends at the base of the neck.

or add some around the mouth, nose, and eye areas. In total, you should have approximately twenty-four to thirty points on the curve. Most should be clustered around the lip, nose, and mouth. Since you might duplicate this curve to make all the rest, you do not want too many points to push and pull around. On the other hand, it is best not to have to worry about inserting points later for extra detail. Most modeling packages that implement lofting or skinning work best when each curve has the same number of points. This is also true when making a spline cage. All the points on each of the splines are manually selected in the proper order and connected as cross-sectional spans. Therefore, if any curves have more points than the others, it is difficult to find a way to connect these extra points.

The total number of curves for one-half of the face should not be greater than thirteen. The face in Figure 6-30 uses eleven splines and twenty-four points on each spline. If you can manage to keep the points and curves to a minimum, you will find

it much easier to animate the face later. Surfaces remain smoother when they have fewer points and curves.

If you plan to use copies of the original curves, the next step is to duplicate the first set. Rather than moving an entire curve away from the original, it is better to select individual points. These should be moved parallel to the first curve's points. Copy the second curve and move its points to continue shaping the outline of the facial features and skull. If your software has layers, then it might be easier to copy the first curve, paste it into another layer, make the first layer visible underneath it, and move the points on this second spline. Once the second curve is completed, you can paste it

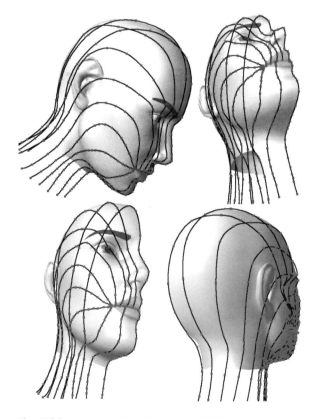

Fig. 6-30 The curves that define the facial features generally follow the direction of the muscles.

back into the first layer. You can get an idea of how most of the curves and points are placed by studying Figure 6-30.

If you are using a three-dimensional head to model from, use the wire preview window to move individual points according to the wireframe's surface. The wire preview can be rotated until the selected point is visible against the edge of the template's surface. This will let you see the relationship of your points to the curves on the mesh.

Duplicate and move the new splines. Detailed areas like those around the wings of the nose and the nostril can be saved for later. For now, make the basic outlines of each section. Later on, polygons can be subdivided and their points moved for all the minute parts.

Check the flow of the curves so that they run evenly in both directions. The connecting spans are viewed by temporarily selecting points in the right order and making a connecting curve between the spline. Figure 6-31 illustrates how you can select points in order and then connect them. Smooth out any severe angles.

After a while, you should notice that the duplicated curves become shorter because they no longer have to cover as great an area. Subsequently, the number of points on these curves squeezes together into a tighter space. Points that are closer together can make the surface bumpier. This type of problem can occur around the cheeks, mouth, and chin. Even though correcting individual points can be tedious, in the end it will save you time.

Once you finish making all of the curves for half of the face, connect each set of points (Figure 6-31). It is very important to keep every section of the connected splines to no more than four points at each corner. As long as each section has either three or four points at the corners, you should not

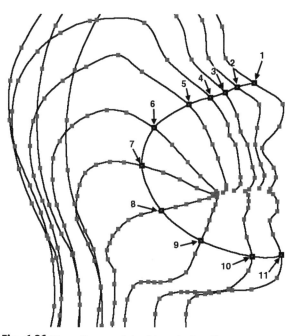

Fig. 6-31 The splines are joined by selecting the cross-sectional points in the right order and making them into a curve. The connecting spans will create a spline cage.

have any problems later. Any part that has fewer than three or more than four points will most likely not surface correctly, resulting in a polygon mesh with holes.

Be sure to select each point in the right order. When they are selected, make a curve from them. This spline will connect the original curves. Continue selecting the cross-sectional points and making curves from them. As soon as you are finished making all the connecting splines, you should have a spline cage that looks somewhat like Figure 6-32. At this point, it would be a good idea to tweak the points on the cage to smooth out any bumps. Compare the spline cage to your templates to see how the points match up.

When you are satisfied with all of the curves and the placement of their points, patch the cage

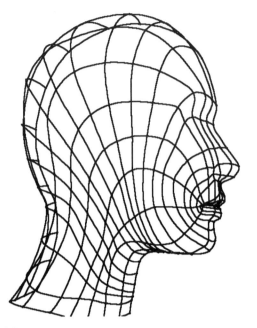

Fig. 6-32 The resulting spline cage. Notice how the cross sections follow the contours of the facial muscles.

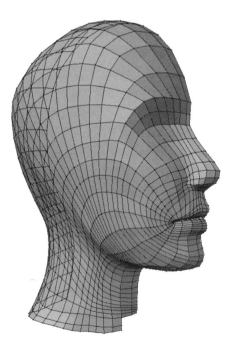

Fig. 6-33 Once the spline cage is patched, the form becomes a solid polygon model.

with a polygon mesh (Figure 6-33). This makes a polygon mesh on top of the spline cage. Software like LightWave 3D uses an AutoPatcher plug-in. The subdivision level should be low so that you can edit parts without worrying too much about detail. A subdivision level of one will give you a basic form that can be edited. Higher subdivision levels would make it too difficult to shape details because this generates many small polygons. You can always subdivide polys later. It is easier to do that than to go back to a simpler shape.

The polygon model should allow you to see a shaded preview. This makes it easier to fix any trouble spots. At this point, you are no longer working with the spline cage, but rather directly with the polygon mesh. You can begin to add points and split polys for details like nostrils, lips, and so on. It would also be a good idea to save the spline cage separately from the model. In the future, you can use it to create other types of faces by changing its basic structure.

Creating the Eye Area

Since the original curves start in the mouth, they are not really facing in the right direction for modeling the eyelids. In order for the lines to follow the direction of the *Orbicularis Oculi,* the circular muscle circumscribing the eye, it makes more sense to cut a hole for the eye. The eyelids are modeled separately and then welded into the eyehole.

Figure 6-34 shows the area around the eye to be modeled. It can be made from a spline cage or from a series of concentric points that are connected to form polygons. Be sure to add an extra row of points for the thickness of the eyelid. These form a shape that extends into the eyeball.

The next step is to cut holes for the eye sockets. Select the points around the perimeter of the eye-

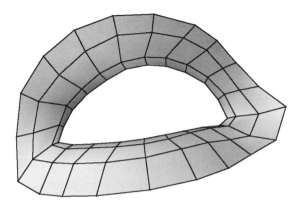

Fig. 6-34 The area around the eyeball is modeled separately.

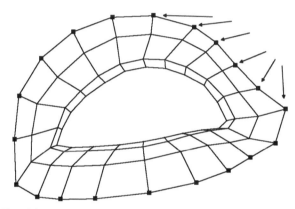

Fig. 6-35 Points along the perimeter of the eyelid mesh are selected and copied.

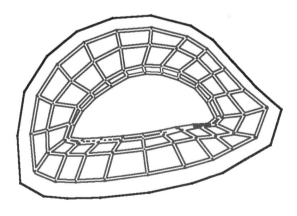

Fig. 6-36 After copying and pasting the points into another layer, they are made into a polygon, which is then enlarged.

lid shape that you just modeled (Figure 6-35). Copy and paste the points into another layer. Select the points in order and make a polygon from them. Make the eyelid model visible underneath this layer. Enlarge the polygon somewhat like the one shown in Figure 6-36.

Make the head mesh visible in the front layer and hide all the polygons except for those around the eye socket. Make the eye socket polygon visible underneath the layer with the face (Figure 6-37). Use a 2D drilling operation to cut a hole for the eye socket.

After drilling the eye socket hole, weld any extra stray points around the opening. Paste the previously modeled eyelid object into the layer containing the head (Figure 6-38).

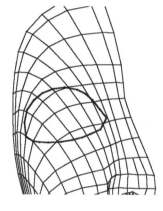

Fig. 6-37 The outline of the eye socket is drilled onto the face mesh and cut away.

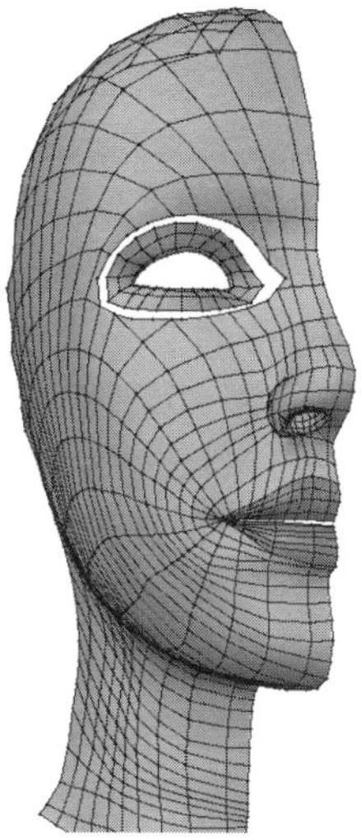

Fig. 6-38 Once the eye socket hole is cut out, paste the eyelid model into the face mesh layer.

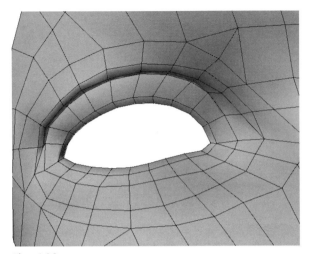

Fig. 6-39 The upper eyelid folds under, creating a line that is modeled by splitting the polygons with extra points.

Select the points around the perimeter of the eyelid object and the edge of the eye socket hole. Create connecting polygons between these two objects so that the eyelids are now part of the same mesh as the face (Figure 6-39). Connect or weld any extra points so that you only have three- or four-sided polygons.

Figure 6-39 shows how the eyelid folds under creating a thick line. It is important to model this

part of the eyelid because it gives a lot of character to the face. Insert extra points in an oval direction around the eyelid, select them in order, and then split the polygons. Once you have several extra, half-oval lines on the lid, you can move them forward and back to form the eyelid fold. Approximately three or four sets of semi-oval lines make up this form. The next step is to model the eyeball.

Making an Eyeball

The eyeball can be a simple primitive ball or sphere. Some prefer to invert the labeled iris surface and form a concave shape on the white eyeball (Figure 6-40). If you decide to do this, make a hole in the middle of the iris for the pupil. The pupil appears black because the inner surface of the white eyeball is colored black. You can select the back half of the eyeball and flip the polygons inward, name the surface, and make it black. Others prefer to keep the iris convex and select polygons in the middle for the pupil surface. In either case, model a transparent cover for the entire eyeball (Figure 6-41). An eye socket should also be modeled. By selecting the points around

Concave Iris

Hole For Pupil

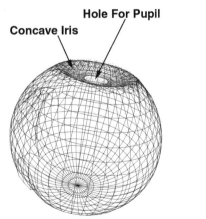

Transparent Cover

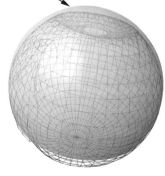

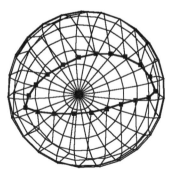

Fig. 6-40 Making the iris concave adds to the illusion of the iris having depth.

Fig. 6-41 A transparent cover makes the eye appear glossy and wet.

Fig. 6-42 The eye socket shares the same points as the inside of the eyelid. It is slightly larger than the eyeball.

Liquid Shape in Eye

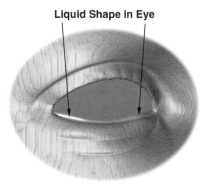

Fig. 6-43 A long, thin shape that runs along the bottom eyelid can simulate liquid in the eye.

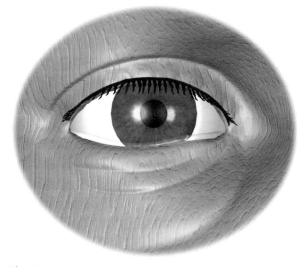

Fig. 6-44 The finished eye.

the inside lid, copying and pasting them into another layer, and then selecting and making a polygon from them, you can proceed to either extrude and reshape the socket or attach polygons to a larger version of a partial eyeball (Figure 6-42).

Another small detail that can be added is the pink membrane in the corner of the eye. This can be modeled from a squashed half sphere. If you want to show a little liquid at the bottom of the eye, then model the shape and attach it to the points along the inside of the eyelid (Figure 6-43).

Through the skillful use of shaders and textures, you should be able to get a fairly realistic eye. Be

sure to give the transparent eye cover a high specular level and glossiness. The liquid in the eye object can have about a 70% transparency and a fractal bump map. The iris can have a real iris texture. Figure 6-44 shows an example of a finished eye.

Extrude Method

The extrude method subdivides the face into vertical slices. The head is built one section at a time. Compared to other methods, which require you to model a face one point or polygon at a time, it is much quicker. This technique is also more accurate and less haphazard than modeling a head out of a cube or sphere by pushing and pulling points.

Before starting, you might want to use a 2D or a 3D template in another layer as a guide. Because it is always a good idea to model in real-world measurements, size the template head to approximately 8.7 inches or 22 cm from the top of the head to the bottom of the chin.

In the side view, draw a series of points to outline the profile of the face (Figure 6-45). Select the dots in order and make a polygon from them (Figure 6-46).

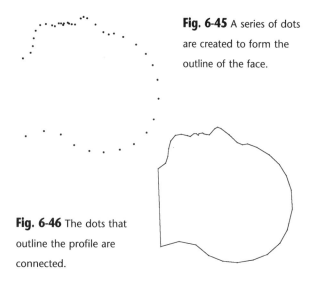

Fig. 6-45 A series of dots are created to form the outline of the face.

Fig. 6-46 The dots that outline the profile are connected.

135

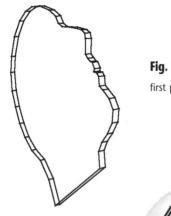

Fig. 6-47 Extruding the first polygon.

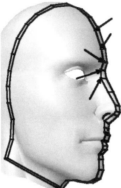

Fig. 6-48 The extruded form against a shaded view of the template. The points are dragged in to form the second profile.

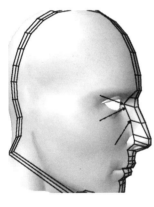

Fig. 6-49 The points along the second extrusion are moved to outline the inner contours of the face.

Fig. 6-50 As each section is extruded, its points are dragged to form the shape of the head.

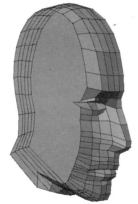

Select the large polygon and extrude it to about the width of half the nose (Figure 6-47). The extrusion should be about 0.26 inches or 6.6 mm.

Select the points along the newly extruded profile and drag them in to follow the contours of the face. Depending on the extrusion direction, shape the profile of the features and the skull located to the right or left of the original profile (Figure 6-48).

Select the second large polygon that outlines the inner part of the head's profile. This is the one formed from the points that you dragged inward. Extrude this polygon about the same amount as the last one.

Select the points along this newly formed profile and drag them in to outline the features that fall along this axis (Figure 6-49). You are now shaping the third profile.

Once you are finished shaping these new contours, select the new, large polygon. This is the one formed from the third contour. Extrude this polygon to make the next slice of the face. Move the points along this new contour so that they are placed against the features of the face. At this point, you are most likely forming the side of the nose, middle to end of the lips, chin, and so on.

Continue to select the newly formed large polygon profiles, extrude them, and shape their points (Figure 6-50). Once you are past the features of the face like the eye, nose, and lips, you can make larger extrusions because you only need smaller polys for details. Try not to fuss too much with detail. You only need to form the general features. Later, you can come back to work on the minute parts like eyelids, nostrils, and so on.

As the extrusions approach the ends of the face near the ear, you should notice a compression of the polygons. Since the same number of polys is moved into a more limited area, they are smaller in scale. You can now start to merge some of these smaller polygons. Once they are unified, you can delete their extra points. Other polygons have a tendency to become stretched during the point-dragging process. These have to be split into smaller ones.

Once you make it to about the same point as shown in Figure 6-51, delete all the large profile polygons. Since you will no longer extrude them, they no longer have any use. Click on the function to automatically merge all the points. This welds all the points that occupy the same spaces and ensure that the face is one seamless mesh of polygons.

You can now connect all the points that form the perimeter around the empty space near the ear (white area in Figure 6-51). Once the points are connected to make a large polygon, subdivide this into smaller ones and move their points to finish the side of the face (Figure 6-52).

Adding details around the eyes, nose, lips, and so on completes the head. The surface can be named and a smoothing algorithm applied to it (Figure 6-53). Refer to Figures 6-14 through 6-18 for modeling the ear. If you want to see what the final head will look like, duplicate, mirror, and merge the middle of the head points.

The Single Polygon Method

Those who want the ultimate degree of control when modeling will find that using single polygons is the preferred method. This requires that one polygon at a time be drawn until the entire face is completed. The approach is similar to creating a mosaic in three-dimensional virtual space. It is also a most time-consuming and tedious technique.

If you are not familiar with using a single polygon creation tool, it is probably better to start mod-

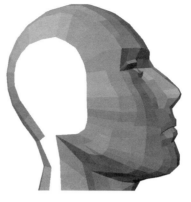

Fig. 6-51 The hole at the side of the face (white area) is subdivided into smaller polygons.

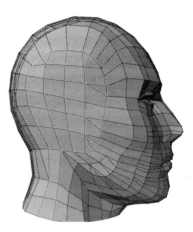

Fig. 6-52 Once the hole is subdivided, its points are pulled out for the final overall shape.

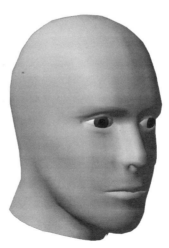

Fig. 6-53 The final head with details and smoothing applied. The ears are added later.

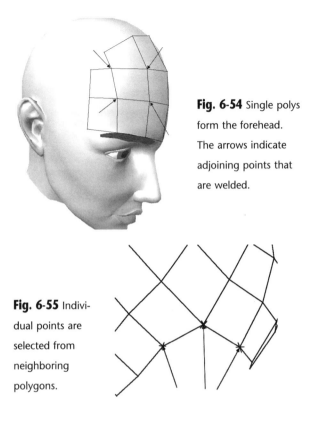

Fig. 6-54 Single polys form the forehead. The arrows indicate adjoining points that are welded.

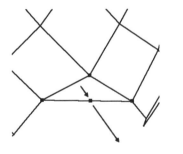

Fig. 6-55 Individual points are selected from neighboring polygons.

Fig. 6-56 Once the triangle is formed, a point is inserted and moved to the right location.

Fig. 6-57 Single points are created for the facial details and connected to make polygons.

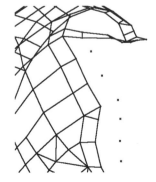

eling a broad area like the forehead. Using a pen tool, start clicking to form a rectanglular polygon. Make your polygons fairly large (Figure 6-54) and do not worry if the polygons are non-planar. Later, they can be subdivided into smaller triangles.

Using two- or three-dimensional templates as guides, move the newly created polygon into the right spot next to the previously created one. After you draw each poly, select both of the rectangle's overlapping points and those of its neighbor and weld them (Figure 6-54). The idea is to create one continuous mesh of polygons with shared corner points.

Moving across the forehead, create the polygons for the top, skull, sides, and back. Because the face will require more detail and thus smaller polygons, you might want to save it for last.

Rather than constantly creating new polys from scratch, you can select three points from adjoining polygons and make a triangle from them. Figure 6-55 illustrates how you can select points from two polygons. A fourth point is inserted on this three-sided poly. This extra point is then moved into the right position (Figure 6-56). This saves you time because you do not have to weld points or move more than one point into the right spot.

Facial characteristics are modeled last because they require more attention to detail. Sometimes, it is better to copy points or create new ones, position them to follow the muscles of the face, and then connect them to make polygons (Figure 6-57). Working with points allows you to work at the minutest level of detail. Specific forms like facial features require this type of attention.

Forming the Eyelids and Eye Socket

The eyelids and eye socket are modeled fairly easily using the polygon mesh. You can use your own

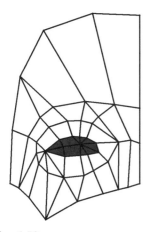

Fig. 6-58 Polygons shown in gray are selected and deleted.

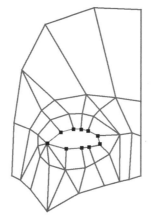

Fig. 6-59 The points around the eye opening are moved according to the template.

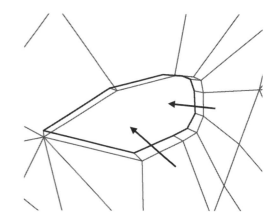

Fig. 6-60 After making a polygon out of the points, extrude it back a little to form the lids.

2D template or the 3D templates on the CD-ROM folder labeled Detailed Parts found in the chapter 6, 7, 8 folder.

To make the eye opening, select the polygons located in that area and delete them (Figure 6-58). Select the points around the eye opening (Figure 6-59) and move them according to your template to make them large enough. Now make a polygon out of the points. Select this polygon and extrude it back a little similar to the one shown in Figure 6-60. To further shape the thickness of the eyelid,

reduce the size of the extruded polygon in the front view so that it looks somewhat like the one shown in Figure 6-61. Use the top view to further refine the inner and outer parts of the eyelid.

The next step is to form the eye socket. If your software has layers, place the eyeball in another layer behind the one containing the eyelid part. It should fit snugly against the inner eyelid. Working in the eyelid layer, extrude the polygon forming the inner eyelid back a little past the eyeball (Figure 6-62). To make it easier to select the eye socket,

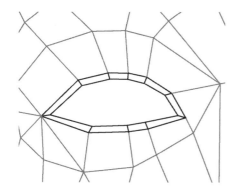

Fig. 6-61 Move the points on the inner and outer lid to match your template.

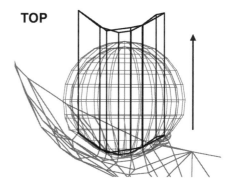

Fig. 6-62 Begin forming the eye socket by selecting the inner part of the eyelid and extruding it back past the eyeball.

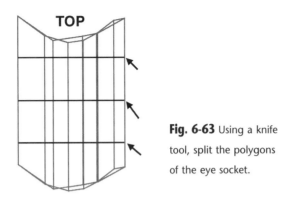

Fig. 6-63 Using a knife tool, split the polygons of the eye socket.

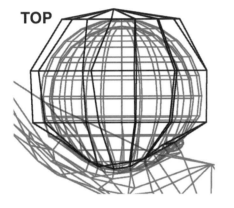

Fig. 6-64 With the "scale" and "move" tools, shape the eye socket to fit around the eyeball.

name the newly extruded polygons and flip them to face inward. You should only be able to see the inside of the eye socket.

In the top or side view, split or subdivide the polygons on the eye socket (Figure 6-63). A knife tool works well for this. Select the points along the lines subdividing the eye socket and use the stretch tool to expand the size and shape of the eye socket. If you use the "scale" and "move" tools, you should be able to form a rough approximation of a sphere around the eyeball (Figure 6-64). The final step is to close up the eye socket. Select the points at the very end, weld them together, and move them to the center and back of the eye socket.

The original inner and outer eyelid polygons, which were extruded for the eye socket, are currently covering the eye opening. These two polygons with more than four sides should be deleted (Figure 6-65). Merge points to get rid of any duplicates.

Finally, it is time to complete the shape of the upper eyelid and the way it folds under when the eyelids are open. Hide all the polygons except for those near the eye opening. Insert points and split

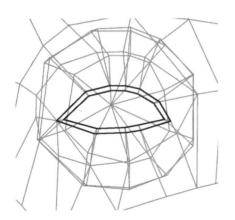

Fig. 6-65 Select the inner and outer eyelid polygons, which are covering the eye opening, and delete them.

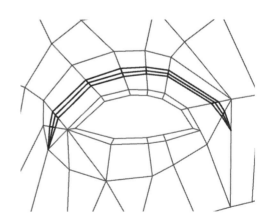

Fig. 6-66 The three black lines mark the location where points are inserted and the polygons split for the upper eyelid fold.

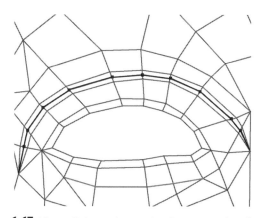

Fig. 6-67 After splitting polygons that have more than four sides and refining the shape around the eye, select the middle eyelid points.

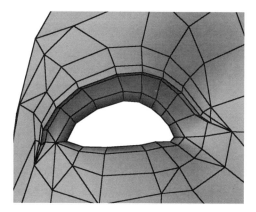

Fig. 6-68 Bring the middle eyelid points forward and down. Select the top line's points and drag them forward a little.

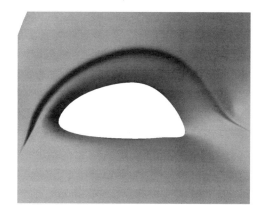

Fig. 6-69 The upper eyelid after applying smoothing to subdivide the polygons.

the polygons for the upper eyelid so that you have three curved lines above the eye opening (Figure 6-66). If necessary, use a template. Subdivide any polygons to improve the shape around the eye and make sure none have more than four sides.

Except for the points at the end where the three upper eyelid lines converge, select the middle line points (Figure 6-67). Move them forward a little and down over the bottom line's points until you see a sharp line take shape in the shaded view window. You are, in effect, folding polygons over each other. Select all the points, except the two at the end along the top line, and move them forward a little but not as much as those for the middle line. Figure 6-67 shows the line that should be seen for the top eyelid fold. At this time, it still has a rough appearance, but that will change once the polygons are subdivided with a "smoothing" command.

To view the eyelid area in more detail, you can apply a "smoothing" command. This will subdivide your polygons so that you can get a preview of what the eye will look like when finished. Figure 6-69 shows the result of smoothing the polygons.

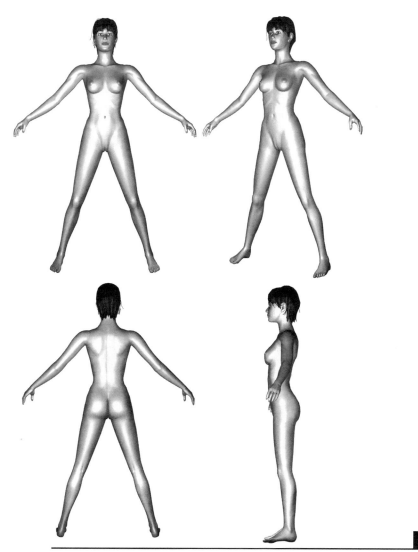

CHAPTER 7

Modeling the Figure

In the previous chapter, a variety of techniques for forming a head were demonstrated. Here we will look at methods for modeling the rest of the figure.

Poly Bevel Extrude Method

A method for modeling a polygon body out of a simple block can be implemented by bevel extruding parts from it. The segmented block is used for the torso and the legs and arms are bevel extruded out of it. The fingers and toes are in turn bevel extruded out of the resulting extra blocks.

The following instructions illustrate this method. I have adapted this technique to modeling a cartoon body. It should work fine for most characters. The advantage to this method of creating a body is that it is fairly quick and uncomplicated. The disadvantage is that bodies modeled this way often lack detail and retain their underlying boxy essence. They also have a tendency to look "cartoony." Of course, this can be an advantage when modeling cartoon characters. It is also useful for beginning students who are just learning the fundamentals of 3D modeling. This method will only work with software that has polygon modeling tools with the ability to smooth polygons. One example of this is the Subdivision Patch function found in LightWave 3D.

Start with a simple long box and subdivide it like the one in Figure 7-1. Reshape the box to look somewhat like a torso. Do not worry too much about detail at this stage. You are just moving some of points around without adding any new ones (Figure 7-2).

Select the polygon on the side of the torso to which the arm would be attached. Bevel or extrude it outward to make it the entire length of the arm

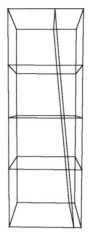

Fig. 7-1 A subdivided box is the object from which the entire body is modeled.

Fig. 7-2 The box is reshaped to look somewhat like a torso.

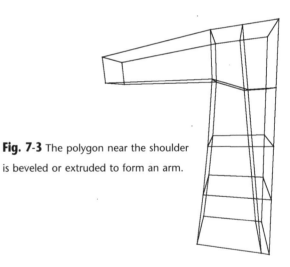

Fig. 7-3 The polygon near the shoulder is beveled or extruded to form an arm.

and hand but not the fingers (Figure 7-3). You may need to delete the polygon that was selected to create the original arm extrusion. It should be at the armpit. This will make the arm and torso hollow and will prevent any errors when smoothing the polygons. Subdivide the arm and move the points in and out to make a general shape of the arm and hand (Figure 7-4).

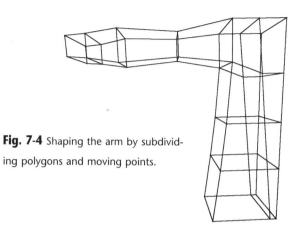

Fig. 7-4 Shaping the arm by subdividing polygons and moving points.

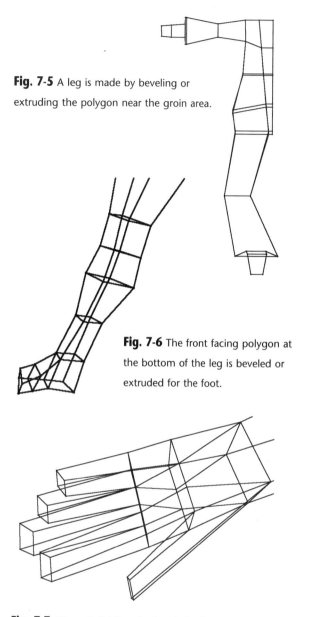

Fig. 7-5 A leg is made by beveling or extruding the polygon near the groin area.

Fig. 7-6 The front facing polygon at the bottom of the leg is beveled or extruded for the foot.

Fig. 7-7 After subdividing the hand, the fingers and thumb are beveled or extruded out.

Create a leg by selecting the polygon on the bottom of the torso and extrude or bevel extrude it down. You might also have to delete the polygon that you selected originally to bevel/extrude. It should be near the groin area. Position the leg and split the polygons of the leg so that you can reshape them (Figure 7-5).

The foot is extruded by selecting the polygon that faces the front at the bottom of the leg. Split the polygons on the foot and move the points to make a rough shape of the foot without the toes (Figure 7-6). The toes will be extruded later from the foot. If necessary, delete the polygon that you had extruded originally for the foot. The bottom of the foot near the heel might have a hole. If so, fill it by making a polygon there.

Now, it is time to extrude the fingers from the hand. Select the points at the end of the hand and make a polygon out of them. This is the polygon that the fingers will be beveled or extruded from. Subdivide the polygon into four sections for each finger. Select each of the four subdivided polygons and bevel or extrude them outward. Adjust the width and length of each finger. If necessary, delete the original four polygons that were used to extrude the fingers from the hand. Leave the tips of the fingers solid. Select the polygon on the side of the hand from which the thumb will protrude. Bevel or extrude it out. Size, shape and move the thumb into the right position. Your blocky hand may now look like the one in Figure 7-7).

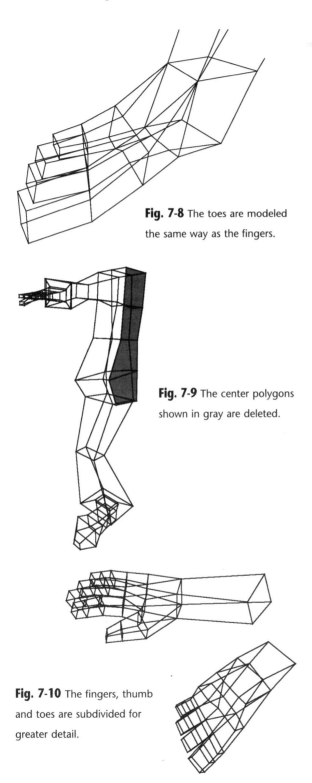

Fig. 7-8 The toes are modeled the same way as the fingers.

Fig. 7-9 The center polygons shown in gray are deleted.

Fig. 7-10 The fingers, thumb and toes are subdivided for greater detail.

Model the toes using the same method as the one for the fingers (Figure 7-8). If you see any gaps between adjoining polygons where the fingers meet the hand or the toes meet the foot, be sure to weld the points. This may require splitting polygons into smaller ones. Some programs such as LightWave 3D require three or four sided polygons for their Subpatch or Metaform smoothing functions.

Since you are only modeling half the body and will need to eventually mirror and weld the two halves together, you should delete the polygons that can be found at the center axis. If those polygon are not eliminated, they could cause problems later when trying to weld points along that seam (Figure 7-9).

At this stage you may want to split some of the polygons and move the points for extra detail in the fingers, thumb, toes, torso, and so on (Figure 7-10). Splitting the polygons near the tips of the toes and fingers often keeps their forms from becoming too pointed when applying smoothing later on. If your software has a smooth shift or bevel option, you can select specific polygons for the muscles such as those on the torso and apply a bevel or smooth shift to them. This will extrude them outward a little. The new polygons can then be scaled and shaped to make the general form of the muscles. Figure 7-11 shows a more detailed version of the model after splitting, beveling and smooth shifting parts.

The head can be made from a block by bevel/ extruding the polygon at the top of the torso. First bevel/extrude for the neck and then from that extrude the head. If you can split polygons and then bevel them out, you can make a fairly good outline of the head (Figure 7-12). Select the polygons along the center axis next to the head and delete these as shown in the previous Figure 7-9.

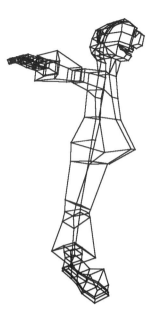

Fig. 7-11 Details and other structures are made by splitting polygons, beveling and/or smooth shifting.

Fig. 7-12 The head is beveled or extruded from the neck polygon and subdivided.

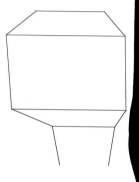

Fig. 7-13 The facial features are roughly shaped from subdivided polygons.

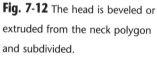

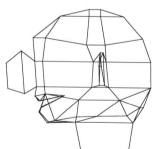

Fig. 7-14 The body is mirrored and welded down the center and smoothing is applied. This simplistic figure was modeled in about 30 minutes.

same x-ax
points after mirrorin
smoothing to the figure
use deformation tools
ging option to shape ex
tions. Once you are sati
you can smooth it aga
would most likely Me
times.

NURBS and Spline
of the Figure_____

Although the following
consuming than the pr
should find these to be
modeling realistic figur
than trying to create a b

of splines. Figure 7-15 illustrates one such model that was built entirely from splines and then surfaced with polygons. Details were added later by splitting certain polygons and pushing/pulling their points. NURBS modelers with hierarchical b-splines (h-splines) also make it possible to isolate specific areas for details.

The following instructions explain how to model the various body parts. Even though the first part here is the torso, it is not necessary to go in the order outlined below. For example, one can start with the legs and end with the head. As discussed before, you might find it a good idea to use either a 2D or 3D template for modeling. Some of these can be found on the accompanying CD.

Rather than building a model piece by piece and then fillet/blending or welding points, some of the more experienced modelers may want to try creating a seamless character by adapting the instructions at the end of chapter nine to their own specific software.

The Torso

When using splines or curves, one should be aware of the Edge to Middle Rule which is simply this. When outlining the profile of a body part in one view, the curve should be in the middle of the object in another view. For example, if you are drawing a curve in the front view to outline the side of the torso, then that same curve should be located in the middle of the torso in the side view (Figure 7-16).

Figures 7-17 and 7-18 illustrate the placement of the front and back torso splines (curves). Each spline starts at the neck and continues below the buttocks to the top of the leg. If your software package does not allow you to rebuild curves, then

...ygons shown
view mode.

ow the natural contours
ines are then connected
h lofting/skinning tech-
miliar with drawing the
se methods without too

s implement some kind
uses lofting or skinning
elers like LightWave 3D
onnected to make spline
e is made, it can be sur-
Rather than trying to
g with hard edged poly-
e smooth flowing curves

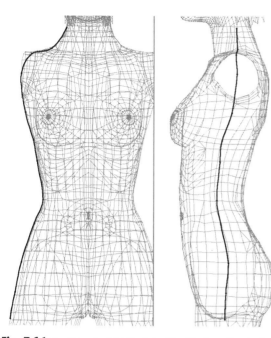

Fig. 7-16 The Edge to Middle Rule. The black outline in the front view is placed in the middle of the torso in the right view.

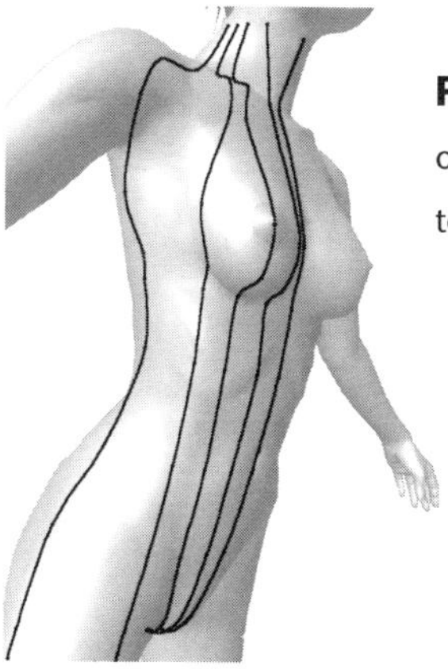

Fig. 7-17 The splines that go on the front and side of the torso.

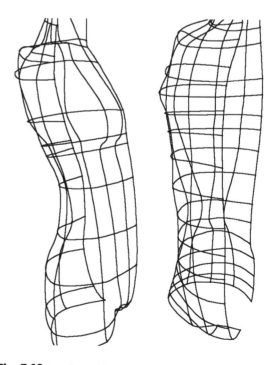

Fig. 7-18 The back of the torso and its splines.

you should start with one curve containing about twelve points on it and then duplicate it to make all the rest. Once you have made all the curves, you will be confronted with several choices. Each will depend on the software that you are using.

If you are working in LightWave 3D, then select each of the corresponding points in order and connect them using the make open curves command (control-P). This will create a series of open splines that act as connectors and will make a spline cage out of the original curves. You can now reshape the spline cage until you are satisfied with the half torso (Figure 7-19). You can now auto patch the spline cage to make it a polygon model. Use the Auto Patcher plug-in for this. Set your polygon level to a low amount such as 1 or 0. This will make it easier to edit the polygons for details. Separate the spline cage from the polygon mesh

Fig. 7-19 A male and female spline cage.

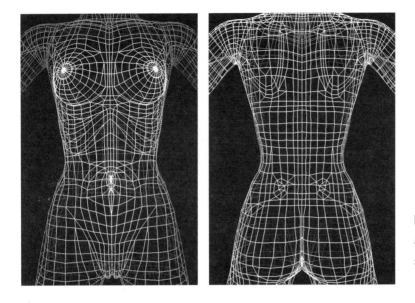

Fig. 7-20 The wire frame view of the front and back torso shows where polygons were split or h-splines added.

and paste it into another layer. The spline cage can be selected by going to the polygon statistics and selecting the ones with more than 4 vertices. Shape the various particulars on the polygon torso such as the nipple, shoulder blade, belly button, ribs, and so on. You can do this by splitting polygons and moving various points. You only need to work on half the torso since the middle points can be aligned to one axis using set value. Later, the total half figure can be mirrored and the points merged along the middle.

The procedure for completing the torso in a NURBS modeler, is similar. Rather than selecting the splines and connecting the points manually, one can simply select them and use a lofting or skinning function to make the NURBS mesh. Half the torso can be mirrored and aligned or attached to the other half. If you prefer to mirror the curves, you can then loft them with the close option on. After lofting, the original splines can be manipulated with history on to change the shape of the torso. If your software has hierarchical b-splines,

then you should find it easier to add details to the torso. Figure 7-20 shows the female torso in wireframe mode to make it easier to see the parts with more detail and how polygons were split or hierarchical b-splines added. Another approach to modeling the torso is to bring the splines from the head all the way down to the waist. This way one can loft all the splines of the head and torso to make them one complete object. The drawback to this method is that it can get confusing having to deal with the points on both the head and torso at the same time. The finished female and male torsos can be seen in Figures 7-21a–d.

The Legs

When modeling the legs you can follow the Edge to Middle Rule by outlining the profile. Figure 7-22 illustrates the first four splines or curves. Notice that by matching the indicated numbers, one can see that when a curve follows the outline in one view, the same curve is placed in the middle of the

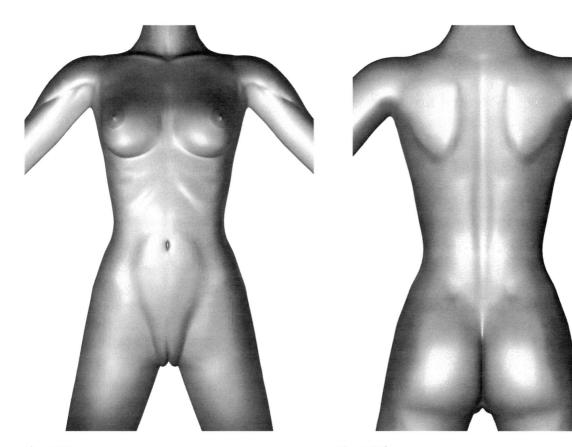

Fig. 7-21a The front view of the final female torso.

Fig. 7-21b The final female torso from the back.

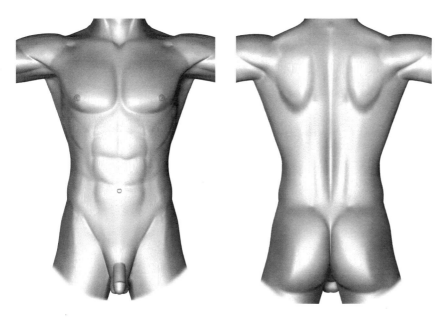

Fig. 7-21c (left) The final male torso viewed from the front.

Fig. 7-21d (right) The male torso from the back.

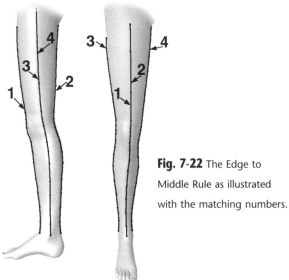

Fig. 7-22 The Edge to Middle Rule as illustrated with the matching numbers.

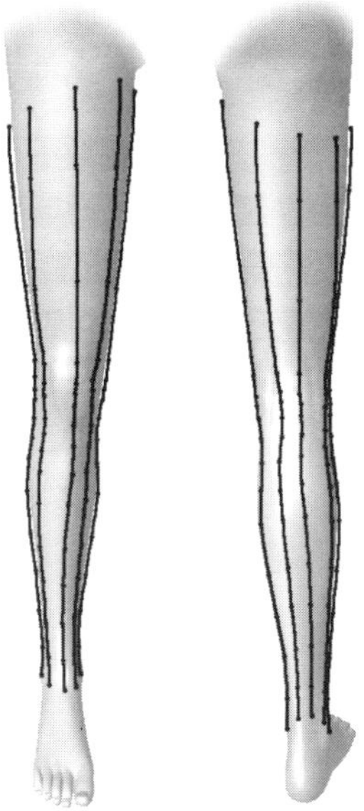

Fig. 7-23 Eight splines define the structure of the leg.

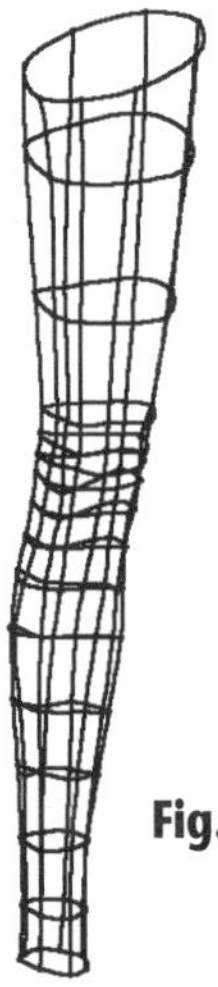

Fig. 7-24 The leg spline cage or lofted spline mesh.

leg in another view. Spline one and two outline the leg in the side view, but are located in the middle in the front view. The opposite holds true for splines three and four. Each spline should have about twelve to sixteen points on it. Again, as mentioned before you can either duplicate curves or rebuild them according to your software.

Once you have finished drawing the four splines, you could loft or connect their points. The problem with using only four is that the shape may not be round enough and the leg will lack detail. Therefore, it is best to add four more splines between the existing ones to give the leg more structure (Figure 7-23). Select each of the eight curves in order and loft or skin them. If you are working with LightWave 3D, then select each individual point in the right order and connect them using the make closed curves command (control-O). Continue connecting all the points to make cross sectional ovals until you have a completed spline cage. You can then auto patch it. Figure 7-

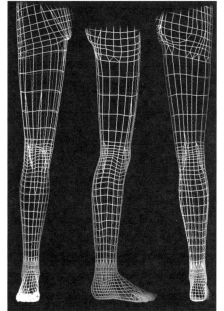

Fig. 7-25 Some wireframe views of the finished leg.

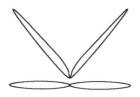

Fig. 7-26 Ovals are drawn defining the shape of an overweight person's legs.

Fig. 7-27 The ovals are lofted.

the general direction of two legs. In this example, the legs of an overweight person will be modeled. After drawing or duplicating the ovals of one leg, you can duplicate/mirror the same ones for the other leg. Loft the circles (Figure 7-27). Edit the model by either moving the points on the original ovals with history on or manipulate the mesh itself.

Create a NURBS plane and move it so it intersects the legs at the waist (Figure 7-28). Select the legs and NURBS plane objects and edit their surfaces by intersecting their surfaces. In other words the NURBS plane will intersect the legs creating a curve on them at the waist (Figure 7-29). Select the leg object and the trim tool. You can now cut away the top portion of the legs. Figure 7-30 illustrates the legs with their tops trimmed away.

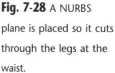
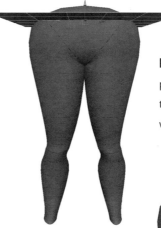

Fig. 7-28 A NURBS plane is placed so it cuts through the legs at the waist.

24 shows the leg spline cage or the lofted NURBS mesh.

Using hierarchical b-splines or polygons, if you are working with them, add detail to the leg such as the knee cap and muscle structure. Figure 7-25 shows the wireframe view of a leg with split polygons or hierarchical b-splines. Modeling the foot is the next step, but before proceeding to this, the following outlines another method for modeling both legs using ovals rather than open spline curves. This technique works very well if you are using high-end modelers such as Maya™.

Figure 7-26 depicts a series of ovals that follow

Fig. 7-29 One surface intersects another producing a line going through the waist. The top of the waist can now be trimmed away.

Fig. 7-30 The heavy legs after trimming the top off.

Fig. 7-31 The legs after fillet/blending the feet to them.

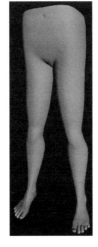

Fig. 7-32 A series of ovals make up the shape of the foot without the toes.

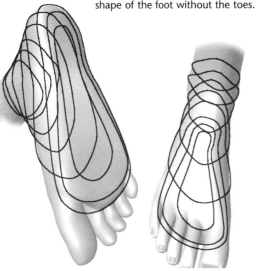

Since the waist area can usually be hidden with a belt or the clothes, you can either fillet blend the lower body to the chest or just place them against each other. The feet can be modeled duplicating the curves at the bottom of the legs. A series of these ovals are then lofted to make the foot and then joined to the legs using fillet blend. The next section explains in more detail the steps to modeling a foot. Figure 7-31 shows the completed lower body with the feet.

The Feet

Figure 7-32 shows the series of oval splines that make up the general shape of the foot without the toes. Approximately 12 to 15 points on each curve should be enough for most feet. The first oval starts at the top and can be a duplicate of the last spline/isoparm or circle found at the bottom of the leg. If you are working in LightWave 3D, then select the points at the bottom of the leg and make a closed curve from them (control-O). This closed curve can be duplicated, moved and shaped similarly to the ones in Figure 7-32.

Once all the ovals are sized, shaped, and placed in their correct positions, then either loft/skin them or in LightWave 3D select their corresponding points and make open curves (control-P). The resulting spline mesh or cage should look somewhat like Figure 7-33. Using the Auto Patcher plug-in, give the spline cage a polygon surface. The open part at the base of the foot, can be closed by making a polygon out of the points around the hole and then splitting it into smaller ones.

The toes are modeled individually by creating open splines along their edges. Figure 7-34 shows the splines for the big toe. The Edge to Middle Rule applies again. In the same way that you outlined

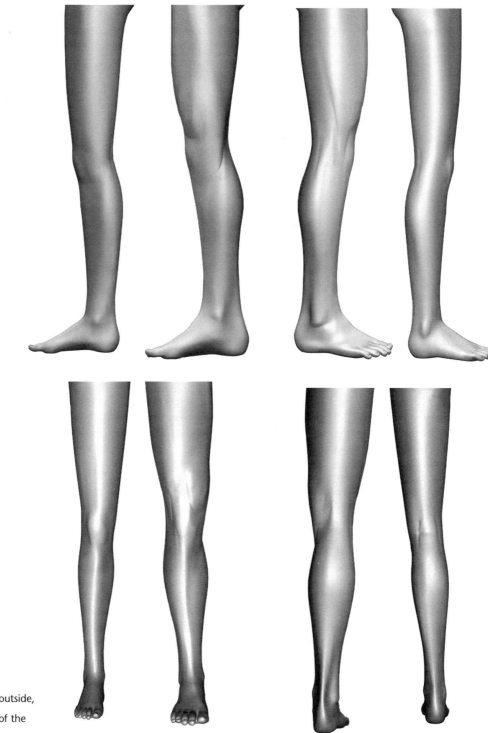

Fig. 7-38 The inside, outside, front, and back views of the male and female legs.

Once the foot and leg(s) are finished, then you can either fillet/blend them to each other or weld their points for a seamless leg. Figure 7-38 shows some different views of the male and female legs next to each other. You can now attach the leg(s) to the torso using either fillet/blends or by welding their points.

The Arms

It is best to model the arms outstretched or at a ninety degree angle from the torso. This will make it easier to outline the length and width. Figure 7-39 shows the first four curves that outline the top and front of the arm. The splines have approximately sixteen points on each. Again, use the Edge to Middle Rule to place the curves in the right positions. As discussed previously either duplicate the splines or rebuild the curves when you are done. All of them should have the same amount of points.

In order to get a more accurate model, it is best to add four more splines. Each of these are placed between the first four curves (Figure 7-40). Select each spline and loft them. Use the closed option to make them connected from beginning to end. If you are using LightWave 3D, then select the points in order and make a closed curve (control-O). Figure 7-41 shows the connected arm curves or spline cage.

If your software has a history option, you can now manipulate the original splines to improve the arm or you can select points on the spline cage or mesh and move them around. Once you are satisfied with the result, you can insert more isoparms for detail if necessary or in LightWave 3D, auto patch the spline cage. Extra details can be added by splitting polygons or on a NURBS mesh inserting hierarchical b-splines.

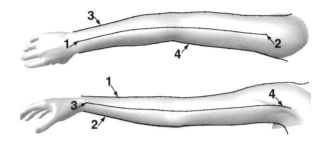

Fig. 7-39 The first four splines outline the arm in the top and front views. Note the corresponding numbers for each view.

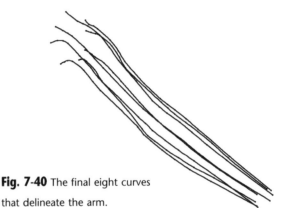

Fig. 7-40 The final eight curves that delineate the arm.

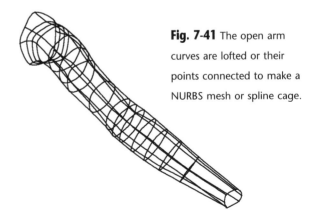

Fig. 7-41 The open arm curves are lofted or their points connected to make a NURBS mesh or spline cage.

The Hands

Next to the face, the hands are the most expressive parts of the body. Great care should be taken to model the hands. A good character animation will show hand as well as facial expressions. Therefore, do not hesitate to add extra details to the hands, since they are often shown close to the camera.

The fingers and hands are modeled separately. You can use approximately 6 curves with about eight points on each (Figure 7-42). Select the curves in order and loft them. In LightWave 3D, pick the corresponding points in order and make closed curves until you have a spline cage (Figure 7-43).

The Edge to Middle Rule applies to the fingers. Figure 7-44 shows how the four splines outline the profile of the fingers. The ones that follow the outline in one view are placed in the middle of the finger in the other view. Each curve should have about eight points on it. As before, you can either duplicate curves or rebuild them, later.

In order to give the finger more structure, you may want to add extra curves between the four. When you are satisfied with the placement of the curves, then select them in order and do a closed loft on them. In LightWave 3D, you can select the corresponding points in order and make closed curves (control-O). The spline cage or lofted wire mesh might look somewhat like Figure 7-45. In LightWave 3D, use the Auto Patcher plug-in on the spline cage.

You now have several options. You can continue drawing splines for the other fingers or you can add detail to this one and then duplicate, size and shape it to make the others. In either case, when modeling additional parts onto the fingers, insert extra splines/isoparms near the joints, and

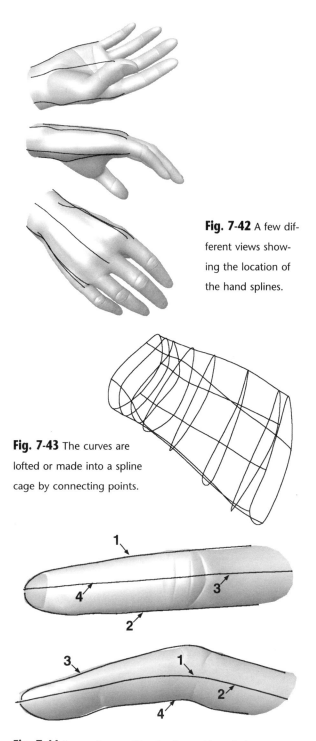

Fig. 7-42 A few different views showing the location of the hand splines.

Fig. 7-43 The curves are lofted or made into a spline cage by connecting points.

Fig. 7-44 Four splines outline the finger. Note their corresponding numbers in both views.

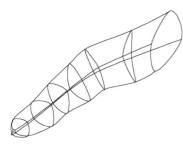

Fig. 7-45 The splines are lofted or made into a spline cage. Some may prefer to draw more than four splines.

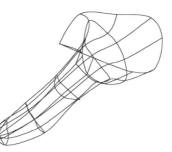

Fig. 7-46 The thumb and part of the palm's curves are lofted or the points connected for a spline cage.

Fig. 7-47 A large hole is trimmed or cut away from the part of the hand where the thumb will be attached.

nail or split polygons. Manipulate the points to make wrinkles, knuckles, nails, and so on.

Once you are finished modeling the fingers, then it is time to do the thumb. The thumb is somewhat more complicated, since you have to also model part of the palm to attach to the hand. Figure 7-46 illustrates the thumb's splines lofted or made into a spline cage.

If you are working with NURBS, then trim holes into the hand for the fingers and thumb. Notice the large hole in the hand for the thumb in Figure 7-47. This is because the thumb contains part of the palm which will be either fillet/blended or welded to the hand.

Once you have attached all the fingers and thumbs to the hand, you can continue improving

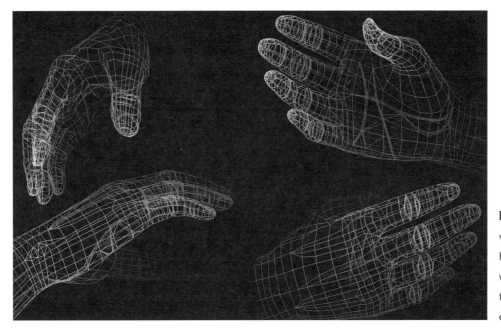

Fig. 7-48 A wireframe view of the completed hands. The lines for wrinkles are close together with the middle points pulled in.

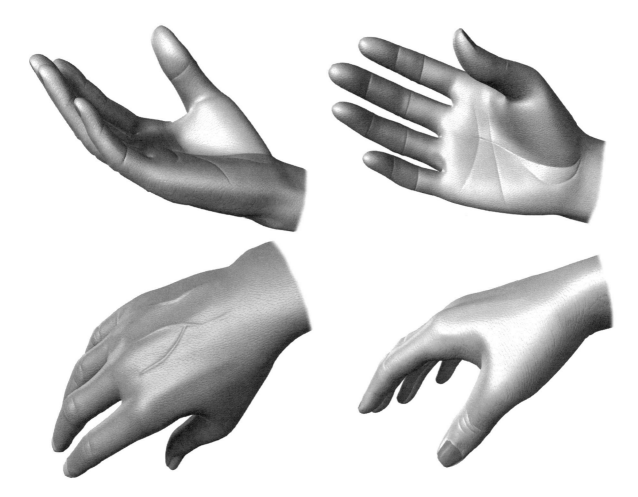

Fig. 7-49 Some shaded views of the completed hand.

it by either splitting polygons, inserting spline/ isoparms or hierarchical b-splines. The extra time that you put into the hand will pay off in the end. Figure 7-48 shows some wireframe views of the hand and the areas that have extra detail. A few shaded views of the completed hand can be seen in Figure 7-49. The arm can now be finished by fillet/blending the hand to it or welding points. The completed male and female arms are seen in Figures 7-50a. and 7-50b.

The arm is attached to the shoulder using the trim, fillet and blend tools. If you are working with a polygon modeler, then cut a section out of the shoulder of the torso and weld the points to the arm. Expect to spend extra time on attaching the arm to the torso. It is one of the tougher areas to model smoothly. Unless you have already done so, be sure to attach all the parts to the body. If you have been modeling a half figure, then be sure to align all the middle points along the same axis using a set value. Rotate the arm down about 45 degrees. Keeping the arms straight out from the

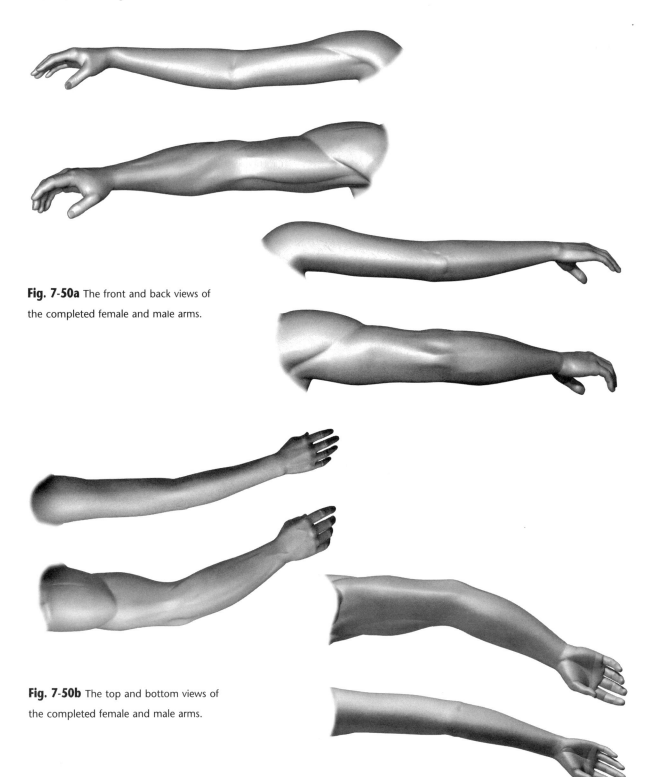

Fig. 7-50a The front and back views of the completed female and male arms.

Fig. 7-50b The top and bottom views of the completed female and male arms.

CHAPTER 8

Completing the Human Figure

A few relevant details should be modeled before moving to the next level. These include hair, eyelashes, and clothes. Realistic hair is very difficult to achieve in computer graphics. The closest that studios have come to creating hair is through the use of fur shaders and particle effects. Some companies offer expensive hair creation plug-ins. At the time of this writing, most artists have to fake hair through the skillful use of textures and a few well-placed strands added to a modeled hair object. Eyelashes can be made as solid pieces with texture maps containing both a positive and negative (alpha) image. Certain artists prefer to model individual eyelashes. This is not as difficult as it sounds and often produces better results than relying on textures. Clothes can be modeled by lofting or connecting splines. If you do not mind skintight clothes, then an easier method is to use parts of the existing body and reshape the mesh or smooth-shift the polygons.

This chapter concludes with a tutorial by one of my brilliant students, Sharon Bilyj, who has taken the spline cage method and adapted it to creating seamless bodies. If you follow her technique, you do not need to attach, weld, or blend segments of the body to other parts.

Hair and Eyelashes

The first method for making hair works well for NURBS modelers. Polygon modelers (like LightWave 3D), which have splines that can be made into spline cages, can also make use of this technique. Using a template of a model's head or placing it in a separate layer, create a series of quarter-moon shaped ovals (Figure 8-1). The sections of the curves that are closest to the head

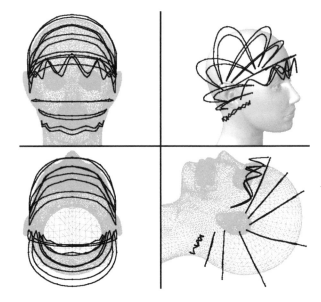

Fig. 8-1 A series of closed curves are placed around the skull for the hair object.

should be partly inside it. The first and last curves at the forehead and nape of the neck can have their points pulled to create a zigzag shape. This should give the hairpiece a more uneven look. If you are modeling longer hair than that shown in the example, continue creating ovals past the neck. As before, you want to have the same number of points on each of the closed curves. Loft or connect the points in order on the closed splines. Shape the mesh or spline cage so that the outer parts are far enough from the head while the inner parts are inside the head somewhat (Figure 8-2). If you are working with NURBS, you can add extra detail by inserting isoparms or h-splines.

Those of you working with a polygon modeler like LightWave 3D can add a polygon surface to the spline cage. The polygon hairpiece is split down the middle so that you only need to concentrate on half of it. Polygons are split and their

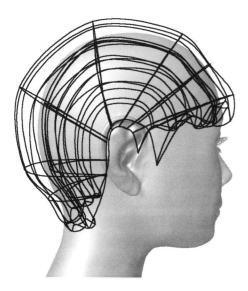

Fig. 8-2 The curves are lofted or their points connected to make a spline cage.

Fig. 8-3 Closed curves are used for the ponytail. Their shapes change according to the varying thickness of the hairpiece.

Fig. 8-4 The resulting spline cage or mesh after the varying curves are lofted or their points connected as open splines.

points moved for extra detail. If you want to add extra parts to the hair like a ponytail, create another set of oval curves. These are shaped for the different areas of the ponytail (Figure 8-3). Loft or connect the points to make a 3D mesh or spline cage (Figure 8-4). In LightWave 3D, you can autopatch the spline cage to make a polygon object. The curve at the beginning of the ponytail is projected onto a NURBS mesh or stenciled to a polygon model. The projected curve is trimmed away and the ponytail fillet/blended to the back of the hair object. If you are working with polygons, weld the end points of the ponytail to the hair object. Another option is to draw a spline for a hair strand and then rail extrude a polygon circle along its length. The polygon circle should have six sides or fewer to save memory. Try to keep the rail extrude object segments as few as possible. Different size polygons can be rail extruded to

make different thicknesses of hair. The end points of the strand are welded.

Now that you have the general shape of the hair, adding individual hair strands of varying thicknesses and lengths will improve the overall look. To save memory, you can usually get by with lofting or connecting the points of three curves (Figure 8-5). Duplicate and reshape the hair strands. The idea is to make only enough to give a general impression of hair. It is similar to an artist painting a brick building without actually drawing each individual brick. Figure 8-6 shows a fair number of hair strands. Most of them appear at the forehead.

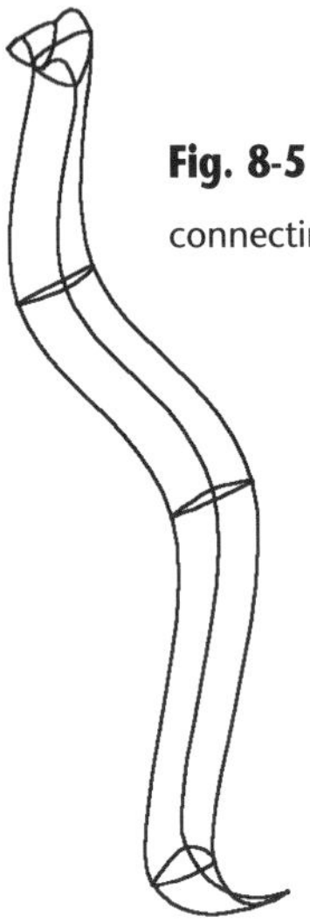

Fig. 8-5 Hair strands are modeled by lofting or connecting the points of three open curves.

nosity and diffuse texture. The skin has a planar bump map of leather texture with high contrast.

Figure 8-9 shows the steps for another method of polygon modeling the hair. Draw the shape of the hair and stencil it on the head. Select the hair stencil and smooth-shift or bevel the hair polygons outward. Move the outside polygons up and out a

Fig. 8-6 Numerous hair strands of varying widths and lengths are duplicated and reshaped.

In case you have been working with only half of a hair model, be sure to align the center points before duplicating and mirroring the object. Any polygons that occur at the center axis should be deleted to avoid errors. Once you have merged the points on the two halves, you may also decide to rough up the model by jittering the points. Figure 8-7 shows the completed hairpiece. The textures used can be found on the CD (Figure 8-8). The stripes are applied as a spherical bump map of about 400%, and the other fur image as a planar lumi-

Fig. 8-7 After texturing the hair, you can get an approximation of real hair. If you use a fur shader, you get better results.

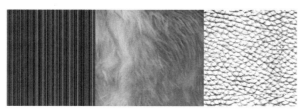

Fig. 8-8 Some examples of people textures. The stripes on the left were used for the hair bump map, the fur texture in the middle was applied as a luminosity and diffuse hair map, and the texture on the right was used as a skin bump map.

Fig. 8-9 The steps for creating a simple polygonal hair object.

strands. Each can be duplicated and stuck into the eyelid or their points can be welded to the eyelid (Figure 8-10). Another method is to model the eyelash shapes (Figure 8-11). Positive and negative texture images are made to map onto the eyelash shapes (Figure 8-12). The negative image acts as a transparency map so that only the eyelash shape is visible while the negative space on the object appears invisible.

Eyebrows can be made by stenciling or projecting an eyebrow shape to the head and then beveling it out a little. Creative texturing should make the eyebrow shapes somewhat convincing. A little realism can be added by attaching a few strands to the eyebrow shape. Figure 8-13 shows a model of an older man with these types of eyebrows and all the other details discussed earlier.

Fig. 8-10 An example of eyelashes modeled as individual hair strands.

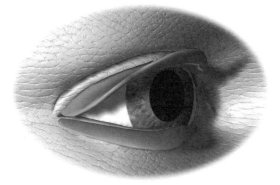

Fig. 8-11 Upper and lower eyelash objects when using transparency maps.

little so that you now have something that looks like a helmet. The hair can now be jittered or a smoothing algorithm applied. If you are working on half a hair model, be sure to delete the extra polygons at the center axis before duplicating and mirroring it for the other half. Adding hair strands should improve its look.

Eyelashes can be made the same way as hair

Fig. 8-12 Positive and negative (alpha) images are used as eyelash textures for transparency mapping.

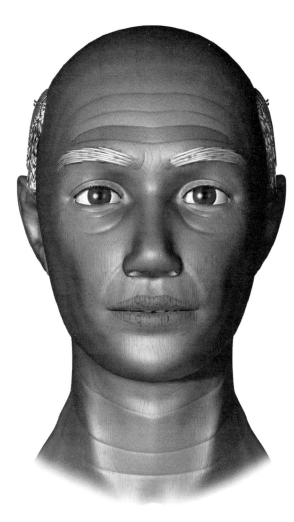

Fig. 8-13 Adding eyebrows and other final touches.

Cloth and Clothes

Although there are plug-ins available for creating realistic cloth, many artists rely on rigid bodies for clothes. At this time, the availability of cloth simulation software is too expensive for most individuals. Therefore, the following information is mainly for those without cloth simulation software.

Figure 8-14 shows a series of ovals that are set up to make a short-sleeved shirt. As before, you can duplicate the curves or rebuild them. Since the shirt is symmetrical, you might decide to only model half of it and later duplicate, mirror, align/attach, or weld points. Loft or connect the points on the ovals to make the mesh or spline cage (Figure 8-15). If you are connecting the points manually, make open curves out of them. Fix the shape of the shirt by manipulating the original curves with "history" on or by moving the points directly on the mesh. Figure 8-16 shows the lofted

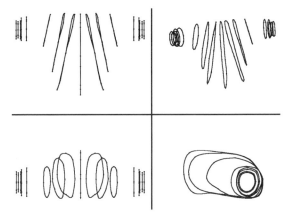

Fig. 8-14 The oval splines can be placed to create a half shirt, or as in this illustration, to make both sides.

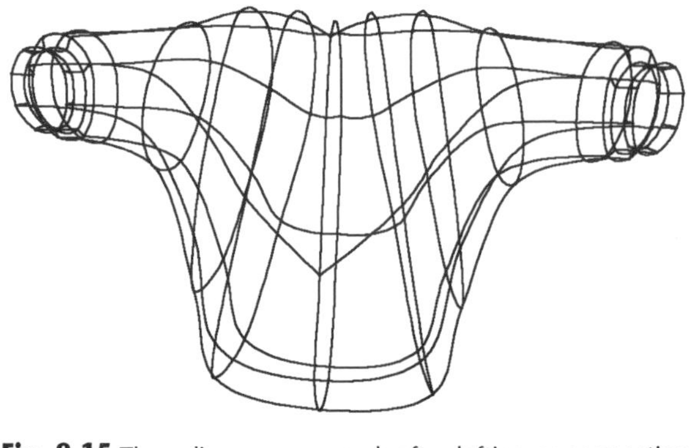

Fig. 8-15 The spline cage or mesh after lofting or connecting the ovals' points.

shirt without detail. It is too smooth so the next step is to add some wrinkles and folds as well as to cut away the top and bottom portions.

When working in a NURBS modeler, you might find it easier to adjust the points on the hull or lattice cage. Once the general shape is completed, you can add more detail by inserting isoparms or h-splines. A sculpting tool like Maya's Artisan is also useful for carving folds into a shirt. To open the top and bottom of the mesh, project a few oval shapes onto the shirt model and trim the collar

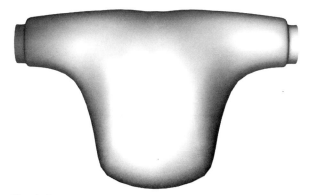

Fig. 8-16 A shaded view of the shirt before modeling, wrinkles, creases, and a collar are added. The top and bottom will have to be trimmed.

Fig. 8-17 The final shirt with a bump texture.

and waist sections. You might also be able to intersect shapes for cutting open the shirt.

If you are working in a polygon modeler like LightWave 3D, autopatch the spline cage and split polygons for the folds. Trim away the top and bottom.

You may decide to add a collar. This can be modeled with open splines that are connected or lofted. The points are then welded to the shirt. Buttons might also add a nice touch. Figure 8-17 shows the completed shirt with texture.

The pants are modeled by drawing a series of ovals like those shown in Figure 8-18. As with the shirt, you may decide to only model half the pants and later attach the two halves.

Select the ovals in the right order and loft them. If you are making a spline cage, then select the points in order to connect them as open curves. You should now have a spline cage or mesh that looks somewhat like Figure 8-19. If you are working in LightWave 3D, then autopatch the spline

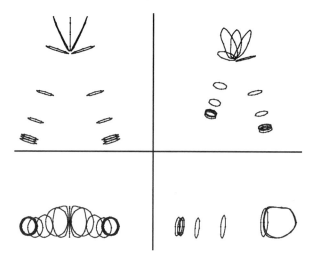

Fig. 8-18 Closed curves are set up for the pants. Some may prefer to only use curves on the left or right side for half the pants.

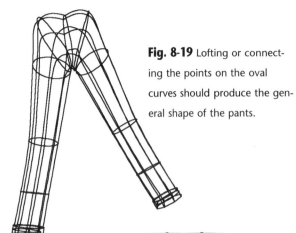

Fig. 8-19 Lofting or connecting the points on the oval curves should produce the general shape of the pants.

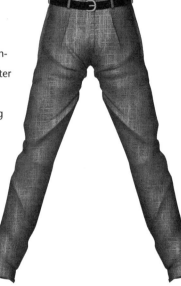

Fig. 8-20 An example of the pants after modeling all the detail and applying a texture.

Once you are done modeling the pants, apply a cloth shader or texture to them. You may find that cubic mapping works well. Figure 8-20 shows the textured pants. Some programs do not allow you to assign specific points to bones. If that is the case, you might have to place extra bones for parts of the clothes furthest from the body. Figure 8-21 illustrates the completed body wearing clothes.

Another method for creating clothes involves the use of stencils. This works well for polygon modeling, but the resulting clothes are often skin tight. The first step is to make a front view screen print or a rendering of your nude model. The other option is to place the model in another layer or template it. Using a 2D illustration program or working within the 3D software package, draw out-

cage. Cut off the top at the waist and add creases and wrinkles by splitting polygons and moving their points in and out. You might also model pockets, belt loops, and a fly.

Those of you working with a NURBS modeler can trim off the top at the waist. A lattice cage around the pants can help to quickly improve their shape, or you might elect to work with the points on a hull. Maya users can add wrinkles with Artisan. If you have h-splines, you can insert extra splines in specific areas for better wrinkles and creases.

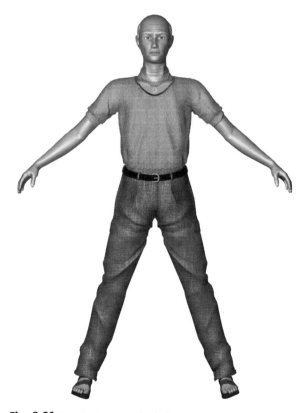

Fig. 8-21 The final man with clothes.

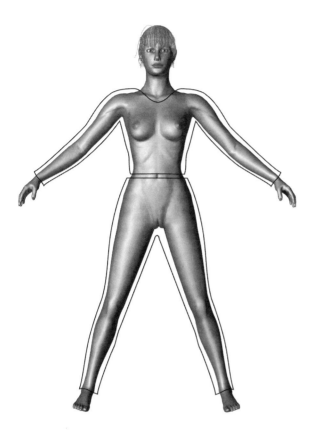

Fig. 8-22 Drawing the outline of the shirt and pants with a template of the model as your guide.

lines of the clothes around the nude model (Figure 8-22).

Extrude the outline of the clothes so that the article of clothing extends in front of and behind the model (Figure 8-23). Use a solid drill to stencil the extruded clothing onto the nude. If you are working in LightWave 3D, make sure that the extruded clothes are in the back layer and the nude in the front. Be sure to name the stencil so that it will be easier to select later.

Once the clothing is stenciled onto the nude, merge any extra points. Normally, you merge points whenever doing a Boolean operation. Select the name of the stencil (article of clothing). Assign

to the clothing a color and other characteristics. Use the shaded view to check the clothing. You might find that some polygons are missing and or that some should be part of the skin. Boolean operations are not perfect. You need to select individual polygons that should be part of the clothing and assign them the same surface as the stencil name.

Select all the clothing polygons, cut the clothing from the model, and place it in its own layer. You can now delete the character and do not save it. Later, you will open your original nude model and place the finished clothing on it. Doing it this way allows you to design other clothing articles for this character, or you might want to let it run around in its natural state once in a while.

Now that the clothing is in its own layer, you can give it some thickness. Use Smooth Shift to offset it a little. It does not take much, perhaps 10 mm. If it is winter clothing, you might use a larger number. Even though the clothes are a little

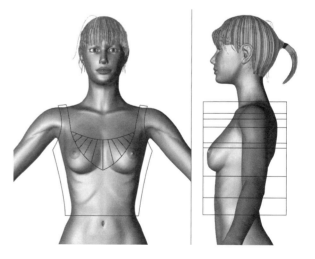

Fig. 8-23 The clothing outline is extruded. Notice that in the front view, some of the points at the bosom are pulled up so that the back of the blouse is not identical to the front.

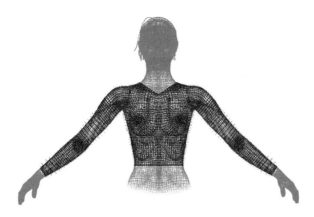

Fig. 8-24 Stenciling the extruded blouse outline to the body using a solid drill operation.

Fig. 8-25 After pasting the clothing into the same layer as the body, textures are applied with cubic image mapping.

thicker, they will still conform to the body (Figure 8-24). If you plan to add pockets, a collar, cuffs, and so on, you can stencil the shapes of these onto the clothes and apply Smooth Shift to them.

Once each article of clothing has its own surface, you can open the original character and paste them in. Assign textures to the clothes and make test renderings (Figure 8-25). When you animate the character with bones, you will find that the clothes will move right along with the rest of the model.

Creating a Seamless Character

Throughout the years, many artists have searched for a method to model seamless characters. Even though constructing models in sections makes it easier to isolate parts by hiding others, the disadvantage is in the extra work involved in putting the pieces together by welding points or fillet/blending segments. The following technique shows that it is possible to create a seamless spline character. The steps are outlined in minute detail in order to simplify the process, which at first seems daunting. Although the directions are geared toward LightWave 3D users, you can try to adapt them to other software programs utilizing NURBS with hierarchical b-splines or hash splines. Before attempting to follow these directions, make sure that your software has the ability to insert splines or isoparms, add points, merge or weld points, and has a method of connecting points that have been inserted on splines or curves.

The reason that I favor using spline cages is because, similar to NURBS, they have much greater flexibility and elegance. Unlike polygons, they can bend like elastic wires. This makes it much easier and quicker to model different body types. Spline cage and polygon modeling are a powerful combination. You get the refinement of NURBS with the adaptability of polygons. Splines define the general anatomy fairly quickly and polygons are used to add detail after the basic form has been modeled.

If you decide to follow the directions, you may want to use the generic male and female templates from the CD-ROM. When placed in another layer, they can be useful guides. Once you have a spline cage, it is recommended that you reshape it for your own individual character. The 3D templates on the CD-ROM are very general but useful for creating the basic forms in the right proportion. When reshaping a spline cage, try auto surfacing it first with a low setting. You can then reshape the spline cage and the polygon mesh at the same time. The advantage to this is that you can see the model in shaded mode.

The Method of Four

The following technique is an extension of the spline cage method for creating 3D models. This system is used to create an entire model made from a single spline cage. Those using this approach will find that models have a smoother appearance, that overall modeling time is reduced, and that new models can be created from the original spline cage quickly and easily. Due to their flexibility, splines are more suitable for adjustment than individual polygons.

When using this method, there are two important considerations. The splines must intersect in a way that forms a four-sided shape because the tool used to create polygons on top of the spline cage, the AutoPatcher plug-in, creates smoother, perfectly aligned polygons when the splines intersect at four points. Shapes bounded by more that four points will autopatch with holes in them. Three-sided shapes can also be used (splines intersect at three points), but you may find that it causes some of the polygons to flip in the wrong direction when autopatching. Flipping the polys or making them two-sided can remedy this easily enough. Another result of three-sided shapes is that some of the polygons can appear darker. This can be fixed by merging points. The second condition dictates that whenever two splines cross each other, they have to be joined by a common point.

If you find that your model has holes in it after auto patching, check for shapes with more than four points and make sure no polygons are flipped. Should you find that this is not the problem, then try merging points and unify the polygons. This will get rid of any stray points or polygons that might have been duplicated by mistake. If this still does not solve your problem, then you might have duplicate points that are not sitting exactly on top of each other. If that is the case, select suspicious looking individual points and weld them.

Remember, you may draw as many splines as you like, but it is best to use as few as possible. This system can be used to model any object, but for the purposes of this tutorial, a human model is created.

Create a spline cage model for the head and torso using the process explained in earlier sections. If you have already modeled a spline cage head from chapter 6, you can use that spline cage for this lesson. Select the points at the bottom of the neck and pull the points down to the upper part of the leg area (Figure 8-26). Insert points at the waist, if you are modeling a male, and at the buttocks, if a female, and connect them with an open spline (control-P). Insert an extra set of points around the groin area and connect these with an open curve (Figure 8-28).

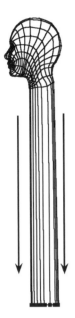

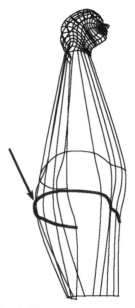

Fig. 8-26 The points are dragged straight down to what will become the top part of the leg.

Fig. 8-27 Points are inserted around the male's waist and connected with an open spline. For the female, the points are added at the buttocks.

Fig. 8-28 Extra points are inserted around the groin area and connected with an open spline. The torso begins to take shape with the waist and groin splines.

Fig. 8-29 After inserting points, the top of the leg is formed with two closed splines.

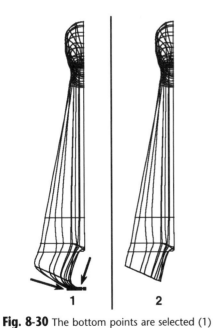

Fig. 8-31 The rest of the torso is shaped with open splines. One open spline is inserted in the groin area joining the previously made open groin spline.

Fig. 8-30 The bottom points are selected (1) and deleted, leaving the truncated leg (2).

Fig. 8-32 Nine points are selected at the shoulder to be dragged outward for the arm.

Right below the groin curve, add extra points for the top of the leg and connect these with a closed curve (control-O). Insert more points near the bottom of the spline cage and make another closed curve out of them for the upper section of the leg (Figure 8-29). Select the points along the very bottom of the spline cage and delete them (Figure 8-30). This will leave you with a leg that is cut off at the top. The rest of the leg will be completed after finishing the torso.

Insert points and connect them with open curves to make the form of the torso. To make things easier after you insert a set of points, use "Set Value" to align them along the *y*-axis. Pull the points on the torso to shape it correctly (Figure 8-31). When you are satisfied with the shape of the torso, select the points at the end of the open groin curve and make an open spline to connect them (Figure 8-31). This encloses the crotch.

Make sure that three of the horizontal splines located on the upper torso are in the area where the arm will be pulled out. Three vertical splines should run down the shoulder area to make a total of nine points from the horizontal and vertical splines (Figure 8-32). The nine points (where they intersect) are selected and dragged straight out from the torso (Figure 8-33).

Begin shaping the arm by adding points and making closed curves (control-O). You may want to "Set Value" the points along the *x*-axis to make it easier to line up the resulting ovals. Another trick is to select the new points and hide everything else, make a closed curve from the visible points, and shape the oval according to your templates. Figure 8-34 shows the closed curve ovals on the arm.

Zoom in on the wrist area of your model and look at Figure 8-35. It shows a set of nine points.

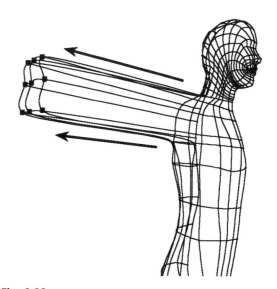

Fig. 8-33 The general shape of the arm after dragging the nine points.

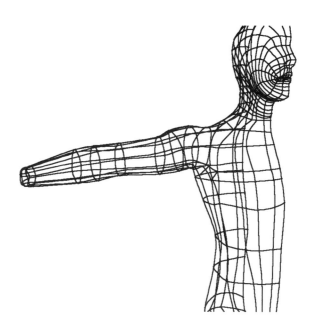

Fig. 8-34 Points are inserted along the length of the arm and connected as closed curves. Using these curves, the arm is sculpted.

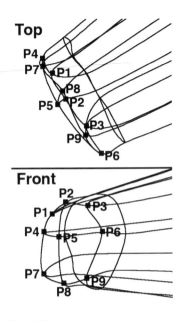

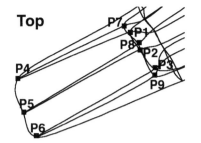

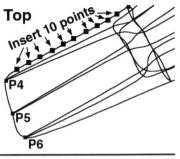

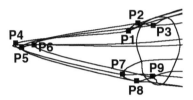

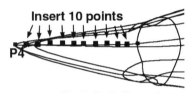

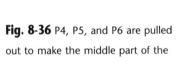

Fig. 8-35 At the end of the arm, nine points are identified. These serve as a reference from now on for modeling the hand and fingers.

Fig. 8-36 P4, P5, and P6 are pulled out to make the middle part of the hand.

Fig. 8-37 On the edge of the middle hand part to the right of P4, insert ten points.

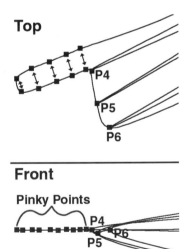

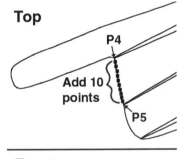

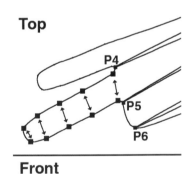

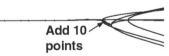

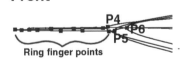

Fig. 8-38 The ten points are shaped into the middle part of the pinky finger. Note the distribution of the points. They are placed across from each other.

Fig. 8-39 Ten points are inserted between P4 and P5 for the ring finger.

Fig. 8-40 Dragging the ten points to make the middle part of the ring finger. Five points on each side of the finger correspond to each other.

This is the region from which you will create the hand and fingers. Using a hand template with the fingers outstretched, move points four, five, and six (P4, P5, and P6) to form the middle part of the hand (Figure 8-36). These points mark the beginning of the fingers.

In the top view, look at the outside spline of the three points that you just pulled out (P4, P5, and P6 in Figure 8-37). Insert ten points on the spline outside of P4. These will be used to form the pinky finger. Move the ten points for the pinky finger shape in the top view. Figure 8-38 shows their placement. There should be five corresponding points across from each other. This is necessary when you add the connecting curves later. These points should be located approximately where the knuckles are.

For the ring finger, insert ten more points between the points labeled P4 and P5 in Figure 8-39. Drag the ten points and shape the ring finger (Figure 8-40). Again, make sure that there are points on either side of the finger that correspond with each other.

Between points five and six (P5 and P6) insert ten points for the middle finger (Figure 8-41). Use these points to shape the middle finger with corresponding points on both sides (Figure 8-42).

Find the spline that is next to point six (P6). It is one of the outside splines. Insert twenty points on this spline (Figure 8-43). These are used to make the index finger and thumb. Use ten of these points to form the index finger and the remaining ten to shape the thumb (Figure 8-44). As with the other fingers, make sure that the points on either side mirror each other.

Now that you have completed the outline for the middle part of the hand and fingers, it is time to pull out points one, two, and three (P1, P2, and

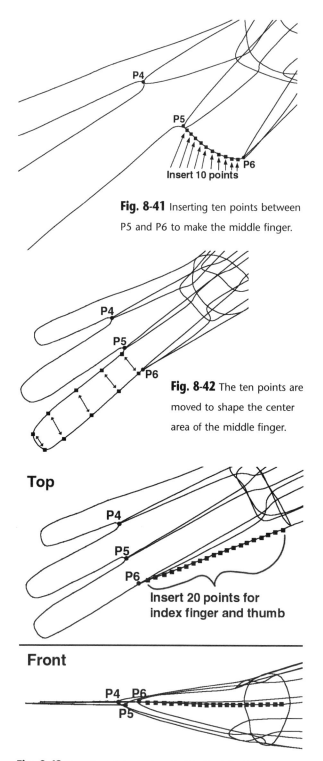

Fig. 8-41 Inserting ten points between P5 and P6 to make the middle finger.

Fig. 8-42 The ten points are moved to shape the center area of the middle finger.

Fig. 8-43 Twenty points are inserted to the left of P6.

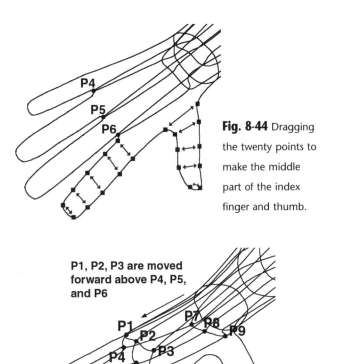

Fig. 8-44 Dragging the twenty points to make the middle part of the index finger and thumb.

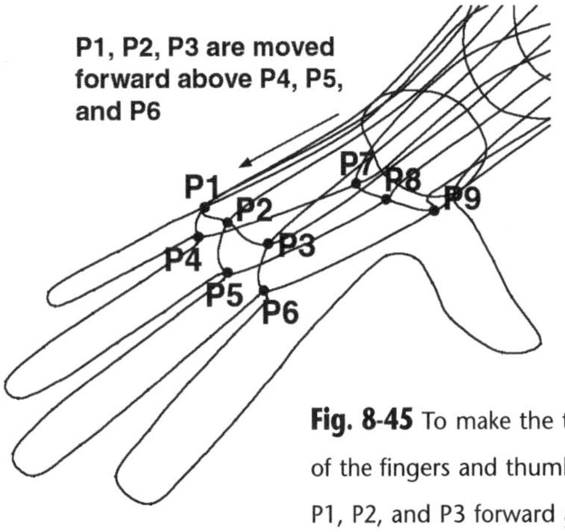

P1, P2, P3 are moved forward above P4, P5, and P6

Fig. 8-45 To make the top part of the fingers and thumb, drag P1, P2, and P3 forward and above P4, P5, and P6.

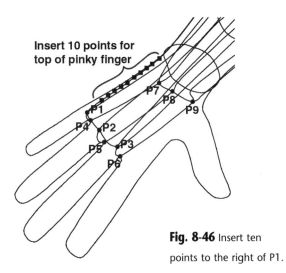

Insert 10 points for top of pinky finger

Fig. 8-46 Insert ten points to the right of P1.

P3), for the top part, and points seven, eight, and nine (P7, P8, and P9), for the bottom section of the hand. The same process of inserting points and shaping the fingers is applied to the top and bottom segments.

Figure 8-45 shows how points one, two, and three (P1, P2, and P3) are pulled forward above the previously moved points four, five, and six (P4, P5, and P6). This is where the top of the fingers begin. On the outside spline of point one (P1), insert ten extra points (Figure 8-46). These are used to shape the top of the pinky finger. Drag the ten points to make the top of the pinky finger (Figure 8-47). The form of the finger is the same as the previously made middle finger, except the outline is a little smaller. Make sure that each set of knuckle points on the top of the pinky corresponds with the knuckle joints of the middle finger.

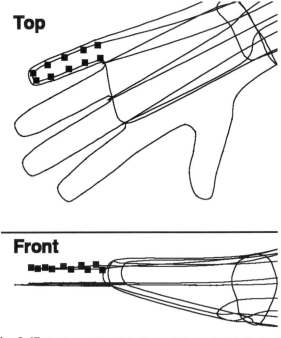

Top

Front

Fig. 8-47 The top of the pinky finger is formed with the ten points.

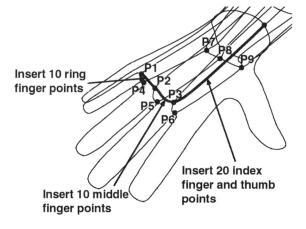

Insert 10 ring finger points

Insert 10 middle finger points

Insert 20 index finger and thumb points

Fig. 8-48 The darker and heavier line represents the area where all the points are inserted for the rest of the fingers and thumb.

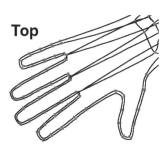

Top

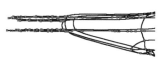

Front

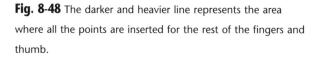

Fig. 8-49 All the points are moved to make the top portion of the ring, middle, index finger, and thumb.

For the next steps, refer to Figure 8-48. Insert ten points between points one and two (P1 and P2) for the top of the ring finger. Add ten more points between points two and three (P2 and P3) for the top middle finger. Next to P3, insert twenty points for the index finger and the thumb. Drag all the new points to shape the top of the ring, middle, index finger, and thumb (Figure 8-49). As mentioned before, it is important that the corresponding points line up with the points on the middle section of the fingers and thumb.

Now shape the bottom part of the hand,

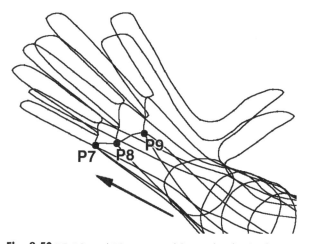

Fig. 8-50 P7, P8, and P9 are moved forward to begin shaping the lower part of the fingers and thumb.

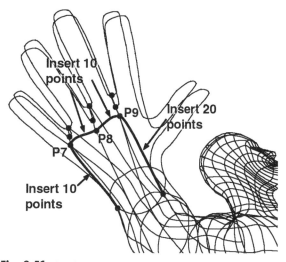

Insert 10 points

Insert 20 points

Insert 10 points

Fig. 8-51 The darker and heavier outline represents the part where all the points are inserted to form the lower section of the fingers and thumb.

181

Top

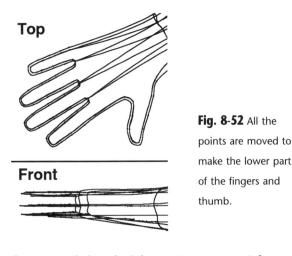

Front

Fig. 8-52 All the points are moved to make the lower part of the fingers and thumb.

fingers, and thumb. Select points seven, eight, and nine (P7, P8, and P9). Drag the points forward somewhat underneath the previously moved P1, P2, P3, P4, P5, and P6 points (Figure 8-50). Insert points at the specified locations in Figure 8-51. Shape the bottom section of the fingers and thumb and make sure that all the points correspond to the previously placed middle and top parts of the

hand (Figure 8-52). At this time, you may want to taper the fingers somewhat by rotating the bottom and top points of the hand, or you may decide to wait until all the points are connected.

Referring to Figure 8-53, you now need to add the hand splines. At the base of the fingers, add six points: three on the right side in-between the thumb and forefinger, and three on the left side, just below the pinky finger. Each of the points is inserted on the top, middle, and bottom finger splines. Select the newly created points and P1, P2, P3, P7, P8 and P9 in the right order and connect them with a closed curve (spline 1). To make it easier, select the twelve points, hide everything that is not selected, and connect.

Add six more points on the left side of the hand where the thumb meets the palm. On the right side of the hand, approximately halfway in-between the base of the pinky and the wrist, insert six more points. Each of these points is inserted on

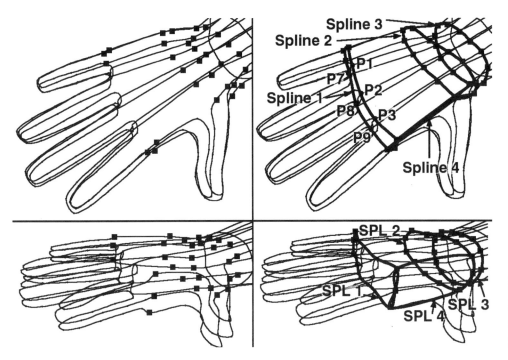

Fig. 8-53 Thirty new points are inserted to make the four, closed hand curves.

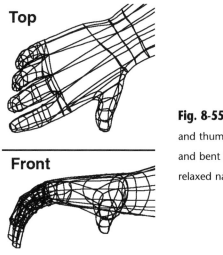

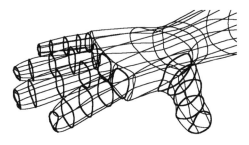

Fig. 8-54 All the finger and thumb points are connected with closed curves.

Top

Front

Fig. 8-55 The fingers and thumb are shaped and bent into a more relaxed natural position.

the top, middle, and bottom finger splines. Add another six points on the bottom and top of the splines that connect to P1, P2, P3, P7, P8, and P9. Connect the twelve points to make another closed curve near the wrist (spline 2). For spline 3, add six points on either side of the hand where the wrist narrows before widening into the palm. Insert another six points on the bottom and top of the splines that connect to P1, P2, P3, P7, P8, and P9. Using the preexisting points from spline 1 and spline 2, where the thumb meets the hand, connect the twelve points to make spline 4.

Connect the points on the fingers and thumb. Figure 8-54 shows the resulting oval curves as darker and thicker splines. They are created by

selecting each of the six previously made points and making closed curves out of them. You can see why it was necessary to align the points on each of the splines for the knuckles. Selecting the six points and hiding the rest make the process easier. While everything is still hidden, fix the shape of the finger at the six points that you just connected.

Now shape the fingers. After you add the finger and thumb curves, the fingers are uniformly sized from the base of the fingers to the tips. The individual points should be adjusted to make the fingers and thumb look more realistic. You can select individual closed curves and hide the rest. Working in point mode, you can adjust the shapes according to your templates. You might also want to bend the fingers and thumb down into their more natural positions (Figure 8-55). After you have finished correcting the points, you are done modeling the hand.

Before proceeding with the leg portion of the model, one more open curve will have to be

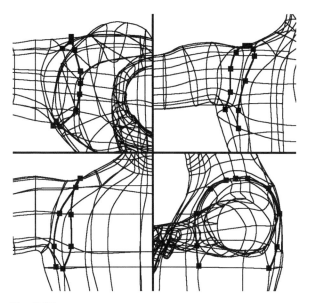

Fig. 8-56 To prevent any autopatching errors, extra points are inserted at the shoulder area and connected with an open curve.

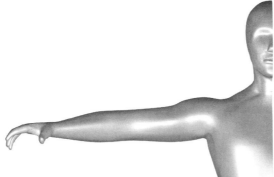

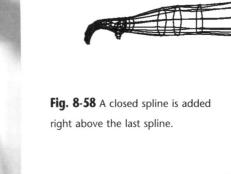

Fig. 8-57 A test rendering of the partially completed figure. At this time, it is still lacking detail, but shows the smooth, seamless quality of this modeling technique.

Fig. 8-58 A closed spline is added right above the last spline.

inserted at the shoulder area. This extra spline prevents any errors like holes in the shoulder blade and chest sections when autopatching. Figure 8-56 shows the area where extra points are added and connected to make an open curve.

At this time, it might be a good idea to check your progress by autopatching the spline cage. This should make it easier to see any hidden flaws. Figure 8-57 shows the figure at this stage. Details like the muscles, nails, and facial features can be sculpted later into the polygons or the spline cage.

Near the bottom of the spline cage, insert points and connect them with a closed curve (Figure 8-58). Select the lowest spline where the upper leg ends and pull it down from the torso (Figure 8-59). Other closed curves are added to the leg in the same manner as the arm and adjusted to form the contours (Figure 8-60). Selecting the

Fig. 8-59 The last spline points are pulled down to the spot where the bottom of the foot will be located.

Fig. 8-60 After adding points, closed curves are made and shaped for the entire leg.

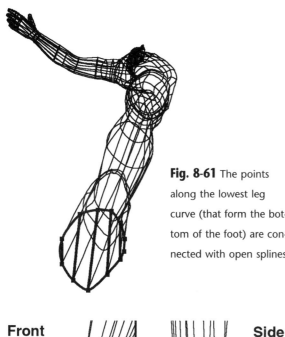

Fig. 8-61 The points along the lowest leg curve (that form the bottom of the foot) are connected with open splines.

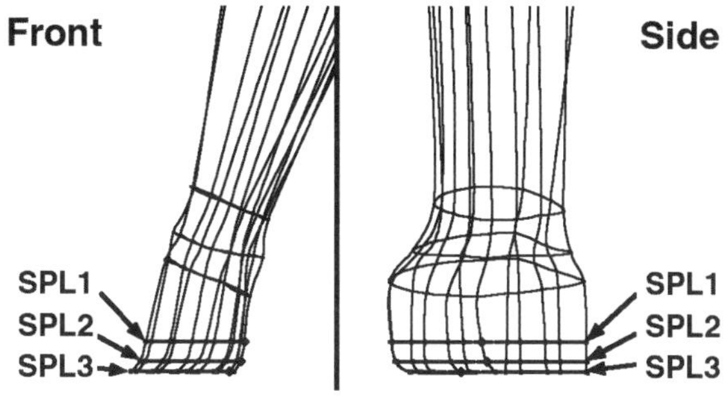

You should already have one on the very bottom.

Begin shaping the three foot splines (SPL1, SPL2, and SPL3) into the back half of the foot. The three front points on each spline are left alone. Figure 8-63 shows the nine points (P1–P9) that you will use to shape the toes. The view is looking up at the partially completed foot without toes.

Figure 8-64 shows the next step, which is selecting points four, five, and six (P4–P6) of the middle spline and pulling them forward to begin shaping the toes. Using the same process as you did for the thumb and fingers, insert ten points between P4 and P5 (Figure 8-65). Do the same thing between P5 and P6. On the side of P4, add ten points. Next

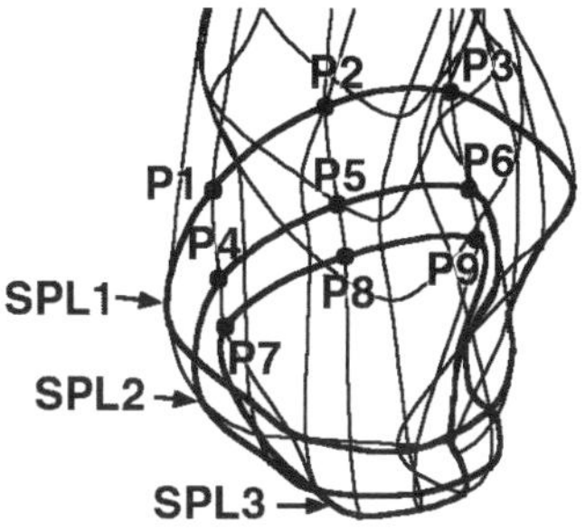

Front   **Side**

SPL1
SPL2
SPL3

SPL1
SPL2
SPL3

Fig. 8-62 Three closed curves, at the bottom of the foot, identified here as SPL1–3, are used to shape the foot and toes.

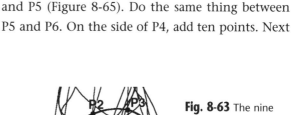

Fig. 8-63 The nine points (P1–P9) on splines 1, 2, and 3 (SPL1–SPL3) identify the top, middle, and bottom of the foot and toes.

closed curves in polygon mode and hiding the rest make it easier to focus on each section. In points mode, the individual oval splines are adjusted to a 2D or 3D template. Connect the points at the bottom of the foot with open curves (Figure 8-61).

Now model the foot and toes. Figure 8-62 shows three splines (closed curves) near the bottom of the leg. These are used to shape the toes in a way similar to the hand and fingers. Insert extra points and connect them to make closed curves for the foot.

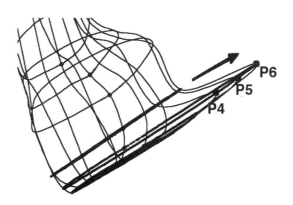

Fig. 8-64 Points four, five and six of SPL2 (the middle spline) are pulled forward to where the toes begin.

185

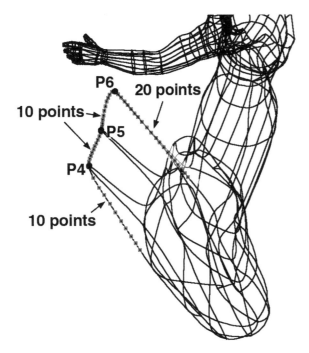

Fig. 8-65 Points are inserted along SPL2. These are used to shape all the toes.

to P6, insert twenty points. The twenty points are used to shape the big toe and the one next to it.

Shape the toes using the points that you just inserted. Notice the placement of the big toe in Figure 8-66. Even though it is in the wrong position, you will see later that this makes it easier to insert extra foot curves. Pull out spline 1 (SPL1),

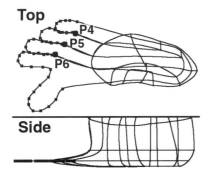

Fig. 8-66 The middle section of the toes are defined.

insert points, and shape it into the top part of the toes (Figure 8-67). The points should correspond to the ones on SPL2. The outline should be slightly smaller than the one for the middle part of the toes. Use spline 3 (SPL3) to insert extra points and shape the bottom part of the toes (Figure 8-68). These are slightly smaller like the tops of the toes. The points around all the toes on SPL1, SPL2, and SPL3 should correspond with each other because they will be connected later. Before starting on the toes, you need to insert some extra curves on the foot.

Figure 8-69 shows where to insert three points to the right of P1 and P7 on SPL1, SPL2, and SPL3. Three other points are added between the big toe and the next one on SPL1, SPL2, and SPL3. The six new points and P1, P2, P3, P7, P8, and P9 (a total

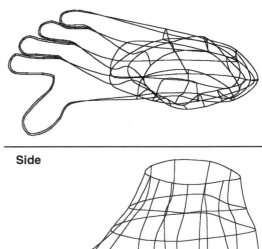

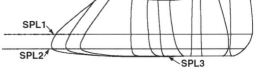

Fig. 8-67 SPL1, the top spline, is brought forward, points are inserted, and the tops of the toes are formed. Note, the top of the toes' outline is slightly smaller than the one for middle section (SPL2).

Top

Side

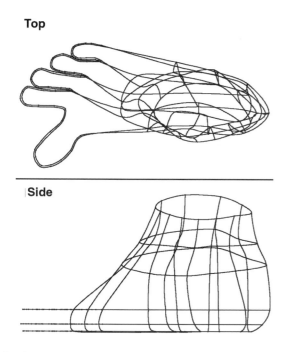

Fig. 8-68 The bottom spline (SPL3) is pulled forward, points added, and the toes shaped. Resembling the top of the toes, it is slightly smaller than the middle section.

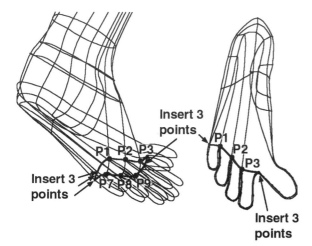

Fig. 8-69 Six new points are inserted to the right of P1 and to the left of P3, next to the little toe, and in between the big toe. The six new points and P1, 2, 3, 7, 8, and 9 are connected with a closed curve. This marks the first foot spline.

of twelve) are selected in order and connected with a closed curve.

Refer to Figure 8-70 to insert twelve more points on the foot and connect these with a closed curve. The third foot spline uses preexisting points located at the base of the big toe (Figure 8-71). These points were part of the points used to create

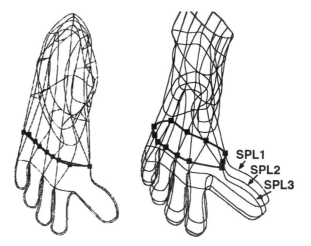

Fig. 8-70 The second foot spline is made from twelve new points.

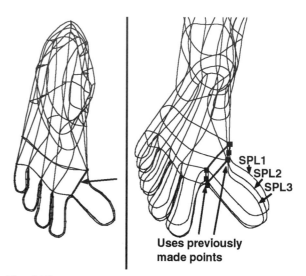

Fig. 8-71 A third foot spline, at the base of the big toe, uses some of the previously created points.

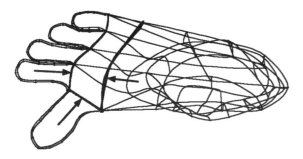

Fig. 8-72 The top view of all three, newly created foot splines.

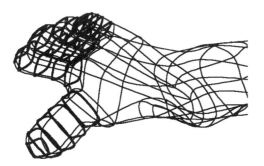

Fig. 8-73 All the toe points are connected with closed curves.

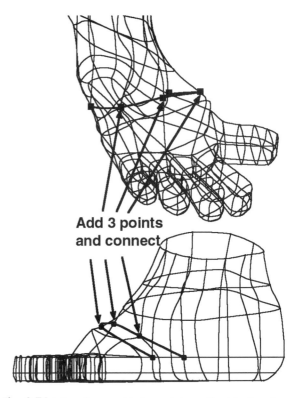

Add 3 points
and connect

Fig. 8-74 A few shapes with five points are fixed by inserting three extra points and connecting them to the two extra ones on the side.

the first and second foot curves. Figure 8-72 shows the three-foot splines that should now be there.

Connect all the corresponding points on the toes with closed curves (Figure 8-73). If you look near the middle of the foot and on both sides, you should see a shape that has five points due to five intersecting splines. If you autopatch the figure at this point, it will leave two holes on each side of the foot. To remedy this, add three more points to the top three splines that connect to P1, P2, and P3 (Figure 8-74). Use an open curve to connect the two side points with the newly made three top points. Look for other five-sided shapes and add extra open curves to make them four-sided or three-sided, if necessary. You might want to autopatch temporarily to find the holes in the foot.

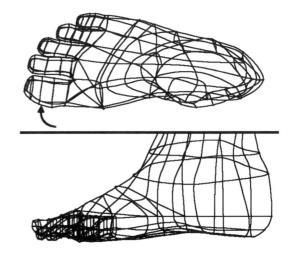

Fig. 8-75 The big toe is rotated into its correct position and all the toes are refined.

The three-sided shapes often autopatch with their polygons flipped. They look like holes but can be fixed later by selecting the polygons and either flipping them or aligning them with the rest.

Select the points on the big toe and rotate it so that it is in the correct position (Figure 8-75). Adjust all of the toe curves to give them a more realistic shape. As with the hand, you can select curves and hide all the rest. Working in points mode, adjust the shapes of the splines. It is better to shape the foot and toes quickly in a general way and then at the end, concentrate more closely on the details.

So far you have been modeling a foot flat on the ground. To align it with the angled placement of the leg, you should select the foot points and rotate them so that the foot is in a position similar to the one in Figure 8-76. Later, after the bones are placed, the leg is rotated so that the foot is flat on the ground once again.

The final modeling touches should be made to the foot and all the toes. Because some of the shapes at the bottom of the foot have more than four points, three extra open curves should be inserted there (Figure 8-77). Check to make sure that each section only has three or four points around it. When you are satisfied, do a test autopatch at 0, the lowest setting. Any holes in the polygon mesh that are not caused by flipped, three-sided polygons could indicate sections with more than four points. Try to isolate these and make your corrections to the spline cage by eliminating extra points or by adding more of them to connect with open curves. When you are finished, be sure to align the head and torso middle points along the *x*-axis. This will keep the model from having holes or creases in the middle when it is mirrored and the points merged.

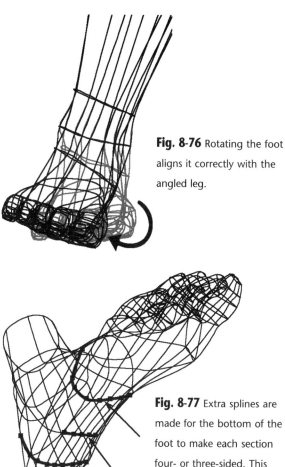

Fig. 8-76 Rotating the foot aligns it correctly with the angled leg.

Fig. 8-77 Extra splines are made for the bottom of the foot to make each section four- or three-sided. This prevents autopatching errors.

Once you are finished with the spline cage model, apply the AutoPatcher plug-in. If you use a low setting like 0, you will find it easier to correct any polygon errors. Applying metaform smoothing remedies the faceted look of the large polygons. In "Polygon Statistics" select "Faces." Cut the selected polygons and paste them to another layer. Save the spline cage model as a file separate from the polygon version. The polygon model might show a few errors such as flipped polygons and a few darker sections. The flipped polygons will

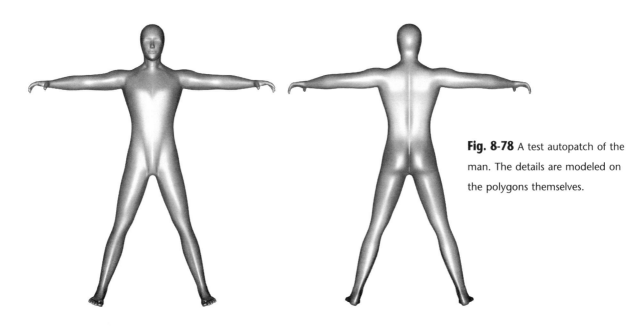

Fig. 8-78 A test autopatch of the man. The details are modeled on the polygons themselves.

show up as holes. Select individual polygons and flip them or try the "Align" command. Merge points to remedy some of the darker patches. Use "polygon statistics" to get rid of any one- or two-sided polygons.

Normally, you would model details, like facial features, skeletal and muscle characteristics, nails, and so on, to the half polygon character or to the spline cage itself. After that, you mirror, set value on the middle points along the x-axis, and finally, merge points on the two halves. Figure 8-78 shows a male model after autopatching, aligning polygons, mirroring, and merging points. It still needs additional detail work.

Adding Detail to the Spline Cage

To save work later, you can add a few details to the spline cage. These can then be refined on the polygon model after autopatching. A word of caution: When adding extra points to the spline cage, make sure that there are no more than four vertices around each shape. If you have more than four,

connect these to others with open curves to create three- or four-sided shapes.

If you are working on a female, shape the breast by creating crisscrossed open curves. These splines cross each other at the tip (Figure 8-79). Points can be inserted along these and connected to make circular closed curves. Pulling the points out will shape the breast.

The eye area should have closed curves around it. These form oval shapes. Figure 8-80 shows the splines that are created from connecting existing and extra points. To make the eye area more detailed, add more circular closed curves. Some of the points can be pulled back to begin shaping the eye socket.

The ear can be formed from the existing spline cage on the head. However, due to its complexity, it is usually easier to model it as a separate spline cage and then weld its outside points to the head. Figure 8-81 shows the open curves that delineate the shape of the ear. These radiate from the inside out like the petals of a flower. The points along

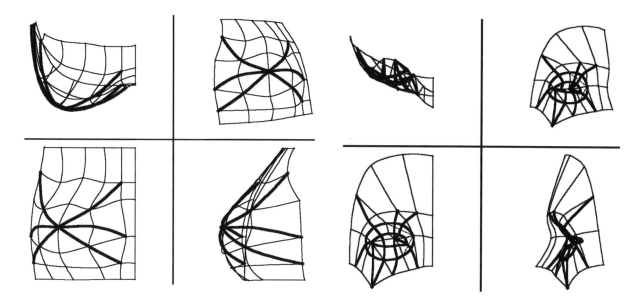

Fig. 8-79 Open curves that form crossing lines are added. Points along these and on surrounding splines are pulled out to shape the breast.

Fig. 8-80 Extra curves are inserted around the eye area. Oval-shaped closed curves define the eye opening and the circular muscle around it.

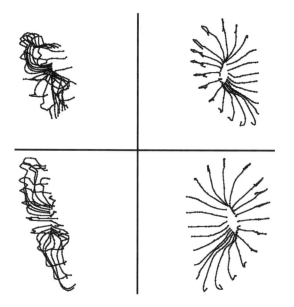

Fig. 8-81 Open curves radiating from the inside define the shape of the ear.

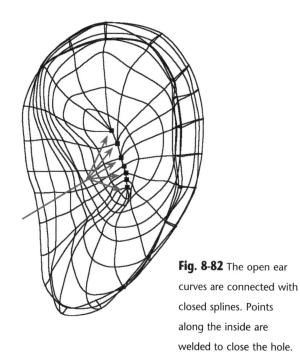

Fig. 8-82 The open ear curves are connected with closed splines. Points along the inside are welded to close the hole.

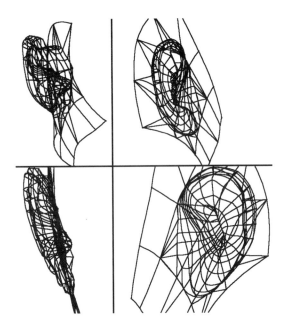

Fig. 8-83 Points along the ear spline cage are welded to the head.

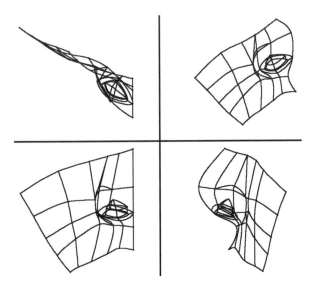

Fig. 8-84 The nostril is made from a series of oval closed curves. The smaller inner curves are pulled up into the nose.

these splines are connected with closed curves (Figure 8-82). To close up the hole in the center, select adjacent points and weld them. Autopatch the ear spline cage to check its shape. When you are satisfied, place it against the head spline cage and weld the points along the ear's perimeter (Figure 8-83). You will most likely have to insert extra points along the head curves. After welding the ear to the head, find any shapes around the ear that have more than four points. Connect these extra points to other points on the head with open curves so that you only have three- or four-sided shapes.

The nostril can be made part of the spline cage. Find or insert points under the nose and connect them with oval-shaped, closed curves. Pull the inner curves up into the nose to make the nostril (Figure 8-84).

This completes the spline cage. Of course, bone structures like the collarbone, knee, elbow, shoulder blade, and so on can also be modeled on the spline cage. Some may prefer to model these directly to the polygon mesh after autopatching. Wrinkles and other minute details can be sculpted onto the polygons themselves.

PART III

Preparing for 3D Animation

CHAPTER 9

Lighting

Light and color are synonymous terms. When writing about one, it is difficult to ignore the other. Painting with color in 3D means painting with light. Light and color are the most relevant mediums in computer art. Light not only varies according to the amount present in a setting but also in relationship to neighboring light sources. Since this book has only black and white illustrations, it is difficult to show the effects of color and light. Therefore, a number of 24-bit color illustrations have been placed on the CD-ROM.

An expert use of light means controlling it not only by selecting the correct light type, and modifying it by degree of falloff, intensity, and color, but also by moderating its influence through the skillful placement of other lights in a scene. These change a scene's character. One example can be seen in Figure 9-1. A strong light source next to an object causes it to lose saturation, thus making it look too light and washed out. If you were to turn down the light's intensity, other areas would become too dark. One solution to this problem is to place a negative light source next to the washed out part of the object, thus cutting down the strength of the first light. The negative light absorbs extra light in a specific part of the scene making it a great tool for localized control. Negative lights have a number of other useful functions that will be discussed in a later section.

Light Types

Some of the most common light types can be viewed in Figure 9-2. Most 3D software packages utilize these in one form or another. Some, like spotlights, are used quite commonly, while others like ambient light are utilized sparingly. Many times a light type is chosen for the quality of its

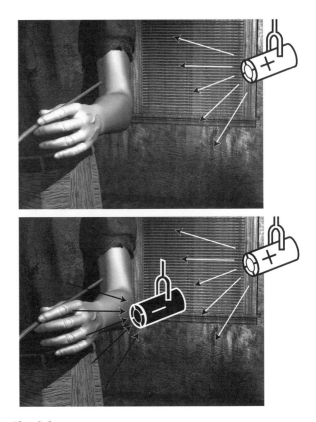

Fig. 9-1 In the upper portion, a spotlight's brightness washes out the fingers and hand. When a negative light is added in the lower half, the extra light intensity is absorbed.

shadows. For example, distant, point, and spotlights produce hard-edged, ray-traced shadows, while linear and area lights create soft-edged, ray-traced shadows.

Ambient light creates a uniform and directionless light source. Since it penetrates every part of a scene, it is often used as a fill light. Most professionals try to keep ambient light to a minimum because of its tendency to make scenes look flat and washed out. Figure 9-3 shows the effect of ambient light. Notice how the scene lacks contrast due to the lack of diversity in the lighting setup. It is usually recommended that ambient light be turned down to about 5% or 10%.

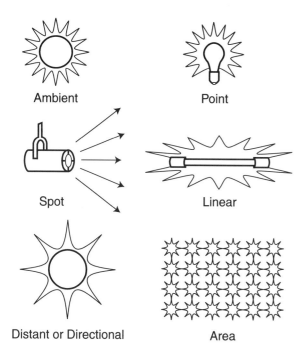

Fig. 9-2 Some common light types. Ambient lights illuminate uniformly in all directions. Point lights are similar to light bulbs. Spotlights cast light in one direction. Linear lights are like a line of point lights. Distant or directional lights are like the sun. Area lights are like a group of point lights illuminating in all directions.

Spotlights are some of the most commonly used light types. This is partly due to the fact that their flexibility gives the user a great amount of control. You can set the spotlight angle to shine on a larger or smaller part of the scene. The direction of the light is easy to handle. In addition, some software packages only let the user create shadow maps or depth-map shadows with spotlights. Unlike most ray-traced shadows, shadow maps are soft-edged. They also render faster. Shadow maps are usually calculated by what areas are hidden when viewed from the light's view. Normally, you would not assign shadow maps to more than one or two lights. Figure 9-4 illustrates the use of spotlights and shadow maps. The scene appears similar to stage lighting.

Area lights are like a rectangular array of lights (Figure 9-5). They send light out in all directions. Due to their ability to create soft-edged, ray-traced shadows, they can produce some of the highest quality renderings. Unfortunately, this comes at a steep price. A scene that would normally render in one minute could take forty minutes with area

Fig. 9-3 Too much ambient light weakens any contrast in the image. Notice how much detail is missing.

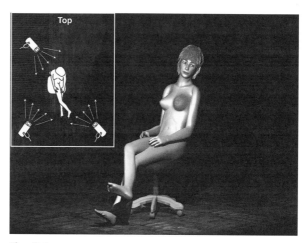

Fig. 9-4 Spotlights are used to make this scene look more dramatic.

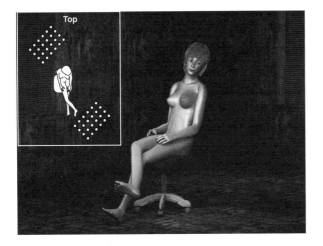

Fig. 9-5 Area lights create pleasing soft ray-traced shadows but the rendering time can be forty times longer than normal.

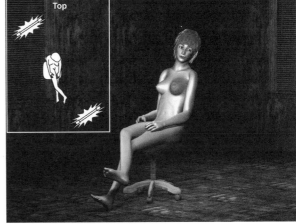

Fig. 9-6 Linear lights yield results similar to area lights except that the shadows are not as soft, but rendering takes only half the time.

lights. Another aspect of these lights is that they can usually be scaled in size.

Linear lights (Figure 9-6) are similar to area lights in that they also produce soft-edged, ray-traced shadows. These lights also have longer rendering times, although not quite as protracted as

area lights. Linear lights are like a row of lights. Normally, these lights can be scaled.

Distant or directional lights are meant to simulate the effects of sunlight (Figure 9-7). Like the sun, their light rays travel parallel to one another in the direction the light is pointing. The light usu-

Fig. 9-7 Distant or directional lights act similar to the sun by illuminating everything equally. Shadows are hard-edged and difficult to control.

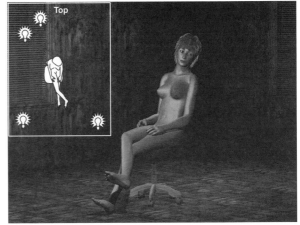

Fig. 9-8 Point lights placed around a scene give soft illumination to objects, although the ray-traced shadows have hard edges.

ally travels through objects. For example, if you place a box in a scene, the distant light would illuminate the interior as well as the exterior. Distant or directional lights have no obvious source and do not decay with distance. Therefore, it does not matter where you place these lights because far off objects receive the same illumination as closer ones. Since distant lights illuminate everything equally, a total reliance on them produces a monotonous lighting scheme.

Point lights illuminate equally in all directions from a central source (Figure 9-8). They can be compared to bare incandescent light bulbs. Careful consideration should be given to the placement of point lights. Used in conjunction with spotlights, point lights can be useful for filling out areas of low illumination as well as reducing light by setting them with a negative intensity.

Lighting Arrangements

Although there is no set formula for placing lights in a scene, basic, classic configurations are used extensively in the real world as well as in computer graphics. The following common lighting arrangements should serve as a starting point to much more interesting and creative approaches. Even though these configurations rely on only four lights, it is recommended that many more lights be added to simulate radiosity, create extra shadows, and enhance the mood through color.

Each object could easily require six lights. Some of these might include a top light, key (main light), fill light (fills out the shadow side), rim light (points from the back toward the camera to outline the figure), a kicker (points in the opposite direction of the key light to outline part of the figure from one side), and eye light (highlights the eyes). Other colored lights could be added to make the object look more interesting. The fill light might be colored blue or purple while the key light could have a warm color such as light yellow.

Figure 9-9 shows a basic light setup in which the color values and emotional impact are weak. Due to the key (main) and fill (softens shadows) lights having similar settings, the objects lack con-

Fig. 9-9 A basic lighting setup. The image lacks contrast due to both the key and fill lights having the same high settings. Increasing the rim light's intensity separates the objects from the background. A lower fill light setting increases contrast.

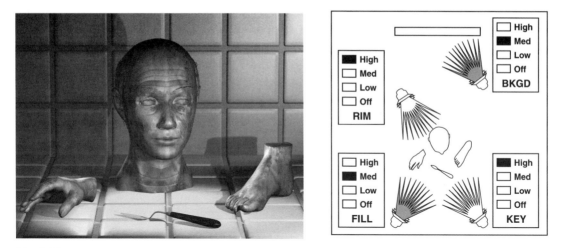

Fig. 9-10 A more dramatic lighting arrangement. The high rim light illuminates the edges of objects and the lower fill light setting adds deeper shadows.

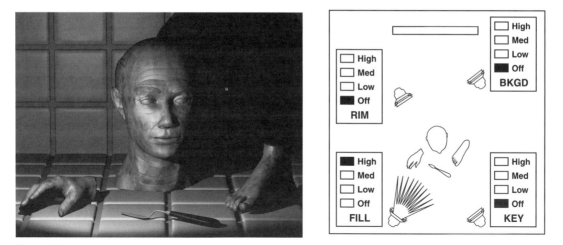

Fig. 9-11 A very contrasty lighting setup. Since the fill light is the only source of illumination, the resulting deep shadows hide much of the detail.

trast and are washed out in areas. A lower fill light setting and stronger rim light (back light) can make this scene more dramatic.

A better lighting arrangement can be seen in Figure 9-10. Having the fill light at a lower setting and the rim light higher helps to define the features of all the objects.

A very simplified lighting setup can be viewed

in Figure 9-11. Only one light is used and it is not even the key light. The dimmer fill light creates deep shadows that obscure most of the detail.

Turning off all the front lights and only using the back lights make objects appear as silhouettes (Figure 9-12). This is a useful device used in broadcasting when interviewing someone anonymously.

A more subdued arrangement can be found in

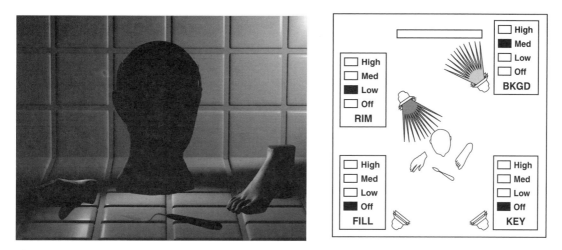

Fig. 9-12 A silhouette lighting scheme. The lack of illumination in front of the subject obscures its identity.

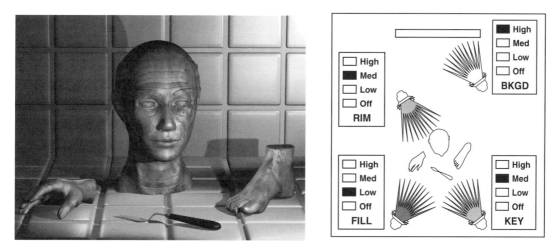

Fig. 9-13 A softer lighting setup. Contrast is good without having the shadows obliterate detail.

Figure 9-13. The front lights have a lower setting while the strongest light is the bounce light in the back. This lighting arrangement can serve as a good starting point for the placement of other lights.

A darker and more mysterious mood can be set up with the fill and rim lights set high (Figure 9-14). A few other well-placed, low-level lights can enrich this scene.

Moving the lights to a lower level and projecting their beams up at the subject can make things look strange (Figure 9-15). It is reminiscent of a child shining a flashlight upward from below the chin.

Nighttime illumination can be created with lights shining down on the subject (Figure 9-16). To enhance this scene, you should place more lights around the objects but with lower settings. Negative

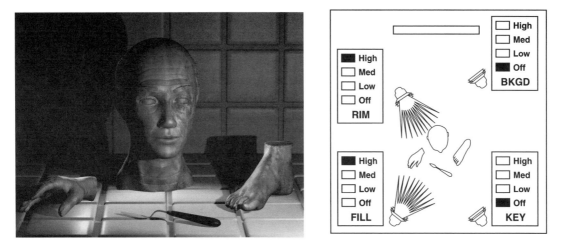

Fig. 9-14 A contrasty lighting arrangement due to the lack of a key light. It can be used to convey a mood of mystery.

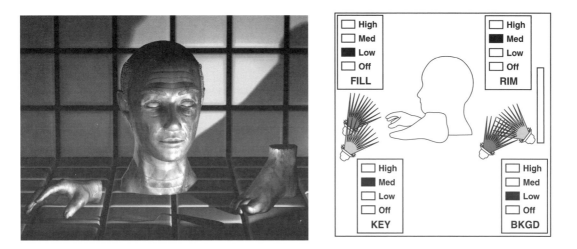

Fig. 9-15 Lighting from below can make objects look eerie. The effect is a favorite with producers of mystery and horror films.

lights can also be combined with the others to soften the bright spots. The standard four-light setup can be enhanced with the addition of one top light.

Lighting Hints

Animation companies, just like movie studios, often use specialists to set up the correct lighting for their scenes. The following section was compiled from interviews with one of my former stu-

dents Patrick Wilson, who now works as a lighting specialist at PIXAR, and Avi Das, a color and lighting artist at Digital Domain. Both of them shed light (pardon the pun) on the inner workings of lighting for animation.

Use Negative Lights

Shadows under the feet are often hard to control. If your software allows you to parent lights to the feet or the bones/joints of the feet, then you can

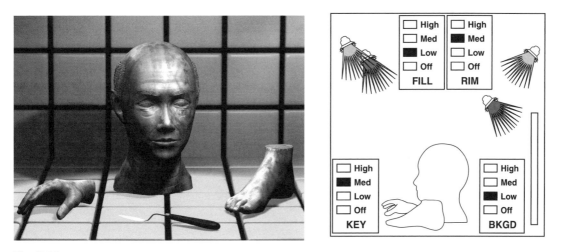

Fig. 9-16 Lighting from the top can simulate indoor nighttime illumination.

create your own shadows without too much trouble. Figure 9-17 shows two pairs of lights. One pair is negative and the other duplicate pair is positive. The positive lights cast shadow maps or depth map shadows, while the negative lights do not project shadows. In other words, "Shadow Type" or "Project Shadows" is turned on for the positive lights while it is turned off for the negative lights.

Figure 9-17 shows the four lights separately for the sake of clarity, but in reality, each set of positive and negative lights occupies the same space above each foot. All the lights have the same intensity, but you can control the value of the shadows by setting different intensities to the negative lights. If both the positive and negative lights have the same intensity settings, they will cancel each other out. The overall illumination stays the same while shadows are cast under the feet. These are sometimes referred to as contact shadows.

Negative lights can also be used to make parts of a scene darker. A good application of this is to place them in corners of rooms or in other spots where you do not want illumination. Figure 9-18 shows the effect of negative lights along the bases

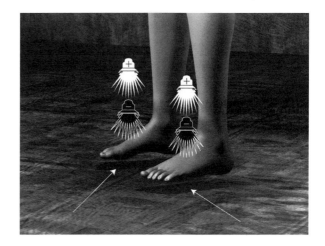

Fig. 9-17 Two pairs of spotlights are parented to the feet. One set has a positive intensity while the other has a negative intensity. Each negative and positive pair has the same settings and unlike the illustration, occupies the same space. This results in shadows under the feet (arrows) without any extra illumination.

of walls and corners of a room. It is as if you were using a sponge to soak up light.

As shown in Figure 9-1, negative lights can be used to cut back intense illumination in a scene. They can keep objects from losing their contrast

Fig. 9-18 To darken corners of rooms or other areas, place negative lights to create shadows.

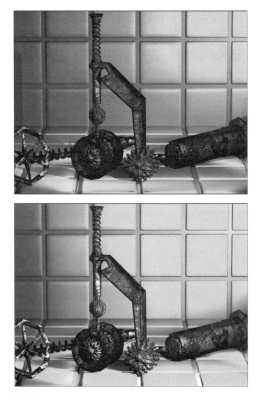

Fig. 9-19 The top image is rendered with hard-edged, ray-traced shadows while the bottom one has soft-edged shadow maps.

and help regulate the values in a scene. Another advantage to negative lights is that they do not increase rendering time. They eliminate all lighting calculations in the influenced area.

Rely Mostly on Shadow Maps or Depth Map Shadows Rather than Raytraced Ones

Rendering shadows using raytracing produces sharp shadows that take a relatively long time to render. Many artists consider scenes with raytraced shadows as cold. You can render shadows much faster while obtaining smooth, soft-edged shadows of equivalent quality (Figure 9-19).

To get a basic understanding of how shadow maps are generated, a few terms need to be clarified. *Z* depth describes how far away objects are in a scene. Normally, *Z* depth information is calculated by how far objects are from the camera. With depth map shadows (shadow maps), the shadows are calculated by how far they are from the light sources that are casting them. The renderer uses this information and the position of the light sources to determine which items produce shadows. It stores all this information in the *Z*-buffer. This extra memory usage means that you often have to limit the number of lights casting shadow maps. Usually, only one or two lights are set to produce shadow maps. Using *Z* depth information makes it hard to get a perfect depth placement of objects. The result is that aliasing problems can appear. This can usually be remedied by allocating more memory to the renderer and setting a higher shadow map size.

Simulate Radiosity with Colored Bounce Lights

Ray tracing creates a ray for each pixel in a scene and traces its path, one at a time, all the way to the light source. A value for each ray is calculated as it travels through and bounces off various surfaces. To minimize rendering time, many renderers trace rays of light backwards from the camera to the light source. This eliminates the extra calculations needed to trace light rays that never reach the camera itself. Ray tracing does not calculate the effects of light as it bounces off one surface and illuminates another.

Radiosity rendering calculates the amount of light that is transmitted from one surface to another. This process continues to follow the light until it is fully absorbed by all the surfaces or dissipates in space. Radiosity calculations require a great amount of memory and raw computing power. Renderings are usually very time-intensive.

To simulate radiosity, place colored bounce lights in your scene. These can be pointed at surfaces that would show light from nearby objects. Figure 9-20 shows the location of several colored bounce lights. These point to the ground surface next to objects that reflect colored light onto it. The spotlights make it look as if various paint tubes are spilling their colored lights onto the tiled floor. A color image of this scene can be viewed on the CD-ROM as CD9-20.

It may take a little extra time to place bounce lights in your scene but the rendering time will be much quicker than a true radiosity rendering. Placing similar colored lights next to surfaces will greatly improve the quality of your renderings.

Ask Yourself: What is the Emotional Goal of the Scene?

Before lighting a scene, think back to situations you have been in. If the scene is going to be romantic, then you might use diffused light with warm shadows. Color sketches can be a great aid in planning the lighting setup (Figure 9-21). They will save you time because you will not have to do

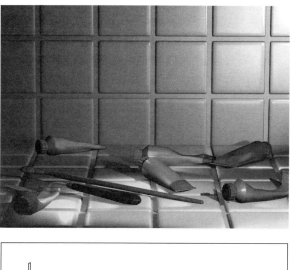

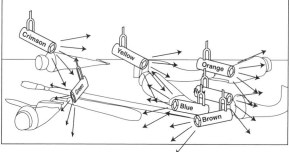

Fig. 9-20 Colored bounce lights simulate radiosity by making surfaces look as if they were receiving light from other objects.

as many test renderings before deciding on the final appearance of your environment. If you are averse to leaving your computer, then sketch the scene in an image manipulation program before starting to light it in 3D.

Use Falloff or Decay and Link Lights to Specific Characters

Limiting the effect of each light gives you greater control over the scene's lighting arrangement. When lights are set to have falloff or decay, they will simulate light in the physical world, which

Fig. 9-21 Sketching first on or off the computer can speed up the process of lighting a scene.

becomes weaker with distance (Figure 9-22). Some software programs allow you to link lights to specific objects so that they affect only these and not adjacent ones. This is very useful for lighting characters. When the character approaches other objects or characters, its lights will not affect them. This is where computer graphics lighting reigns over set lighting. In a set, a light illuminates everything in its path unless stopped by a flag.

Use about six lights per character. Some of the lights that shine on the shadowed parts of a character can be colored blue or purple for a richer look. Consider using the complementary (opposite on the color wheel) color to the key light. All lights should have a hint of color because pure white light rarely exists in our world.

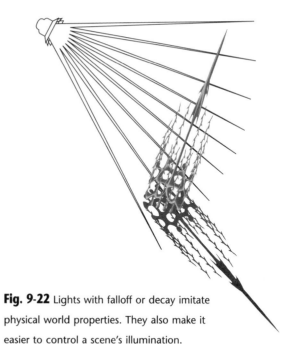

Fig. 9-22 Lights with falloff or decay imitate physical world properties. They also make it easier to control a scene's illumination.

Illuminate Scenes with a Variety of Lights

Try not to skimp on the number of lights in a scene. When you consider all of the various types of lights like bounce, fill, rim, kickers, negative, key, background, and so on, you could easily end up with fifty to one-hundred lights in a large scene. Localized lights with falloff or decay, and lights assigned specifically to individual objects, may add up, but they allow a greater degree of control. Typically, a scene might have no fewer than thirty lights (Figures 9-23, 9-24, and 9-25). Each light has a reason for its existence, otherwise, it is a waste of ren-

Fig. 9-23 Over thirty lights are used in this scene. They consist of positive and negative spot and point lights and one area light on the floor. The lights can be seen in Figures 9-24 and 9-25.

Fig. 9-24 The lights used in Fig. 9-23 as viewed through the camera. A number of lights are behind objects and other lights and are out of camera view and cannot be seen.

Fig. 9-25 An overview of all the lights used in the Fig. 9-23 scene. Positive and negative lights often occupy the same space. The lights appear to be stacked on top of each other when in reality they are spaced along the z-axis.

dering time. Usually, only one or two lights are set to cast the main shadows. Negative lights provide a few other areas of shadow while contact shadows (Figure 9-17) add a few more. Color images showing examples of indoor lighting with over thirty lights can be viewed on the CD-ROM as CD9-23a and CD9-23b.

When starting to light an interior, use a very low intensity, overall light to establish the basic ambience. This ambient light can vary among slight purple, blue, or even green. Fluorescent lights radiate a greenish hue. Then begin to add brighter lights with local influence only. Vary the cone angles and penumbras (soft edges of lights). These lights should dissipate after a specified distance as in real life. One example is a bar scene in which many lights with differing falloffs allow shadows to occur between lights. If there is a row of lights along a corridor, the intensity and the falloff or decay can vary as well. This prevents the lighting from looking flat and produces a visually

interesting setting. In the physical world, the light bulbs vary in age with some more intense than others. The older ones have a slightly cooler temperature. These have more decay (lower falloff setting) and warmer colors. To break up a uniform look, project a slight noise pattern through some of the lights. This technique is discussed in the next section on light gels.

Outdoor scene lighting can sometimes be accomplished with far fewer lights. The first step involves setting up the ambient light. It should be at a very low setting and its color should be context-specific. A bright daylight exterior has an unsaturated blue ambience. This kind of light scatters as it penetrates the atmosphere. The key light, which in this case simulates sunlight, is set up next. A yellow/orange distant light works unless you want it to cast shadow maps. Your software may limit you to using a spot light. The key lighting colors are generally warmer and less intense for sunrise and sunset scenes. Once this is established,

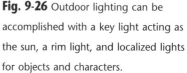

Fig. 9-26 Outdoor lighting can be accomplished with a key light acting as the sun, a rim light, and localized lights for objects and characters.

point a complementary colored light (blue to purple) from the opposite direction toward the key light. The intensity should be about 30% to 40% and fill in the shadow side. Once this basic lighting has been established, look for areas where local lighting effects should happen. For example, Figure 9-26 depicts an outdoor scene with two characters with their own set of lights, which include the key, fill, and kicker lights. Extra lights are placed around the scene to bring out specific details like trees, grass, and so on. Negative lights are placed in parts of the scene to soak up extra light or to create more shady areas. This scene can be viewed in color on the CD-ROM as CD9-26.

Another application of local lighting can be found in city scenes. Two white buildings next to each other at 45-degree angles to the sun's rays have one of their sides in the shadows. One building can reflect a pale yellow light onto the other building's shadow side creating a slight radiosity effect. This can be achieved by placing a light inside the building that is reflecting luminosity and pointing it at the one receiving the light. If the building that is reflecting is of a different color, then the bounce light projects the wall's hue onto the other building.

Midday scenes are generally accomplished in a similar manner, except for the change in color and intensity of the key and fill lights. Unlike early morning or late afternoon, when the key light reflects the sky with warm colors, midday light has a light blue color. For a very bright day, you can increase the luminance of your objects. This brings down the shadow densities. The effect is similar to days when you have to squint your eyes. To make it appear as if sunrays bounce off the ground and illuminate the underside of objects, place a low-intensity fill light under the ground. Point it up and turn off its shadows and set a falloff. The color of the light could be pale brown. Sometimes it only takes three or four lights to illuminate an outdoor scene.

209

Fig. 9-27 Light gels can be placed in the path of a spotlight or mapped to the light itself. The light becomes a slide projector.

Fig. 9-28 The use of light gels in an underwater scene. The animated gel texture is placed on the top light to create patterns on the swimmer and on the bottom surface.

Try Using Light Gels

For more realistic lighting, try incorporating light gels in your scenes. Gels are patterns, images, textures, gradations, and so on that are placed in front of lights. For example, in computer graphics a fractal noise shader or texture can be projected from a spotlight. The light acts similar to a slide projector. The fractal noise breaks up the light, simulating real-world spotty, inconsistent lighting (Figure 9-27).

In cinema, lighting gels are sometimes referred to as gobos or kukalories. Any cutout or semi-transparent image can be placed in front of a light source. A good use of gels is found in underwater scenes. Figure 9-28 shows the effects of a gel placed on a top light. The mapped image has a slow texture velocity, which makes the underwater patterns move. An animation of this underwater effect can be viewed on the CD-ROM as CD9-27, and as an image file labeled CD9-27b. Another important ele-

ment of underwater scenes is the use of blue fog to make objects fade quickly in the distance.

Animation companies like PIXAR create animated shaders for light gels. For example, a shader consisting of a tree with branches and moving leaves is projected on the ground producing an active shadow.

Use Volumetric or Fog Lights for Dramatic Effects

Volumetric or fog lights can be seen as they move through space. In the physical world, tiny airborne particles reflect light in the air. Light streaming through the window of a dusty room, or a lighthouse illuminating a hazy night, are just a few examples of volumetric lighting. If you are looking for a way to make lighting more dramatic, you might try volumetric lighting, but be prepared for very long rendering times (Figure 9-29). A color image of volumetric lighting can be viewed on the CD-ROM as CD9-29.

Since volumetric lighting can greatly increase rendering time, you may decide to try this technique for faking volumetrics. Using an object for the light and applying some creative texturing, you can cut back rendering time to a fraction of what it takes to render real volumetric lighting.

Fig. 9-29 Volumetric lighting can enhance the mood of a scene but it does increase rendering time greatly.

Fake volumetric lighting can be accomplished by modeling the shape of the light beam (Figure 9-30). A transparency map is created for the object. It consists of a light to dark gradient seen in Figure 9-30. This map is used to soften the edges of the object. The lightest areas show the object clearest while the darker ones obscure it. A fractal noise pattern of white and gray is applied to the object. The transparency is set to 60% and the transparency map is placed on it as a negative image. Edge transparency and glow are also applied to the object. The result is viewed in Figure 9-31 and in color on the CD-ROM as CD9-31.

Mood Lighting

Lighting and color play an important role in establishing the mood or emotional quality of a scene. Before setting up lights, visualize the type of illumination that you desire. Use reference materials if you need to. Studying the works of artists like

Fig. 9-30 Fake volumetric lighting can speed up the rendering process dramatically. The volumetric light object on the left has the transparency map (shown on the right) applied to it. Its surface has transparency with fractal noise, edge transparency, and glow. Fig. 9-31 shows the result.

Fig. 9-31 The fake volumetric effect after surfacing. Rendering time was minimal compared to real volumetric light rendering.

Rembrandt, Monet, Caravaggio, Vermeer, Parrish, and many others will prove to be an invaluable resource to draw from. The following suggestions for lighting may serve as a starting point or at least show some ways to light a specific scene.

Romantic Scenes

Warm colors like red, orange, and yellow are usually associated with feelings of affection and passion. Soft warm lights and shadows with low contrast can give the scene a glowing quality. The key light is placed high above while the fill light is set lower to soften the density of shadows.

Crime Scenes

Cool colors play a primary role here. Blue can make the scene look cold. An almost white, harsh key light conveys an uneasy feeling. Design your lights in a way that will produce deep pockets of shadows. Lighting for a scene like this can be a mix of the naturalistic and pictorial. Naturalistic lighting uses logical sources of lights while pictorial lighting is for aesthetics. Backgrounds should be out of focus to convey a sense of insecurity and danger. A wash of green light on background walls and objects can make the scene look unhealthy. Dark shadows and strong contrast play an important role in scenes like these. Avoid using warm colored lights.

Fantasy Scenes

Fantasy scenes can be designed in a great variety of ways. The lighting design is mostly pictorial. The entire lighting setup should be directed toward an aesthetically pleasing environment. Pastel colored lights can be used. All lights and shadows should be soft. Extreme light and dark values should be avoided. Of course, all of this depends on the mood that you are trying to establish.

Corporate Scenes

Office space should feel emotionless and sterile. Since most office spaces use fluorescent lights, a pale green key light from above can simulate this. The scene should have very little contrast, which can be accomplished by increasing ambient lights or fill lights. A scene like this can have an enormous amount of light; therefore, shadows should be soft and almost non-existent, especially for thinner objects.

Horror Scenes

Lighting for horror scenes can be similar to crime scene lighting. There should be high contrast with many shadows. The difference between the two is that in horror scenes, warm luminosity can be emitted from key and fill lights. Light gels are very useful here to project extra objects into the scene. This makes the environment appear to contain more than is actually modeled. For example, a dead tree with branches stretching out ominously with a noose swaying in the breeze can be projected onto a dimly lit, bloody red wall. Volumetric lights coming through a window can also give the scene an appearance of mystery and drama. All of this makes the scene appear disturbing or chilling.

Hostage Scenes

Try to imagine a scene where a hostage is bound to a chair and is being interrogated by terrorists. You can place a key spotlight inside a modeled light bulb hanging right above his head. It would cast a very harsh light, creating deep shadows under his eye sockets and chin. The light can be parented to the modeled light bulb, which, in turn, might slowly swing back and forth creating a disturbing play of light and shadow on the man's face and body.

The light should have a narrow cone angle and soft penumbra (edge angle) so that it does not influence much beyond the prisoner himself. The falloff should be enough so that the far reaches of the room are dark. The walls can be seen through the use of soft blue fill lights. A window with bars can let some light into the room. A kicker light, consisting of harsh white or blue light, placed about three-quarters behind the prisoner can be used to separate the prisoner from the background. It adds a sense of isolation to the prisoner.

Other characters can be seen as silhouettes against dimly lit, blue walls. They would look mysterious, unknown and dangerous. A very faint light, of about 20% of the key light's intensity, can be placed under the floor directly beneath the key light. It bounces up light from the floor and creates underlighting on the character for close-ups.

CHAPTER 10

Surfacing Techniques

3D animation involves building virtual environments. This means a lot of modeling followed by texturing. Knowing how to apply surfaces in a creative way will make your work look better and can save rendering as well as modeling time. Texture mapping can be the simple application of a color or image to an object. It can also be a very complicated process when trying to simulate special effects like those discussed in chapter 5. Surfacing often takes the place of complex modeling. Bump mapping is used to make fine details like wrinkles or hard-to-model crevices. Transparency mapping acts as a substitute for building complicated models like trees covered with leaves.

Texture Types

Surfacing normally means utilizing image maps or procedural textures. Image maps are digitized real-world images of brick, wood, fabric, and so on. They can make objects look photo realistic. The disadvantage to using them is that when seen in close-ups, they can show up as irregular surfaces due to the appearance of their individual pixels. To avoid this problem, high-resolution images can be utilized, but they require greater memory usage. Making the textures seamless so that they can be tiled is another solution, but the drawback is that a discernable pattern often arises on the surface of objects, which can make them look artificial.

Procedural textures, which are sometimes referred to as shaders, are images generated by mathematical formulas. They can take the form of two-dimensional or three-dimensional surfaces. 2D procedurals can be generated in an image-editing program and then saved as image maps. 3D procedural texture maps are defined in terms of points in three-dimensional space. Sometimes, these are

referred to as solid textures. They exist on the surface of the object as well as on the inside. Unlike 2D procedural textures, which are projected only on the outside surface of an object, 3D procedural textures are distributed throughout the object. If the object were sliced in half, you would find the texture inside of it. A procedural texture can be given parameters to vary its appearance in ways that are difficult to achieve with an image map. For example, an animated fire texture can look like it has flickering flames, or a water texture can be made to generate pond ripples. Unlike repeating image maps, procedural textures usually contain a random noise function, which makes them appear to lack any visible order. The disadvantage to procedural textures is that they are not very useful when trying to simulate realistic physical objects.

Rather than choosing either image maps or procedural textures, why not combine the two? Applying both to a surface can result in an interesting texture. The two can be used in any combination. For instance, you could use the procedural texture as a bump map and the image as a surface map. Figure 10-1 shows the image and procedural surfaces and a mixture of the two. One is an image of wood while the other approximates the look of wood grain through a random noise pattern.

Surface Appearance

Without using any textures or shaders, surfaces can be set to have different appearances. Luminosity, diffuseness, specular, reflectivity, transparency, environment and bump mapping, and more can modify the quality of objects.

Luminosity or incandescence denotes how much a surface appears to be illuminated of its own accord. Objects seem to have an internal light.

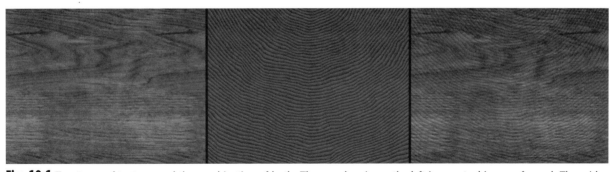

Fig. 10-1 Two types of textures and the combination of both. The wood grain on the left is an actual image of wood. The middle one is a procedural texture that approximates the look of wood grain. The image on the right is a union of both.

Figure 10-2 illustrates a sphere with various degrees of brightness. Luminosity scatters light evenly across a surface and makes the object appear flat like a disk. This can be useful when you need to project an image on a surface and you do not want the object to appear shaded.

Diffuseness reacts to light in different ways, depending on the position and orientation of the light source. The ability to scatter light across a surface is a characteristic of diffuseness. Figure 10-2 shows how various percentages of diffuseness affect the appearance of a sphere. The angle and position of the light source also plays an important factor here. Mapping an image on the diffuse level allows you to keep the original color of the object. The texture appears as a grayscale image while the object retains its assigned color. Hard-looking metallic or reflective surfaces are made with lower diffuse levels.

Specular levels control the appearance of highlights on a surface. They determine how shiny an object appears. Figure 10-2 depicts the specular degrees on a sphere. The higher settings make the ball appear shinier. Rather than scattering light evenly across a surface, specularity concentrates and focuses it on specific areas according to the light source. A specular map can be applied to a surface to control which areas should be glossy and which should be matte. For example, you can make a specular map for a face in which the parts that stand out more, like the nose, lips, forehead, and so on, can be painted lighter, and, in turn, make those parts of the skin look glossier. Coloring the specular highlights with the same hue as the object makes it seem more metallic.

Reflectivity controls the mirror-like appearance of a surface. This can come about in several ways. The first method uses ray-traced reflections in which each pixel on the screen has a ray whose path is traced back to the light source. The characteristics of surfaces are calculated as the ray bounces off or travels through various objects. Ray tracing can yield very accurate reflections and refractions but it does require longer rendering times. One way to speed up ray-traced reflection renderings is to turn down the recursion depth or ray recursion limit. This relates to the number of times that a ray is allowed to reflect off a surface. Usually a setting of 2 is enough for most circumstances. Reflection maps offer an appealing alternative to ray tracing reflections. You can reduce rendering times greatly by applying an image map

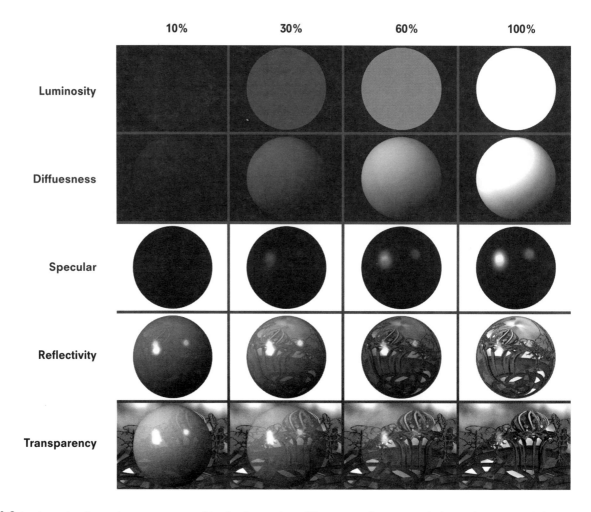

Fig. 10-2 A sphere showing various percentages of luminosity or glow, diffuseness or the way in which a surface scatters light, specular or shininess, reflectivity, and transparency.

of a background or a simple noise pattern to your software's reflectivity options. Figure 10-2 shows a reflection map applied to a sphere in various degrees. The image is applied onto the ball with reflective surfaces as if the environment is being reflected. Few surfaces have mirror-like qualities. Therefore, if you want more realistic reflections, blur the reflection image map and turn down reflectivity to a lower percentage.

Transparency determines how much light is allowed to pass through an object. Figure 10-2 illustrates various degrees of transparency. The lowest setting makes the sphere appear more opaque. Except for the specular highlight, the highest transparency setting renders the ball invisible. Objects with transparency often refract light, which is the bending of light as it passes through objects. A judicious use of refraction keeps rendering times from becoming too lengthy. Transparency maps, which will be discussed later, are indispensable tools for artists who are trying to work under limited memory conditions.

Mapping Methods

Most software programs use a similar paradigm for mapping textures. The most common are planar, cylindrical, spherical, cubic, and front projection (Figure 10-3). UV coordinate mapping is another method that will be discussed later. Since most objects are not simple primitives, it may take some

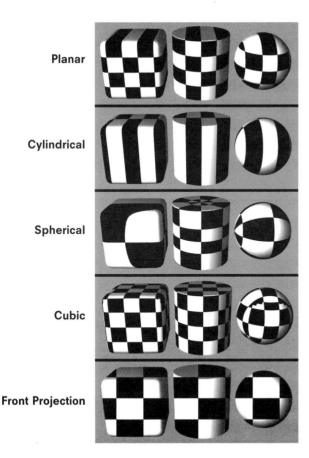

Fig. 10-3 Five types of texture mapping.

experimenting with different image map types before deciding which system works best.

Planar image mapping (Figure 10-4) projects an image onto a surface similar to a slide projector. Normally, the texture can be applied on the *x*-, *y*-, or *z*-axis. If you modeled a car and it was facing forward on the *z*-axis, you could apply a decal to its hood using the *y*-axis. The doors could have decals applied to them on the *x*-axis and the front and back of the car could have maps applied using the *z*-axis.

Cylindrical image mapping (Figure 10-5) wraps a texture around an object similar to toilet paper around a roll. The map connects the two edges at the opposite end. Cylindrical image mapping is not used that often because it does not work too well with most complicated models. Using the previous car analogy, you would wrap the tailpipe on the *z*-axis. A can sitting on the dashboard could have its map applied on the *y*-axis. The tires could have a texture mapped on the *x*-axis.

Spherical image mapping (Figure 10-6) is similar to wrapping cloth around a ball. The texture at the specified axes is pinched. This compression at the poles distorts the mapped image. Usually the *y*-axis is used to map a texture on a spherical object like the surface of a planet.

Cubic image mapping (Figure 10-7) projects an image on all three axes at the same time. Along with planar mapping, cubic mapping is one of the more useful techniques for applying textures. It works well for applying maps on complex objects because it does not distort the image. The one drawback is that it can show seams where the separate maps meet. When all else fails, try cubic mapping.

Front projection mapping (Figure 10-3) is like taking a background image and projecting it

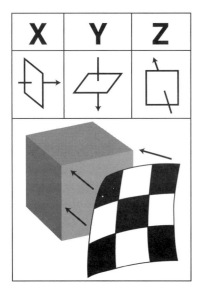

Fig. 10-4 Planar image mapping.

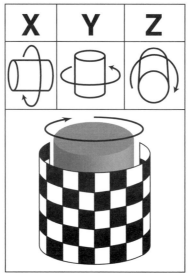

Fig. 10-5 Cylindrical image mapping.

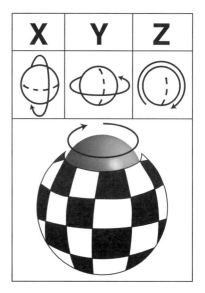

Fig. 10-6 Spherical image mapping.

directly on an object. The texture does not distort and matches precisely the same surface used as a background image. The size of the texture remains the same as the background image. An example of utilizing front projection mapping occurs when you have a background image of trees and a dog is supposed to run out from behind them. Create a plane and place it in front of the background and somewhat to the side. Then use front projection mapping to map the same texture on this foreground plane. The trees match both the background and the plane, and you can now have the dog run out from behind the trees imaged on the foreground plane.

UV coordinate mapping (Figure 10-8) is very useful for precise mapping on curved surfaces. Unlike the other mapping features, which treat all objects as if they were simple shapes, UV coordinate mapping allows you to match a texture to the structure of the geometry. The space of a surface is defined by a U-horizontal value. It usually stretches

from 0 on the left to 1 on the right. The V-coordinate space normally defines the vertical value and stretches from 0 at the top to 1 at the bottom. When a model is deformed during an animation, the UV coordinate mapped texture stretches and bends right along with it. Another way to identify U- and V-axes is to think of the U-axis as longitude and the V-axis as latitude. UV coordinate mapping is so precise that it allows pixel-to-vertex matching. The textures behave like elastic surfaces similar to rubber gloves on a surgeon's hands.

Fig. 10-7 Cubic image mapping.

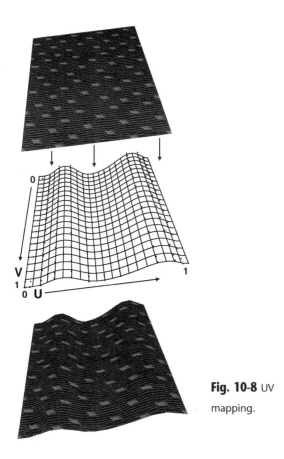

Fig. 10-8 UV mapping.

Bump Maps

Bump maps offer an appealing alternative when trying to model every single detail on an object. Simple models can look very complicated with bump maps. The position that surface normals face is changed during the rendering process so that light reflects in several directions from the surface. This simulates the way in which light reflects from rough objects. Lighter areas are rendered as elevations while darker areas appear as depressions, although this can easily be reversed by typing in a negative value for the texture amplitude. In reality, the surface remains flat and the elevated areas cannot project shadows. An easy way to spot bump

mapping is to look along the edge of an object. The surface appears flat while other areas that face toward the camera look bumpy. Bump maps should not be confused with displacement mapping. A displacement map actually alters the geometry of an object by moving its points in three-dimensional space.

Bump maps increase rendering times. Figure 10-9 shows a few simple objects without any surfacing on them. Figure 10-10 illustrates the same objects with only bump mapping applied to them. The second image was six times longer to render than the first. To save rendering time, you can fake bump maps by using photos that appear bumpy or altering even-looking ones. Most image editing programs have emboss or other filters to make surfaces appear bumpy.

Specular Maps and Diffuse Maps

Whenever you apply a bump map to an object, try to add a specular map along with it. The specular map causes highlights to appear in the lighter areas

Fig. 10-9 The image without any maps.

221

Fig. 10-10 The same objects after applying only the bump maps shown in the bottom row.

of the texture. It does not map a color to the surface but makes parts of the model appear shiny. The type of light source and surface present also govern specularity. Therefore, highlights only occur near hotspots and not evenly across the entire surface.

Diffuse maps are very useful for aging or making a surface appear grimy because they darken the colors of a surface. A diffuse map does not apply a color to a surface, instead, it causes variations in the object's color. Figure 10-11 illustrates the same objects that previously had bump maps applied to them. With the addition of specular and diffuse dirt maps, the scene appears to have more individuality.

Creative surfacing requires more than just applying digitized photos or using built-in shaders (pro-

Fig. 10-11 The final image after applying specular and diffuse grime maps.

cedural textures). People once were fascinated with images of shiny spheres reflecting the surrounding environment. Earlier computer images were too flawless and did not relate to the imperfect world. It takes artistry to make a model look old, worn, dirty, and weathered. Many artists strive to create images that do not look as if they were computer-generated. They try to make animations or images that are super-realistic or computer art that has a personal style. In either case, they try to avoid making images that appear artificial and imitative.

One of the first steps for making worn out, dingy, dusty, and weather-beaten surfaces is to create brushes in your favorite image-editing program. You can start by selecting parts of rusty, peeling, dirty, moldy, or any bumpy surface. Use a soft-edged feathered selection and copy it to a new file with a transparent background. You then define a new brush from the pasted texture. Another option is to use filters on it to make it a noisier texture or to roughen it up some more. Using a feathered selection will keep the edges soft so that one brush stroke can blend into another. Painting selections with a "quick mask" option allows you to create crosshatch and streak-effect brushes. To get you started, there are some predefined brushes on the CD-ROM, which can be used in Adobe Photoshop. They can also be viewed in Figure 10-12.

When you paint a surface with grime brushes, be sure to set the brush to fade after a certain number of pixels. It also helps to have a digitizing tablet and pen to vary the size of the brush stroke by pressure. Another technique you can use is to paint decay textures with black grime brushes first, and then follow with white dirt brushes. This erases parts of the surface and makes it look more uneven.

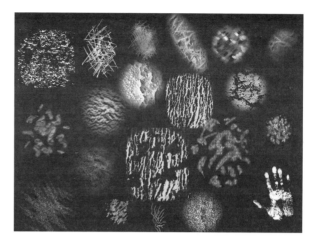

Fig. 10-12 Some grime brushes for creating worn surfaces.

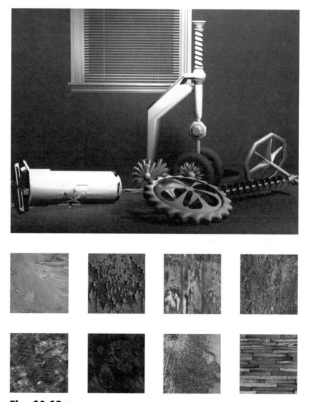

Fig. 10-13 The objects unsurfaced. The textures at the bottom will be applied to them.

223

Fig. 10-14 The same objects after adding the floor and grime textures.

Besides having a collection of grime brushes, you should also have a library of textures that show wear-and-tear on various surfaces. Photos of brush strokes, rust, dirt, peeling paint, dust, corrosion, and so on are invaluable materials. These images can be switched with one another so that they can be used as bump maps or as specular, diffuse, and image maps. Figure 10-13 shows a pile of junk in a room before the surfaces at the bottom are applied to everything. Figure 10-14 illustrates the same room and junk after applying only the surfaces shown in the previous illustration. A color image of this picture can be found on the CD-ROM as CD10-14. The same maps are used on different objects but applied in various ways. For example, if one texture is used as a diffuse map on an object, it might be applied as a specular map on another. Objects often have multiple texture maps applied

to them. Several bump maps as well as other types are applied to the same object. By making some less opaque, the ones underneath show through in places.

Characters look more interesting when you apply grime, paint, and other textures to them and to their clothes. Figure 10-15 and color image CD10-15 depict an artist before and after applying various surfaces. Some were created using grime brushes while others were developed from photographs and painted textures.

Transparency Maps

When it no longer matters how many polygons are in a scene because computers can render and display everything in real time, then transparency maps will become obsolete. In the meantime, they

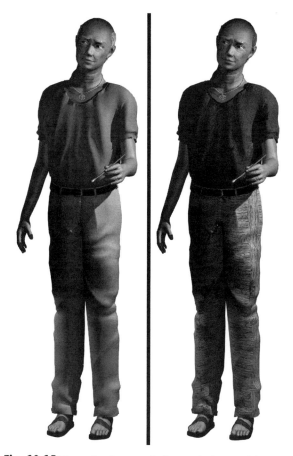

Fig. 10-15 The artist character before and after applying textures.

are an important part of complex scene building. This is especially true when it comes to outdoor scenes with trees and plants. Anyone who has ever modeled a tree or used a tree generator knows that once the leaves are added, the polygon count can easily exceed 35,000. Moreover, this is only for one tree. Imagine a scene filled with dozens of trees and plants. Most desktop computers and even some workstations are not equipped to handle this many polygons.

Transparency maps are composed of two images. One image contains the actual rendered object while the other is a negative image that blocks out everything except for the rendered object. Figure 10-16 shows tree renderings and their matching negative images. The negative images are identical to the corresponding tree pictures, except they are white. They act like a cutout because everything within the white area displays the rendered tree image and everything that is black is transparent. When the positive and negative images are mapped onto an object, only the areas that fall within the white parts will be visible while the black areas are rendered invisible. Other objects can be seen behind the black portions. The positive image is applied as a planar map to a flat polygon. The negative picture is added as a transparency texture with the exact same settings as the positive version except that it is specified as a negative image.

To create a transparency map, you can render a 3D object like a tree (some can be found on the CD-ROM in the chapter 10 folder), or you can use photos and illustrations. Once you have your positive image, select it. For example, if it is a tree, you can usually render the original with an alpha channel. This makes it easier to select only the tree and its leaves. If you are using a photo or illustration, select only the tree and its parts. Fill the selected area with white, inverse your selection, and fill the background with black. Save this as your negative image.

The object used for mapping can vary in shape. Figure 10-17 depicts some commonly used forms for transparency mapping. A simple rectangle works fine in most circumstances. You can use the dimensions of your image maps to determine the height-to-width ratio of your rectangle. The direction that your plane faces determines which way you should map the image and its transparency map. For example, if the plane faces toward the front, use planar mapping on the *z*-axis. Two rec-

Fig. 10-16 Complicated objects like trees can be made using transparency maps. The image of the tree and its alpha channel are mapped onto flat polygons. The only part of the image that is visible is the tree showing through the white part of the alpha map.

tangles that intersect each other like those in Figure 10-17 can be used if the camera moves in your scene. The object will always appear three-dimensional because the image is mapped on both the *x*- and *z*-axes. The plane that faces to the right has the image and its corresponding transparency mapped on the *x*-axis while the plane that faces forward has the exact same images mapped on the *z*-axis. Another option for scenes in which the camera moves is setting the flat planes to always face toward the camera. Depending on your software, this might require a plug-in or a script that tells the object to use the camera as its target. The half-cylinder shape shown in Figure 10-17 works fairly well in scenes with some camera movement. The only disadvantage to this form is that it distorts the object somewhat, and the camera can only be moved half way around it.

The fourth form in Figure 10-17 is a combination of 3D and 2D. A tree trunk and its branches are modeled and then flat planes are placed facing in different directions. Since all the planes are

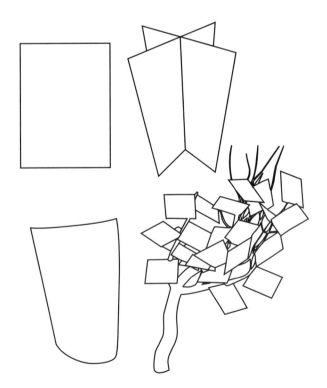

Fig. 10-17 Commonly used objects for applying transparency maps. The tree trunk and branches are part of a 3D model.

Fig. 10-18 The tree on the left illustrates the effect of transparency maps, while the one on the right shows the texture without the negative alpha channel.

turned in various directions, the camera is free to move anywhere. Figure 10-18 and the color image CD10-18 show the tree rendered without its transparency maps. Memory usage is fairly low and the leaves have a great amount of detail on them. If you plan to use this type of approach, make one plane (a rectangle or square) facing up in the top view. With planar mapping, apply the image and its transparency on the *y*-axis. Move the pivot point of the rectangle to the end where the image is supposed to come from a tree branch. Clone the rectangle and place all the copies around the tree with the pivot point touching the tree branch. Now rotate all the copies in different directions. Since the pivot point is against the tree branch, each plane can be revolved without separating from the tree. If you tried to map onto planes facing various directions, the images would distort. Since the rectangle was facing up on the *y*-axis originally, the image mapped correctly and remained constant no matter which direction it was revolved toward.

If you use high quality renderings for your image maps, it is very difficult to tell whether transparency maps or 3D models are utilized in a scene. Figure 10-19 can be used as a test to see which of the two trees was rendered from a 3D

Fig. 10-19 Transparency maps are very difficult to distinguish from 3D objects. Which of the two trees is the transparency map and which is a 3D model?

227

Fig. 10-20 The answer to the question asked in Fig. 10-19.

Fig. 10-22 The same scene from Fig. 10-21 and what it looks like before rendering.

Fig. 10-21 A scene filled with transparency maps. Some can be viewed in Fig. 10-22.

Fig. 10-23 An underwater scene with transparency-mapped objects.

Fig. 10-24 The transparency-mapped planes and the two 3D objects near the camera. Skeletons were placed inside the 2D as well as the 3D objects.

tree. One of them is a rendering of a flat plane while the other is the actual tree. The answer can be found in Figure 10-20.

Figure 10-21 illustrates a rendering of a complicated scene with many transparency maps. The color image can be seen on the CD-ROM as CD10-21. To view some of the actual objects in the scene, refer to Figure 10-22. By keeping the environment memory usage low through transparency maps, you can utilize more characters with greater detail.

Objects that appear closer to the camera can be left as 3D models while those that are further away can be simple planes with transparency maps. Figure 10-23 shows a complicated underwater scene with many plants, most of which are flat planes as seen in Figure 10-24. Only the two plants closest to the camera are left as three-dimensional objects. To have the plants move slowly with the underwater currents, skeletons were placed in the subdivided planes (Figure 10-25). The chapter about lighting referred to this animation and can be found as CD9-27.

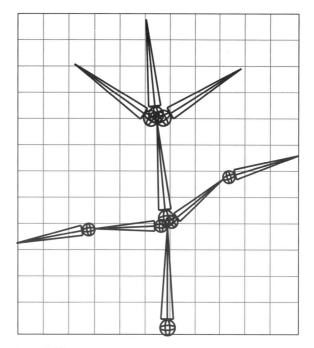

Fig. 10-25 The skeleton inside the flat, subdivided plane moves the transparency-mapped object.

229

Fig. 10-26 Displacement maps can be used to deform the actual geometry of objects. In this example, each of the grayscale gradient textures are used to make different landmasses.

Displacement Maps

Displacement mapping deforms geometry based upon an image or a procedural texture. Unlike bump mapping, the silhouette of the object is consistent with the rest of the surface. Displacement mapping is very useful for creating terrains, billowing cloth, water ripples, flickering flames, and many other effects. The surface of an object is displaced according to the intensity of the pixels in the texture map. The lighter parts of the image cause greater displacements. Figure 10-26 displays a few textures used as displacement maps along with the terrains that were derived from them. Notice that the lighter parts of the images create greater elevations in the terrain.

If you plan to create a terrain using displacement mapping, be sure to experiment with various amounts of texture amplitude. A negative value works well for reversing the elevations. To get enough detail, use a high-resolution plane that has been subdivided many times. For example, a NURBS plane can have a setting of 22 for its U and V directions if the texture's measurement is 512 × 512 pixels. If you are working with polygons, triple the plane before displacing its surface. Once you are satisfied with the appearance of the displaced geometry, you can usually save the transformed object. The terrain model can then have additional alterations applied to it like smoothing.

The following tutorial shows how displacement mapping can be used for many special effects. Perhaps you have seen it utilized in a movie when a character was trying to push through a solid object like a wall. The wall appeared to bulge and take on the character's shape. A variation of this effect might be cloth deforming from a person pushing against it. Although the method outlined here has you displace a faceted object with a face, it can easily be adapted to recreating the previously described effects.

Fig. 10-27 A pin device for making impressions.

Fig. 10-28 The needle object.

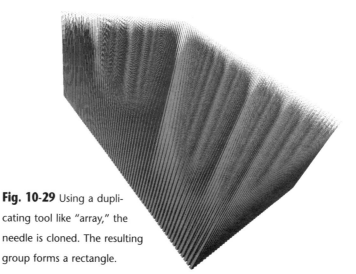

Fig. 10-29 Using a duplicating tool like "array," the needle is cloned. The resulting group forms a rectangle.

This tutorial has you create a gizmo composed of hundreds of tiny pins. When you push against the mesh of flat pins, it deforms outward on the opposite side, making an impression of the shape of your hand or whatever might be pressing against it (Figure 10-27). For those who are too lazy or do not have the time to make everything from scratch, you will find all the objects and textures on the CD-ROM.

The first step is to create the gizmo that will be deformed. Later, you can substitute this with anything, perhaps a wall or cloth. Make a flat pentagon on the *y*-axis. Its size can have radii of 2.7 mm on the *x*- and *z*-axes and 0 mm on the *y*-axis. Extrude the pentagon up 13.5 cm on the *y*-axis. Select the points at the top of the extruded object and either weld them together or scale them down to 0. The object now has five sides at the bottom and comes to a point at the top (Figure 10-28).

This needle object will have to be cloned many times. If your software has an array option, set it to duplicate the needle fifty times on the *x*-axis and

seventy times on the *z*-axis. The subsequent cube-like form is made up of these needles (Figure 10-29).

In an image-editing program, create a grayscale gradient that starts with white on the left and becomes black on the right (Figure 10-30). Cut off the front part of a head so that you only have the face, which looks like a mask. You can use any object, but this tutorial refers to it as a face. Position the face to look straight at you in the front view (*z*-axis). Apply the gradient texture on the *x*-axis and set it to size automatically to the full scale

Fig. 10-30 A grayscale gradient is mapped to the face on the *x*-axis.

231

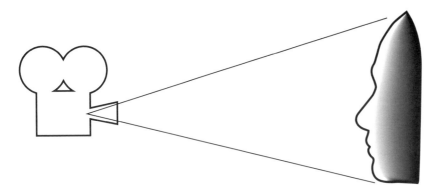

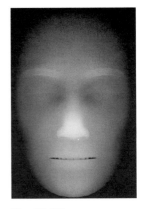

Fig. 10-31 A grayscale gradient is mapped to the face on the *x*-axis. The side view should show the closest portion to the camera as the lightest part, and the farthest as the darkest.

Fig. 10-32 The face is rendered with only a 95% ambient light.

of the face (Figure 10-31). Position the camera to look directly at the face and set its focal length to about 75 mm to avoid distorting the face.

Turn off all the lights except for ambient lighting, which is set at 95%. This creates an even dispersal of light with no shadows. Render the face with a black background. Notice that this type of lighting, combined with the gradient, produces an interesting effect. It makes objects appear smooth with an inner light. This technique is useful for showing x-rays, smooth stone, ghosts, and so on.

The rendered image is now used as a displacement map. Turn the needle object so that the sharp points are facing down on the *y*-axis. The top view should have the dull ends facing toward you. Now comes the fun part. Apply the displacement map (the rendered face) to the needle object on the *y*-axis. The texture amplitude should be about 100%, but you may have to try different settings. You should see the face pushing up through the needles. If you want the needles to appear metallic, apply a reflectivity map to their surfaces and set it to ray trace the backdrop. The reflection map looks like fractal noise that has been filtered to look like

bumpy glass. This can be made by creating a cloud texture and applying an ocean ripple filter to it. Reflectivity may have to be turned down to about 80%. To speed up rendering time, turn down the ray-trace recursion limit to 1 or 2. The rendering can be sped up even more by turning off "trace reflection." Figure 10-33 shows the final image.

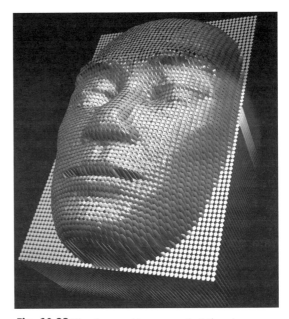

Fig. 10-33 The face pushing up against the pins.

The next step is animating the displacement map. To have the face appear to push through the needles, set an envelope on the texture amplitude. For a 30-frame animation, you can have the amplitude set at 0 at frame 1 and 100%, or whatever is desirable, at frame 30.

The animation can be made even more interesting by having the face change expressions after it is pushed up. Create an animation of facial expressions using the previous 95% ambient light setup. For the first thirty frames, the face should be still because that is the part where it pushes up against the needles. Import a movie or image sequence and apply it as a displacement map. Use the same envelope that has the face push through over thirty frames. When you render the animation, it will apply all of the facial expressions as displacement maps throughout the sequence. An animation of this effect can be found on the CD-ROM as CD10-33. Images from it can be seen in Figure 10-34.

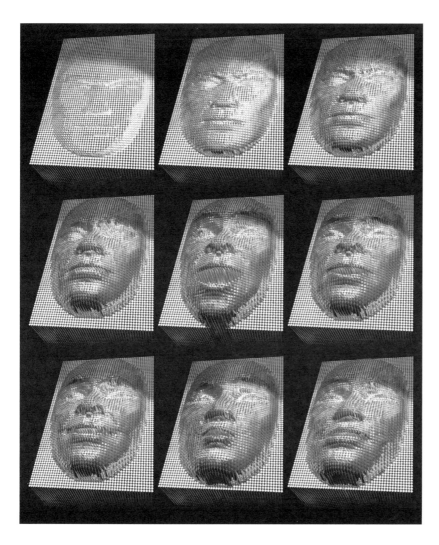

Fig. 10-34 Images from the pinface displacement animation.

PART IV

Character Animation Fundamentals

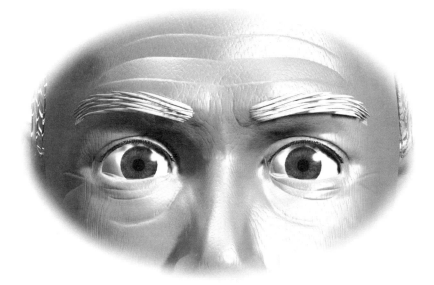

CHAPTER 11

Expressing Emotion with Facial Animation

When animating emotion, relying only on facial animation has little substance if it is not combined with a relevant body posture. The attitude of the body should support the expression on the face (Figures 11-1 and 11-2).

Normally, the facial expression will show up first, which is then followed by the movement of the body. The two occurrences are only fractions of a second apart, but nevertheless, should be animated in that order. For example, if a person perceives something, the eyes are the first to move, followed by a turn of the head, then the shoulders, and finally, the rest of the body.

Although the posture of the body reflects the mood on the face, this discussion will focus solely on the drama of facial expressions. The muscles of the face are close to the skin and reciprocally connected. To see this, close one eye and you can observe the upward movement in the corner of the mouth. One of the most important aspects of facial animation is that the combinations of various head muscles convey emotion. Even though you have to model the various expressions as single

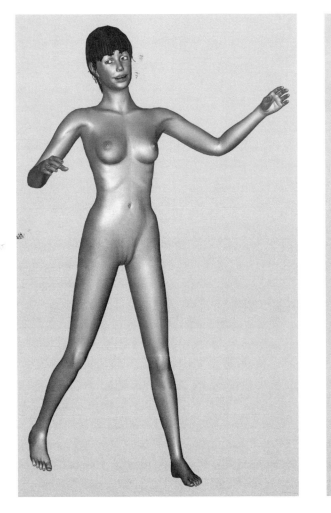

Fig. 11-1 (left) Happiness is expressed through a combination of bright eyes, upturned corners of the mouth, raised eyebrows, a lively stride, straight back, and raised shoulders and arms.

Fig. 11-2 (right) A coy demeanor can be displayed by biting down on the lower lip, casting eyes downward, bending the neck, and keeping the limbs close to the body.

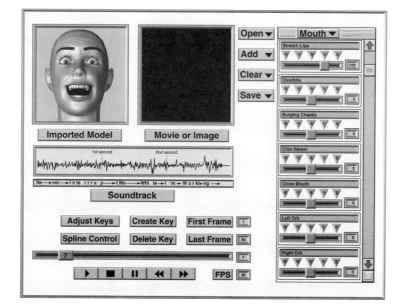

Fig. 11-3 Modeling the various expressions individually allows you the flexibility to combine them in numerous ways. Many programs such as this one use sliding buttons to blend the various expressions.

occurrences, it is the assemblage of these during the animation process, that yields the appropriate emotional state. Animated singly, the individual expressions by themselves create only mild drama.

So far, the discussion for manipulating geometry has centered on using images, procedural textures (displacement maps), and skeletons. Another method involves moving the actual points on an object to create variations of the original geometry. These, in turn, become morphing targets that allow you to shape-shift one object into another. The process is called metamorphosing or more commonly, morphing. It provides greater control for changing the appearance of a model than displacement maps or skeletons. The reason is that the animator can use all the modeling tools available to change any point on an object. The transformed models are poses or different states into which the original object morphed.

For example, you start with a base model in which the face is neutral and all the muscles are relaxed. Using the various modeling methods like a magnet tool, you can pull and push points around the mouth to model the same face smiling. This new facial pose is saved as a morph target. Returning to the neutral face, you can move the points on the eyelids to close the eyes. The new morph target is saved as one of the eye expressions. Continuing this process and always starting with the base neutral face, you can shape a number of expressions and save each one separately. The software allows you to blend the various expressions using percentages of each. Therefore, the face can be animated with a range of different emotions over a specific time period.

Most mid- to high-end software packages offer some kind of shape-shifting tool (Figure 11-3). These often use sliding buttons, which can generate various percentages for each facial movement. If eye, mouth, nose, eyebrows, jaw, and other movements are modeled separately, you can achieve a diversity of expressions and phonetic shapes for speech. Because the muscles on the left and right sides of the face vary in strength, some

239

features are modeled as separate left and right shapes. When modeling the following expressions, a hand-held mirror becomes an indispensable tool.

One way to illustrate the entire morphing process is through explaining how it is implemented in a specific software package. One of the better-known methods is found in LightWave 3D. It uses an operation called "Endomorphs." After modeling the various expressions or morph targets, all the information is saved in a single object file called an endomorph. Because all the information for the various states is stored within one base object, the original model can be changed without adversely affecting the morph targets. If you decide to add detail to the base model, the change works its way through all the various poses and modifies their point counts accordingly. Unlike some other software packages, you do not have to worry about keeping the same exact number of points on each separate morph target. Facial animation can take place directly in the scene without having to work in a separate box like the one shown in Figure 11-3.

Since there is no need to worry about point counts, you can start with a simple model, sculpt the various expressions, and then subdivide the base model later for a more detailed character and its various morph targets. A word of caution: The simple base model should have enough lines on it to shape creases in the forehead and make wrinkles on other parts of the face when the mouth, nose, and eyes change their appearance (Figure 11-4). Changes to the point counts should be made only on the base object and not on any of the morph targets.

In LightWave 3D, you start with the simple model and activate the "SubPatch" mode. This smoothes out the model and makes it fairly easy to

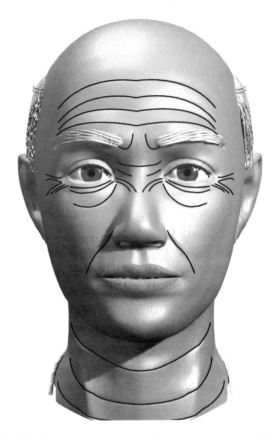

Fig. 11-4 Each black line on the face represents a set of three or four parallel lines. The middle line(s) of each set is moved to make wrinkles and creases.

change its appearance. Working in "Modeler," activate the morph map mode by clicking the "M" button. Select "(new)" from the pop-up menu next to the "M" button. When the "Create Morph Map" dialog appears, enter a name like Mouth.Smile. The period after the word "mouth" will later create an individual tab in the "MorphMixer" panel of "Layout." These tabs are used to separate the various groups such as mouth, eyes, brows, nose, and so on. Clicking "Relative for Type" means that the changes are relative to the base object. The "Absolute" button is used when the entire object changes shape (like a person shifting into an animal). Click "OK" or press "Enter" to close the dialog box. Use the various modeling tools to change the appearance of the object.

Select the base model again from the pop-up menu next to the "M" button. The object will revert back to its original shape. If you want to create more morph targets, select "(new)" from the pop-up menu next to the "M" button and after naming the new morph map, change its shape. When you save the original model, all its morph targets are saved with it. The next step is to work in the "Layout" portion of the program to create an animation by blending the different shapes.

Before explaining the morph mixing process in "Layout," there is another method that should be discussed which allows you to take separate morph targets and integrate them into one base model. This is useful for those who have separate models and morph targets created in earlier versions of the software.

Open the assorted models that have served as morph targets and place them in their own layers. Make the base object active in the foreground layer. Display one of the morph targets in a background layer behind the foreground base model. Use the floating "Layers" palette to set the foreground and background layers. Select the plug-in named Bkg-to-MORF. In the dialog box, name the morph target and be sure to place a period in the middle of the name so that morph mixer displays it later as an individual tab defining its group. This will work as long as the morph target has the same point count and order as the base object. Continue this process with the other targets by making the base object active in the foreground layer and displaying the next target in the background layer. You can test the targets in "Modeler" by clicking

the pop-up menu next to the "M" button and selecting the various map names. You will see the base model transform into the different shapes.

After saving your endomorph model, bring it into "Layout." For the object, click the "Item Properties" button and under the "Deformations" tab, click the pop-up menu button named "Add Displacement." Select the "Morph Mixer" plug-in. Open the plug-ins option panel by double clicking it in the list. Click on the various tabs that separate the grouped targets and use the sliding buttons to set the degree of morphing that you want. Create a key and go to another keyframe along the timeline. Use the "MorphMixer" sliders to change the appearance of the model and keyframe the new pose. You can use the left and right arrows to move from one keyframe to another.

Dialogue can also be paired to facial expressions. Open the "Scene Editor" panel, click the "Audio" button and select "Load Audio . . ." The imported audio file appears as a graph along the timeline. Scrolling through the scene will play the sound. Lip movements can then be matched to the words or music.

The Basic Shapes

Despite the fact that the human face is capable of hundreds of expressions, you can model approximately forty basic features to achieve most countenances. Each of these has been divided into the following separate group: brows, eyes, nose, mouth, and jaw.

Before you begin to model the various expressions from the original face, be sure to add enough points and curves in specific areas that will be used for wrinkles and creases later. Some parts of the face that should have extra splines are the fore-

Fig. 11-5 The brows are depressed and brought in causing a horizontal wrinkling at the root of the nose.

Fig. 11-6 Inner brows are raised for looks of grief or surprise.

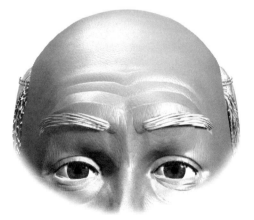

Fig. 11-7 Raising the eyebrows brightens the eyes and wrinkles the forehead.

head for wrinkles, the base of the cheeks near the nose wings running to the corners of the mouth, above and below the eyes, the corners of the eyes, and the bridge of the nose. Figure 11-4 shows a face with lines indicating where extra curves should be modeled. Each dark line suggests where you should have three or four extra curves running parallel to each other. For example, if you have three parallel lines for one crease, you would move the middle line in to make a depression in the skin. The lines do not have to be visible when the face is in a normal, relaxed mode. When it is time to model a certain expression that causes wrinkling in those areas, then you can move the points on the lines.

The Brows

The following list describes basic brow movements:

- Brows depressed and contracted (Figure 11-5): Lowering the eyebrows creates a slight fold over the eyes and a wrinkling at the nose. Compressing the eyebrows moves them toward the center, forming a puckering in the middle of the forehead.
- Inner brows raised (Figure 11-6): Raising the inner ends causes a puckering in the middle of the forehead.
- Brows raised (Figure 11-7): The left and the right eyebrows are modeled separately in a raised position. This results in transverse folds along the forehead.

The Eyes

The following list describes basic eye movements:

- Upper eyelids closed (Figure 11-8): Both upper eyelids rotate down for the blink.
- Eyes look down (Figure 11-9): Both eyes look down.

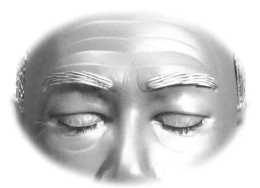

Fig. 11-8 A blink lowers only the upper eyelids.

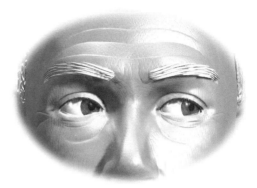

Fig. 11-11 Normally, the eyes move in tandem.

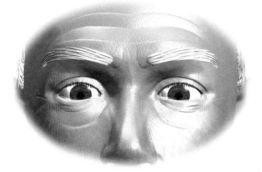

Fig. 11-9 The basic eye movements can be modeled separately.

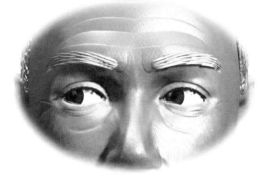

Fig. 11-12 Eye movements make the animation look livelier.

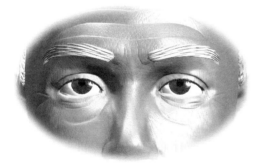

Fig. 11-10 By combining the four basic eye movements during animation, the eyes can be rotated into almost any position.

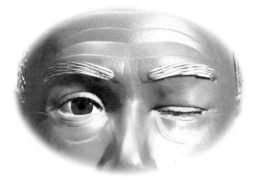

Fig. 11-13 The eyewink moves both the upper and lower eyelids together.

Fig. 11-14 The left and right eyelids are raised separately.

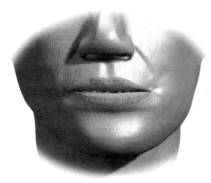

Fig. 11-15 The jaw is modeled in both the left and right horizontal positions.

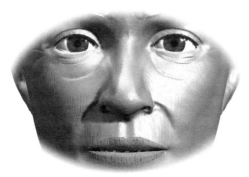

Fig. 11-16 The wings of the nose are moved up and out. Each side is modeled separately.

- Eyes look up (Figure 11-10): Both eyes look up.
- Eyes look left (Figure 11-11): Both eyes look left.
- Eyes look right (Figure 11-12): Both eyes look right.
- Upper and lower lids close (Figure 11-13): Both the lower and upper eyelids meet in the center for the wink. The right and left eyelids are modeled separately.
- Eyelids raised (Figure 11-14): The upper eyelids are raised. Both are modeled separately.

The Jaw

The jaw has four basic movements. You only need to model the left and right motions (Figure 11-15). The up and down directions are modeled as part of the various mouth movements.

The Nose

Simplifying the nose movements to the left and right nostril dilators should take care of most animator's needs (Figure 11-16).

The Mouth

Of all the parts, the mouth has the most flexibility. This means that many mouth positions can be modeled. The following are the most basic ones:

- Stretching the lips (Figure 11-17): The left and right side of the mouth is stretched. It is also very important to show the neck muscles straining.
- Bite down on the lower lip (Figure 11-18): The lower lip is sucked in and up under the upper teeth.
- Blowing out to expand the cheeks (Figure 11-19): Exhale through the mouth while keeping the lips together.
- Lip thinner (Figure 11-20): The lips are made thinner by moving the jaw up.
- Closed mouth (Figure 11-21): Modeling the face with the mouth slightly open makes it easier to

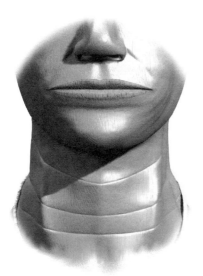

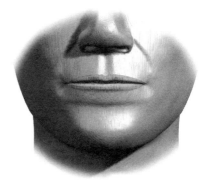

Fig. 11-20 Raising the chin thins the lips.

Fig. 11-17 Drawing the lips to the side results in straining the neck muscles.

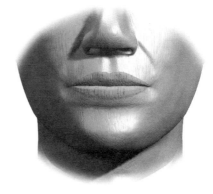

Fig. 11-21 The lips are brought together to close the mouth.

Fig. 11-18 The jaw is moved up and the lower lip in so that the upper teeth bite down on the lower lip.

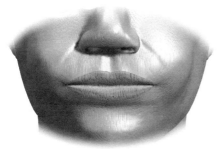

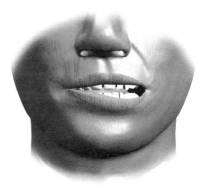

Fig. 11-19 Blowing out with the lips closed produces bulging cheeks.

Fig. 11-22 The mouth corners form an orb. This can be very useful for punctuating speech.

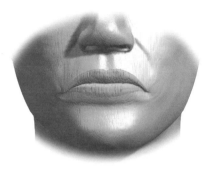

Fig. 11-23 The left and right corners of the mouth droop down.

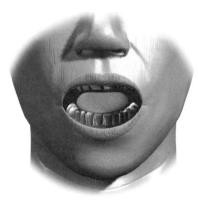

Fig. 11-24 The mouth opens in a heart shape for speech, breathing, astonishment, yawning, and so on.

Fig. 11-25 The lower lip is pushed up and out to form a pout.

select the lower or upper lip points. Closing the mouth in a relaxed attitude can be used in place of the original slack-jawed model.

- Orb right and left (Figure 11-22): Both sides are modeled separately. This mouth pose appears more often than it would seem.
- Depression of the corners of the mouth (Figure 11-23): Each side is modeled separately.
- Open mouth (Figure 11-24): The mouth opens in the shape of a heart.
- Extending the lower lip (Figure 11-25): Pushing out the lower lip in a pout.
- Big grin (Figure 11-26): The jaw drops and the corners of the mouth move back and up.
- Lower jaw drops down (Figure 11-27): Only the jaw moves down while the upper lip stays the same.
- Upper lip is elevated (Figure 11-28): The upper lip rolls up and out to reveal the upper teeth. The lower lip stays in the same position.
- Inward pucker of lips (Figure 11-29): The lips are brought together to form a small "o" shape.
- Outward pucker (Figure 11-30): The lips push forward and out.
- Smile (Figure 11-31): The lips part slightly to form a smile when the corners of the mouth are brought up.
- Sneer (Figure 11-32): The upper lip curls up to display the canine tooth.
- Tongue between teeth (Figure 11-33): The tongue comes forward between the teeth while the lips part slightly. This is an important pose for making the "l" and "th" sounds.
- Tongue touches roof of mouth (Figure 11-34): While the mouth is open, this pronounces "r" sounds.

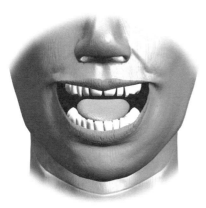

Fig. 11-26 The corners of the mouth are retracted up and out while the jaw drops to form a big grin.

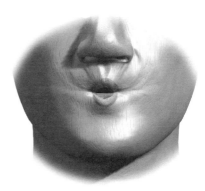

Fig. 11-29 The lips pucker inward.

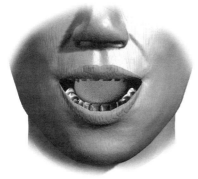

Fig. 11-27 The jaw drops to open the mouth.

Fig. 11-30 The lips pucker outward.

Fig. 11-28 The upper lip is raised.

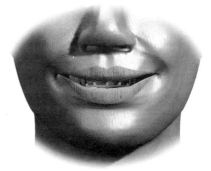

Fig. 11-31 A smile is formed when the corners of the mouth are retracted and the lips part slightly.

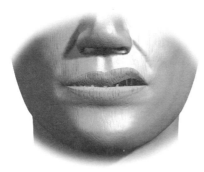

Fig. 11-32 A sneer is formed by curling the corner of the upper lip.

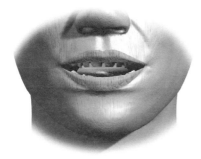

Fig. 11-33 The tongue is inserted between the teeth with the lips parted for "la" and "th" sounds.

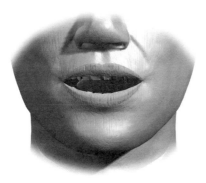

Fig. 11-34 The tongue touches the roof of the mouth while the lips part for "rar" sounds.

Blending Expressions

After you finish creating all the basic facial expressions, it is time to load them into your shape-shifting editor. Blended shapes are created by combining mouth, nose, eyes, eyebrows, and other expressions. By altering the percentage of each, you can achieve countless facial expressions of varying subtlety.

Figures 11-35 to 11-41 illustrate some of the expressions you can attain by blending the base objects. The examples are only meant to be a rough guide.

Direction of the Muscular Pull

A muscle is composed of a bundle of fibers that work in a mutual association to perform common duties. Muscles never act alone. When one muscle or a set of muscles contracts, other opposing muscles become active and regulate or change the behavior of the contracting ones. It is this combination of movements that results in the complicated harmony of the facial muscles. Figure 11-42 illustrates the directional pull of the various muscle groups to achieve specific expressions.

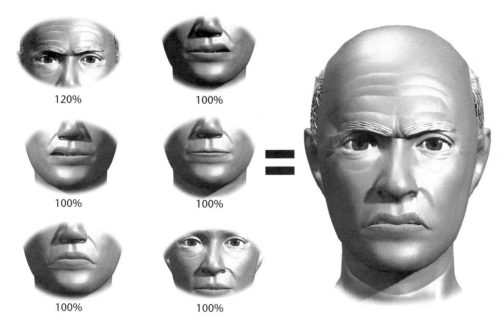

Fig. 11-35 The original shapes are blended in different percentages.

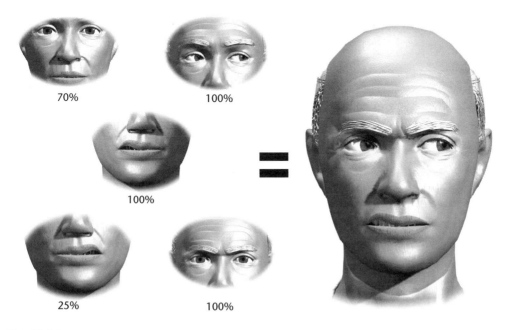

Fig. 11-36 A look of disgust is the result of blending varying percentages of the above base expressions.

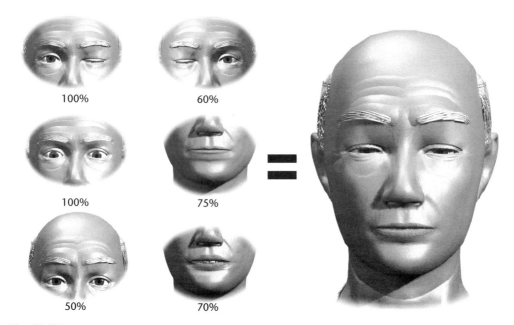

100%   60%

100%   75%

50%   70%

Fig. 11-37 A contemplative look comes from combining the above target shapes.

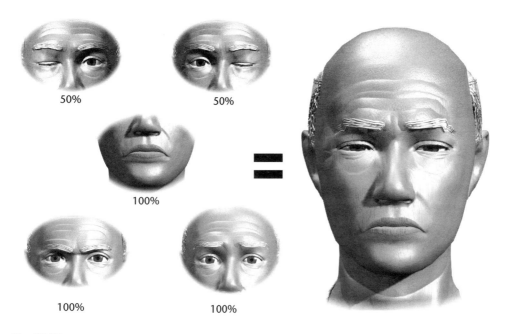

50%   50%

100%

100%   100%

Fig. 11-38 A sad expression is achieved by combining the above base objects.

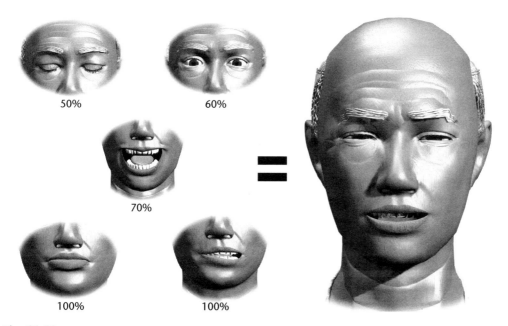

Fig. 11-39 Sometimes unexpected expressions can be formed by the most unlikely combinations. In this case, a tired look is the result of the implausible mouth shapes shown above.

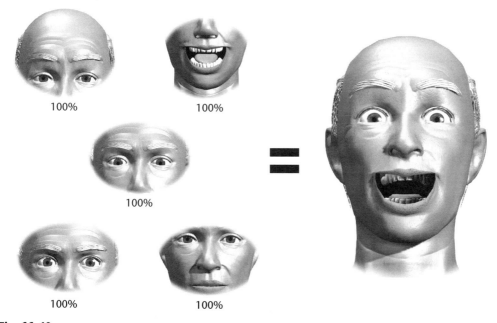

Fig. 11-40 A few target shapes can create a very expressive look like one of surprise.

40%

55%

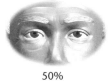

40%

56%

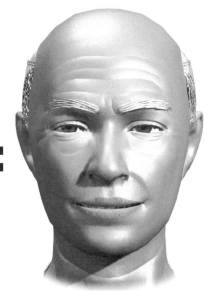

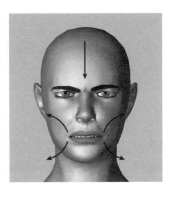

50%

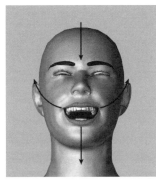

60%

Fig. 11-41 A coy aspect.

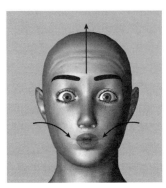

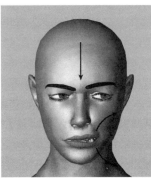

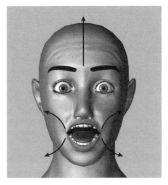

Fig. 11-42 The muscles combine to create aspects of anger, hysteria, fear, surprise, and suspicion.

CHAPTER 12

The Elements
of Action

Animation often involves the production of basic, everyday actions such as walking, runing, blinking, and breathing. There are many tools available to computer animators for simplifying the daunting task of convincingly animating such movements. Some of these include extracting parts of previously animated actions and applying them to other characters, importing video as a template for animation, applying motion plug-ins such as two-legged walk cycles, using motion capture, and so on. Although these devices can sometimes be useful, there is nothing greater than relying on your own experiences and creativity. Experience helps you determine the correct timing for specific motions, while creativity applies the right amount of exaggeration to make the movements more noticeable, interesting, and dramatic.

Fig. 12-1 Besides a powerful computer and software, a stopwatch and mirror are indispensable tools for the animator.

The Importance of Timing

In addition to having a great computer and outstanding software, the animator often relies on two simple tools: a stopwatch and a mirror (Figure 12-1). It is a well-known fact that timing is the most crucial element in animation. Usually, beginning animators rely very heavily on a stopwatch for measuring the cycles of movements. After becoming more familiar with these cycles, the seasoned animator develops an intuitive sense for the correct temporal order of things.

Good animators should also be good actors. They are often called upon to playact for each other. However, more often, they have to role-play for themselves. It is not uncommon to see them stand up for no apparent reason, perform an imaginary action, and then sit back down to continue their work. Thus, a mirror is the other indispensable tool. This is especially true when doing facial animation. Animation students should learn to make faces in a mirror and pantomime without

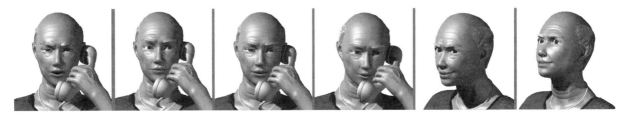

Fig. 12-2 Animating eye movements is an important part of making a character lifelike.

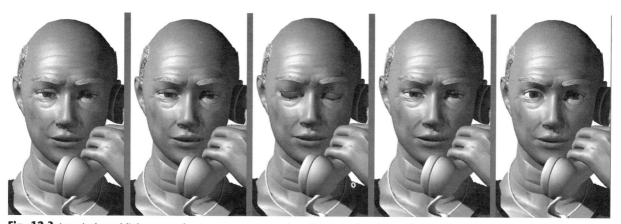

Fig. 12-3 A typical eye blink occurs about every two seconds and lasts for five frames from open eyes to half closed, then fully closed, back to half closed, and finally, fully open again.

feeling self-conscious if others are watching. Your digital puppets are a reflection of your own acting abilities.

Before considering animating a character's gestures, you should be aware of three basic movements that occur throughout an animation. They are eye movements, blinking, and breathing. Without these, your digital actors will appear lifeless. Be sure to apply them for the duration of the entire animation.

Eye motions are constant. The individual that you are animating has eye movements according to its thought patterns and in response to what is occurring around it. A simple back and forth eye motion takes about one-third of a second or ten frames at thirty frames per second. Tracking the movement of something can vary according to the speed of the object. There are no set rules that apply to eye movements. Figure 12-2 shows a few frames from an animation in which eye movements indicate the thoughts running through the character's head.

Blinking is an important part of an animation that should not be ignored. Unlike the squint, only the upper eyelids are rotated down. Normally, a person blinks about every two seconds (every sixty frames). Typically, the blink will run over the course of five frames. For example, frame 59 starts the blink with the eyes half closed. Frame 60 shows the eyelids closed. The next frame has the eyes half open and frame 62 returns the eyes to the open position again. Figure 12-3 shows the 5-frame sequence for blinking. For rapid blinking, skip the half-closed eye frames so that the eyelids go from wide open to closed and back again to wide open. For slow blinks like someone falling asleep and then waking up suddenly, try closing the upper eyelids over a longer time like three frames instead of one. The eyelids can remain closed for three or more frames. The speed at which they open depends on how fast you want the subject to wake up.

Breathing is also an important part of animation that should not be ignored. If your characters exhibit breathing throughout the animation, it will give them an incredible amount of life. The "breath of life" is a saying that applies very strongly here.

The enclosed CD-ROM contains a short animation of a woman breathing (CD12-4). When she inhales, notice how the stomach draws in between

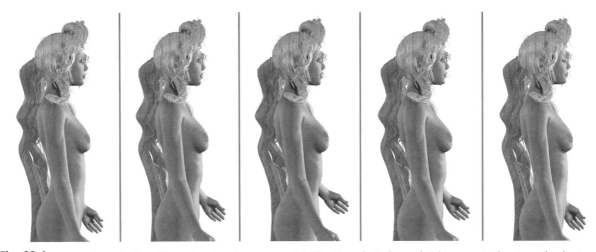

Fig. 12-4 Excerpts from the breathing animation. Frames one, 15, 30, 45, and 60 show what happens to the stomach, chest, and shoulders during inhaling and exhaling.

frames 1 and 30. The chest does just the opposite. It expands between frames 1 and 30. The shoulders rise up over the first thirty frames while the head is raised slightly. Between frames 30 and 60, the opposite occurs. The stomach area returns to its normal relaxed state while the chest settles back down upon the exhalation. The shoulders also drop. Figure 12-4 contains frames 1, 15, 30, 45, and 60 from this animation.

Figure 12-5 depicts the key bones that are moved to simulate breathing. The stomach bone is sized smaller while the two chest bones are enlarged and rotated upward. The shoulder bones are moved up. Most of the time you can repeat the same motions with these bones. Sometimes, depending on the action in the scene, you may have to vary the breathing time. This can usually be done in your software's motion graph.

Besides eye movement, blinking, and breathing, weight transfer is another factor that needs to be considered. A person never stays immobile but will often shift weight from one foot to the other.

This means the center of gravity moves. A more detailed discussion about balance can be found in the next chapter under the subheading, "Equilibrium."

Rendering in Movie or Image Format

Before rendering an animation, consider the two forms that you might want as the outcome. Most software gives you the option of rendering as a movie file (QuickTime , AVI, and others), or as a set of individual images (bmp, pct, psd, tif, and others).

If you are doing test renderings, then you might use a movie format with video compression of thousands of colors. These are easy to play back without having to go through a conversion procedure. The disadvantage of generating movie formats is that extended rendering times can jeopardize your final animation. If there is a power interruption during the rendering process, you will most likely lose the entire animation, thus wasting valuable time.

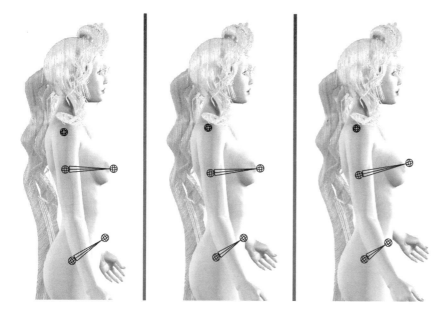

Fig. 12-5 Frames 1, 15, and 30 show how the stomach bone decreases in size while the chest bone increases and rotates up. The shoulder bone moves up.

Many studios prefer to output files as individual images. It is a safer process. Should the operation be interrupted, you still have the images that were completed before you stopped rendering. Then it is a matter of starting the rendering at the frame where you left off.

Using a video editing program, the image sequences can be converted into a movie format. To view the movie in real time on your computer, make a movie out of all the images. In order for the movie to play in real time, be sure to set the still image duration to one frame not thirty. Use any compression that you want and set the frame rate at thirty frames per second. If you set your color depth to a thousand or less, your computer should have an easier time playing it back. Make the movie and view the animation running in real time.

Sound Syncing

One of the best ways to understand timing is by having to synchronize sound to mouth movements. Matching facial expressions to your sound track might seem at first to be an impossible task. If you can plan ahead by making a graph of your sound and labeling it with the words and frame numbers below, you should be able to do a fairly good job of pairing the two.

Figure 12-6 has a sound graph coupled with the individual phonemes identifying the portion of the graph in which the various vowels and consonants occur. The frame numbers at the bottom are the most important part of keying the location of each phoneme. A sound-editing program is used to chart the location of phonemes and frame numbers. Depending on your software, you may have to label these by hand after playing through each part of the sound several times.

Once you have a sound chart plotted with the frame rate, activate the shape-shifting option of your software. Set your facial blend shapes to correspond with the labeled frame numbers on the sound chart. Be sure to use a mirror to mimic the mouth forms. The facial expressions that you mod-

257

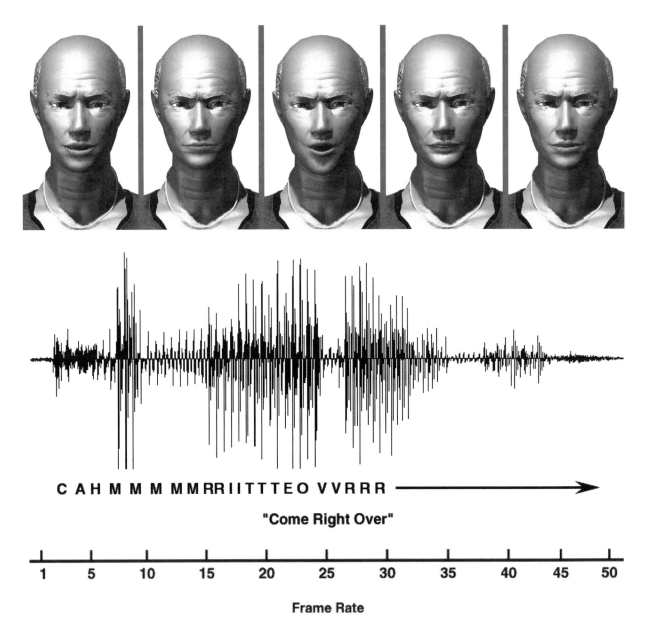

C A H M M M MMRRIITTTEO VVRRR ⟶

"Come Right Over"

1	5	10	15	20	25	30	35	40	45	50

Frame Rate

Fig. 12-6 A sound chart plots the phonemes and matches them to the frame rate. Shape-shifting software is used to blend facial expressions according to the corresponding frames.

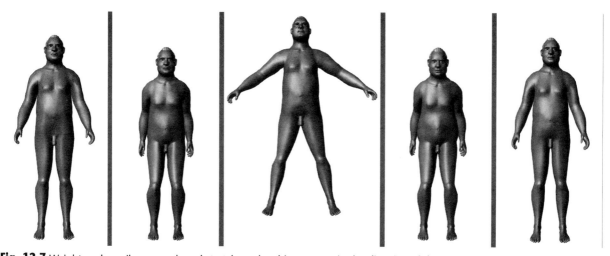

Fig. 12-7 Weight and recoil, or squash and stretch, make objects move in the direction of the motion. When its progress is halted, it will compress. In this case, observe the expansion and contraction of the cartoon character's lower torso.

eled in the previous chapter should work fine for dialogue. An animation of sound syncing can be found on the CD-ROM as CD12-6.

Weight and Recoil

Secondary action means that all parts do not arrive at a destination at the same time. Weight and recoil, also referred to as squash and stretch, uses secondary action. On the CD-ROM there is an animation of a cartoon character jumping up and down (CD12-7). When it lands, the resulting expansion of bodily mass and the swinging of arms are the secondary actions that follow the primary activity of the body landing. Although weight and recoil is more of a traditional cartoon effect, it is still very useful for teaching new animators basic lessons. Many professionals use weight and recoil to convey a feeling of weight for their characters. The next chapter covers overlapping (secondary) action in more detail.

Figure 12-7 shows an excerpt from the CD12-7

animation. The entire sequence lasts only forty frames. A heavyset cartoon character is shown jumping up and landing. In cartoon fashion, he expands like a balloon when bending down and when landing. When he propels himself into the air, he stretches.

Moving several bones accounts for the expansion and contraction. You should plan ahead by strategically placing these bones in anticipation of squash and stretch. One bone is placed in the front and center of the lower torso. Two other bones are set on the left and right sides of the lower torso.

Figure 12-8 depicts front and side views that outline the figure and the placement of bones during the jumping sequence. At frame 1, the bones are in their set position. Frame 10 shows the figure bending forward and down in anticipation of the jump. The two side bones are moved apart and the front bone is placed forward and down. This causes an expansion of the lower torso. In frame 20, the body is in the air stretching upward. The three bones are brought up and in a little to propel the

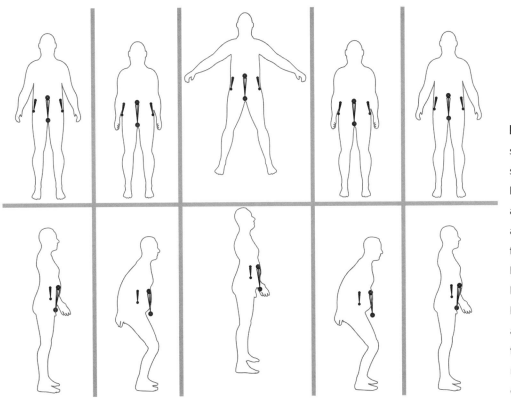

Fig. 12-8 The two side and front, squash and stretch bones are moved according to the action of the heavy figure. When he bends down or lands, the two side bones are moved apart while the front bone is moved forward and down.

lower torso in the direction of the jump. The greatest exaggeration occurs when he lands at frame 30. The two side bones are separated the most and the front one is brought forward and down. The final frame (40) returns the bones to their normal position. Besides moving bones, you can size them during the sequence. It all depends on how much weight and recoil you want to show.

You can also depict weight by indicating a visible struggle to move it. In the case of the weight and recoil animation, the fat male character has to wind up or tighten like a spring before becoming airborne. He does this at frame 10 by bending down somewhat.

Other means of showing heavy weight can be accomplished by the sudden stopping of weight and the jarring that results. This can be communicated through overlapping actions showing objects vibrating after the termination of the main action. When a heavier object lands or collides with something else, the effects of weight and gravity take longer to end than if it was light in weight. In a similar fashion, the heavy character takes longer to recover from the effects of gravity while the lighter one seems less affected by recoil. The featherweight seems to have springs on his feet and appears to float in the air. The heavy one exhibits drooping, tension, and strain.

The center of balance is lower on heavier characters. This can be depicted by the sagging of hips, shoulders and the forward bending of the spine. Heavy objects show more resistance to movement.

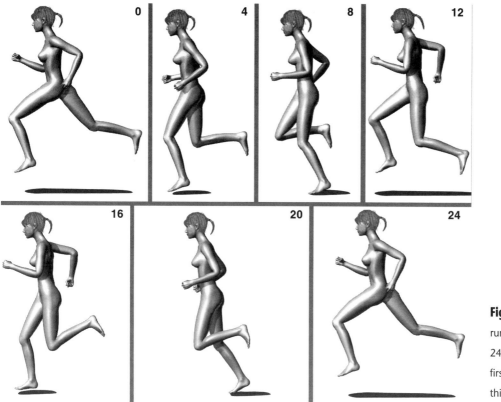

Fig. 12-9 A 24-frame running cycle. Frame 24 is identical to the first frame, which in this case starts at 0.

More tension is built up from the effort of trying to move. A ponderous creature moves slower with a jarring walk.

Animating a Two-Legged, Running Sequence

One action that is fairly simple to animate is the run. It teaches some important lessons. One of them is repeating animation: When one cycle is complete, it can be duplicated with motion graphs. The other important lesson involves weight and recoil: When the foot comes down, it acts like a spring to propel the body up and forward. As mentioned before, the character's size determines how much distortion (squash and stretch), if any,

occurs during the landing and lifting-off interval.

A fairly fast running sequence is illustrated in Figure 12-9. It portrays a lightweight female moving at a fast pace. The entire cycle lasts twenty-four frames with the last one repeating the first. You can view the animation on the accompanying CD-ROM as CD12-9. Since this is a light character, she practically floats in the air without distorting when landing. The stationary camera also adds to the illusion of speed. If you decide to have your camera follow and track your character, then the action will appear to be slower.

The animation was recorded using a wide-angle lens with a 15mm focal length. As mentioned before, a wide-angle lens can show a greater amount of the scene. Thus, the running figure

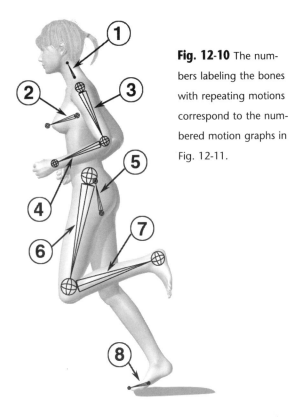

Fig. 12-10 The numbers labeling the bones with repeating motions correspond to the numbered motion graphs in Fig. 12-11.

appears to cover a greater distance as she approaches and leaves. A longer lens such as a 100mm shows less environment and the figure appears to speed by faster because there is less ground to cover before leaving the shot.

If your software has motion graphs, you can use the following directions as a guide for setting up a running sequence. Figure 12-10 illustrates the bones that use repeating motions. They are numbered according to the motion graphs in Figure 12-11. The recurring cycles in the graph are labeled with the word, repeat. The frame numbers at the bottom are an important indication of when to keyframe each one. Usually, for the repeating command to work correctly, you should use the same value for the first and last frames. In the case of the neck bone, frames 0 and 12 have the same numer-

ical value. The neck is rotated forward at frame 4 and back to its original position at frame 12. The amount of rotation depends on the size of your character. Therefore, it is labeled a relative rotational value without any visible numbers.

Secondary or overlapping motions can be seen with the breastbones. As the figure lands, the breasts move down slightly at frame 4. To give them extra bounce, the same keyframe is set at frame 10. At fourteen they rotate up a little. Using the same principle, you can also apply secondary motions to the hair, clothes, shoestrings, and so on.

When two limbs such as the arms and legs have repeating motions, they are usually opposite each other. Note the right and left upper arm bones. Their graphs are reversed. When one limb rotates forward at a specific frame, the other rotates in the opposite direction. This is the way bodies create balance.

The toe bone is labeled number eight. It is used to flex the foot after it hits the ground. As the body is propelled up and forward, the foot bends on the ground to accommodate the weight shift. The front of the right foot bends at frame 6 and returns to its normal position after leaving the ground at frame 12.

The only bone in Figure 12-11 that does not have rotational values is the parent bone. It controls all the other bones and is used to move the entire body in specific directions: in this case, the up and down motions when the body lands and takes off. This up and down movement can also be repeated.

The reason you use a parent bone instead of moving the body itself is that the body is moved only in the direction of the run. It only needs two keyframes for a straight path: one at the beginning

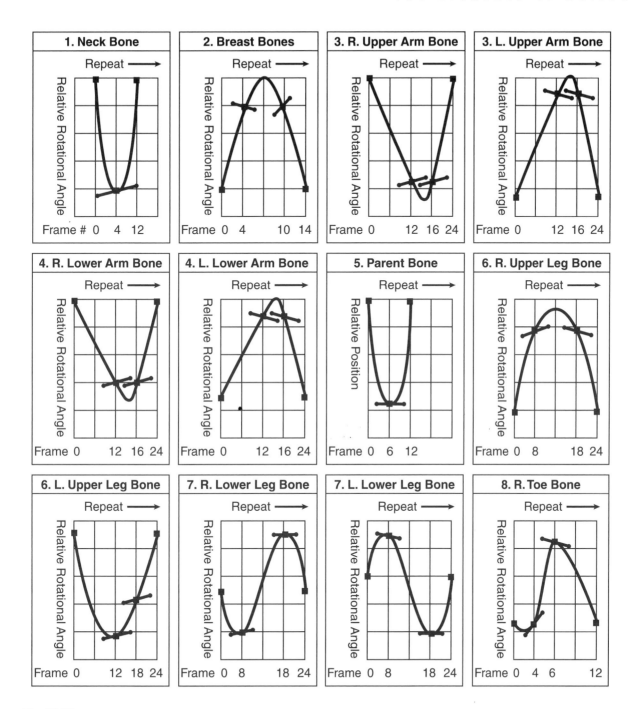

Fig. 12-11 Each motion graph corresponds to the numbered bones in Fig. 12-10. The rotational angles are relative because each software package has its own value system and the size of your character may differ from this one. The frame numbers should serve as a keyframing guide. Every one of these bones has repeating motions. Note the Parent bone. It is not rotated but moved up and down to control the leaping and landing of the body.

and the other at the destination. The further you move the body, the larger the strides appear to be. The figure also appears to be quicker because it covers more ground in the same amount of time. Of course, if you want the character to run along a curving path, you could set several keyframes for the body. Before propelling the character, make sure that all the limbs move correctly. Test animations can be made of your subject running in place. Once you are satisfied, then move the body to propel the character forward. Be sure to angle the body forward a little.

Animating a Four-Legged Running Sequence

A study of character animation would be painfully incomplete without considering the work of the great pioneering photographer Eadweard Muybridge. In his photographic volumes *Human and Animal Locomotion* (Dover Publications), he provided an invaluable resource for animators.

Muybridge introduced stop-motion sequences in the nineteenth century. He designed three batteries of cameras with twelve lenses for each battery. The three batteries were placed at right angles to each other. All were focused on one subject. On each of the three twelve-lens cameras, every lens was exposed for a fraction of a second in succeeding order. When a model was photographed, thirty-six negatives were obtained. Each one contained a different stage of action from three different views.

During his many slide lectures, Muybridge demonstrated the fallacy of animal poses in ancient and modern art. He often shocked his audience by revealing their true movements in his stop-motion photographs. It was shown that even

pigs showed grace and agility when they were galloping.

The photographs directly influenced famous artists like Eakins, Remington, Degas, and Duchamp. The impact of his work on artists, art students, animators, and illustrators can hardly be overstated. To this day, no body of work documenting human and animal movements equals that of *Human and Animal Locomotion*.

Figure 12-12 illustrates the four-legged movement of a puppy running. The animation can be viewed on the CD-ROM as CD12-12. The puppy's movements are similar to the gallop of other four-legged creatures. As might be expected, there are some differences. The puppy's legs are stubby, thus impeding much of his drive.

Overlapping action can be seen in the flapping of the ears and wagging of the tail. The entire running cycle continues for eighteen frames. The last frame repeats the motions of the first. The bones responsible for most of the movements are listed in Figure 12-13.

The parent bone is responsible for the upward and downward mobility of the body. This makes it easier to move the body from one point to another without worrying about having it go up and down at certain points.

Rotations for opposite limbs like the left and right upper back legs, except in a few instances, occur at the same frames with reverse values. For repeating movements to work, be sure to study the photographs of Eadweard Muybridge and jot down notes for the rotational values. One other benefit found in the third volume of *Human and Animal Locomotion* is Muybridge's timing charts. These are the travel records of each photographed subject. You can match the time to the specific plate and know how fast the person or animal was moving. Once

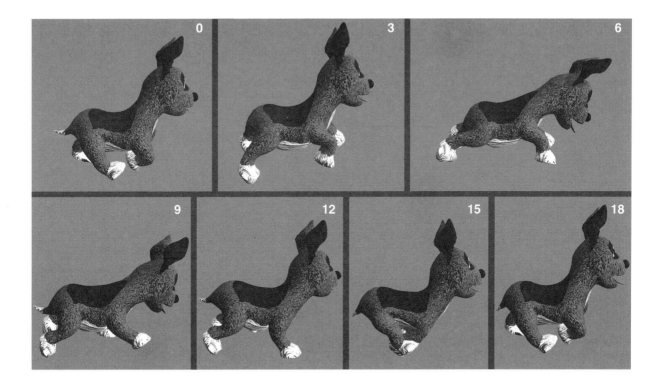

Repeating Rotation or Movement of the Bones						
Parent	✓	✓	✓	✓	✓	Same as 0
R. & L. Upr. Back Leg	✓	✓	✓	✓	✓	✓ Same as 0
R. & L. Midl. Back Leg	✓		✓	✓	✓	✓ Same as 0
R. & L. Back Paw	✓		✓		✓	Same as 0
R. & L. Frnt. Upr. Leg	✓	✓	✓	✓	✓ Same as 0	
R. & L. Frnt. Lwr. Leg	✓	✓	✓	✓	✓ Same as 0	
R. & L. Frnt. Paw	✓				Same as 0	
Frame Number	0	3	6	9	12	15	18

Fig. 12-12 A four-legged running cycle. Frame 18 repeats the motions of the first frame.

Fig. 12-13 This chart outlines the rotations of the bones responsible for most of the motions. The first and last frames have the same values.

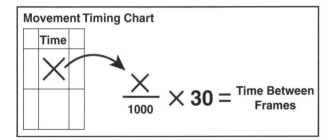

Movement Timing Chart

$$\frac{x}{1000} \times 30 = \text{Time Between Frames}$$

Fig. 12-14 Using Muybridge's timing charts, you can apply this formula to find out the frame rates for all his photographed movements. The *x* stands for the time that he recorded in his charts.

you have located the time, use the formula in Figure 12-14 to calculate the frame rate for each image.

The following is an example of implementing this formula. Plate 709 shows twelve frames of a galloping dog. The chart in the back of volume three records the number 41 for the time. Utilizing our formula, you divide 41 by 1,000 to get .041. The number .041 is multiplied by 30 giving us a frame rate of 1.23. This means each of the twelve photos is spaced 1.23 frames apart. Applying this to an animation means that the second frame is keyframed at 1.23. The third pose is keyframed at 2.46, and so on. Most people round off the keyframe rate. In this case, if you want your dog to run faster, space each frame by one. If you want it to go slower, use two.

Pose-to-Pose Animation

If you decide to use Eadweard Muybridge's stop-motion photographs as a guide, you will be animating in a style referred to as pose-to-pose, pose planning, or pose-extremes animation. For this type of animation, a sequence of photographs, sketches, or video serves as a template to assist the animator in planning each pose for the duration of the action.

Figure 12-15 illustrates pose planning according to plate 272 from Muybridge's book. His chart lists the time of the stumbling and falling sequence with the number 161. Applying the formula to this number means that each photograph represents 4.83 frames. Rounding this off to five frames, we

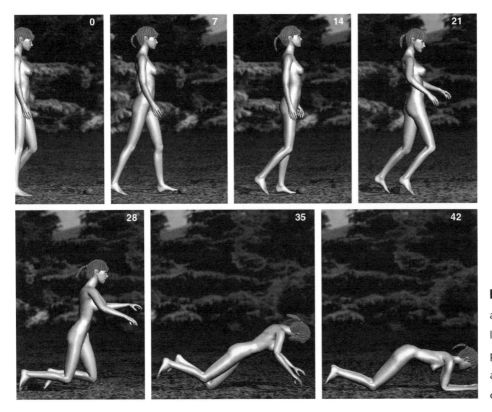

Fig. 12-15 Pose-to-pose animation uses key poses like those from time-lapse photography or sketches, and then positions the character accordingly.

get the keyframes 0, 5, 10, 15, 20, 25, 30, 35, 40, 45, 50, and 55. In other words, the entire action lasts for fifty-five frames.

The illustrations in Figure 12-15 represent selections from the CD12-15 animation on the CD-ROM. Only six frames spaced at every seventh frame are seen in the illustration. The animation was shot with a long lens (100mm) bringing the background closer to the viewer and compressing the entire environment.

Beginning animators should find pose-to-pose planning easier to use than straight-ahead animation, which is more improvisational. Straight-ahead animation will be discussed in the next section. Pose planning means that you plan ahead by creating a kind of blueprint. Most of the action is controlled by following the poses in photographs, videos, or sketches.

Pose planning is useful for repeating actions like walking and running. When you have scenes of extreme drama in which you want your digital actors to strike key poses, try using pose-to-pose animation. If you want your character to end in a certain position at a specific time, and the first and last frame poses are extreme, then pose them that way at the beginning and at the end. Select a few keyframes between the beginning and ending positions. Place your models at those keyframes in the attitudes that you think they should be in. Playback a test animation to see how the software interprets these key poses. Make your adjustments accordingly. For example, if you want your character to sit in a chair, you could pose it standing in the first frame. Once you decide the length of time that it takes to have the character sit down, then place him in a sitting position at the final frame. Now create some of the keyframes between the first and last by posing the character in the act of sitting down.

A word of caution about pose planning. If you position parts of your character at keyframes that are very close together, you could end up with jerky movements. For more fluid motions, space the keyframes apart. This is especially true with secondary or overlapping actions. Another common mistake is for animators to keyframe all the parts at the same time (say, every fifth frame). Overlapping actions should occur at different times than the main motions. When the upper arm swings forward at frame 5, the lower arm might lag a little and end its motion at frame 8.

While the animation is running, movements should never appear to come to a dead stop. Except when they die, it is not natural for biological entities to become immobile. The next chapter discusses methods for avoiding this problem. One of these is to set the same keyframes twice, spaced anywhere between three to twenty or more frames. This gives limbs and other parts a little extra bounce. Bending the curve on the motion graph between the two identical frames controls the amount of bounce.

Straight-Ahead Animation

This is a more spontaneous method of animating one move after another. It is recommended for experienced animators who are familiar with proper timing. Straight-ahead animation means that actions are acted out during the process and that they are based on a set of loosely drawn storyboards. Every activity is an outgrowth of subsequent ones. This can lead to unplanned and innovative effects. It is frequently an unplanned performance.

Many professional animators who create straight-ahead animations, pantomime some of

Fig. 12-16 Straight-ahead animation means that a great deal of the performance is unplanned. This leaves a lot of room for impromptu actions.

Fig. 12-17 Usually a rough storyboard and the playacting of the animator is all that is used for straight-ahead ani-mation.

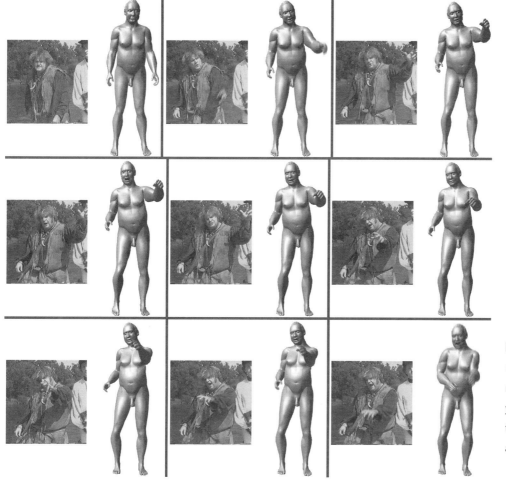

Fig. 12-18

Rotoscoping in animation means having your character follow the motions of an actor or cartoon.

the movements before keyframing them. This gives them an idea of the timing and direction of their characters. Facial animation is often practiced this way in a mirror and then animated.

Figure 12-16 shows an example of a straight-ahead animation found on the CD-ROM as CD12-16. It is based on a loosely drawn storyboard as depicted in Figure 12-17. This is a sketchy plan of action, which is given more substance and detail during the animation process.

Pose-to-pose and straight-ahead animation can be combined. You can set up key poses in the shot and then animate toward each one in a straight-ahead manner. When animating toward the first pose, you may decide to alter it according to the direction you find yourself moving.

Rotoscoping in 3D Animation

Rotoscoping is a method of importing a movie, image sequence, or animation and then having a digital character follow the movements in an imported file. Figure 12-18 shows an example of a computer graphics actor imitating the moves of a real actor. The rotoscope animation can be viewed on the CD-ROM as CD12-18.

For some people, rotoscoping is an invaluable guide for realistic movements. Many gaming companies use motion capture for lifelike action moves while others use rotoscoping. Most beginning animators have problems with correct timing. Rotoscoping helps them to overcome this difficulty. It gives them a guide that has correct timing built into it. All they have to do is follow the actions of the videotaped person, animal, insect, and other character.

Once students becomes more comfortable with the animation process, they may find it unnecessary to always follow filmed action. Their sense of timing will have developed to the point where they can act out certain movements. Although they may become experts in human movement, they will most likely still depend on observing the motions of other creatures like whales, ostriches, and other animals. Some major animation studios have developed libraries of different creature movements. Their animators can use these videotapes for rotoscoping or studying specific actions.

If you decide to use rotoscoping, try not to match each movement to every frame of the video. This would result in too many keyframes, making the action look choppy at times. For example, if the videotaped actor's arm moves down over a period of thirty frames, you might keyframe your character's arm at frames 0, 15, and 30. You would not keyframe it every step of the way down. When a motion stops, be sure to add a little bounce by keyframing it twice at the end and spacing the two keyframes anywhere between three to twenty or more frames apart.

Emphasis or exaggeration is an important part of animation. When rotoscoping, it is easy to over-

look. This can result in movements that are too soft. Use rotoscoping as a general guide, but be sure to punctuate motions with distinct mannerisms. Magnifying specific actions makes your animations less mundane and even adds some personality to your characters.

Rotoscoping can also be helpful for facial animation. Your character can follow the speech patterns of the videotaped person. This method is more useful if your software can display the sound graph as well as the video images.

The foremost animation software packages have some kind of method for displaying either movie or image sequence files. Some have you load movie scenes into an image plane or as a background image. Others allow you to map image sequences onto an object like a rectangle. If you decide to map an imported video file onto a rectangle, then be sure to model it to the same proportions as the imported images. The rectangle can also be two-sided so that you can see the mapped images from either side. If you are using numbered sequences, convert your movie files in a video-editing program. Number them: *Name.000.bmp, Name.001.bmp, Name.002.bmp,* and so on.

The file format varies according to your software and hardware. When you move your time slider, the image numbers should match the frame numbers.

Animating a Walking Sequence

Creating a walking sequence involves one of the most basic keyframing skills that every animator must master. It seems simple enough until you try to go through it and find the timing to be wrong, the movements robot-like, the feet slide, and so on. You can learn a lot when trying to make a char-

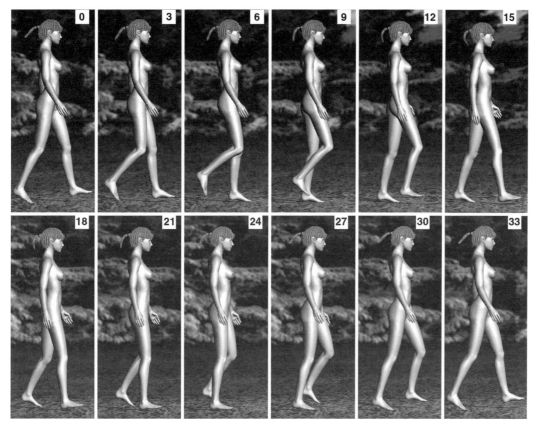

Fig. 12-19

A 33-frame
walk cycle.

acter walk. This is the reason that I ask all my animation students to create a walking sequence. Granted, there are software packages and plug-ins that can create automatic walking sequences. If you rely on these, then it is important to add small nuances to make the character more individual. Depending on your software package, you may decide to use partial Inverse Kinematics. IK can be restricted to the lower half of the body, which requires a way to anchor the feet to the ground to prevent sliding. The upper part can use Forward Kinematics with repeating motions.

The following method makes use of repeating motions. The feet and knees are moved with a manipulator handle that can be anchored. Some software packages use IK spline handles to control the IK chain. Whatever your software package calls these manipulation objects, you will need to make sure that the feet can be locked to the ground at certain points of the walking cycle. Sometimes this is referred to as sticky posing, which allows you to stick one or more IK handles to a location in space while you move other IK handles.

The moment that a foot hits the ground, it should lock until it is time to lift it again. The forward motion of the body makes the locked foot roll on the ground. Due to its anchor at the toes, the heel comes up while the toes remain in the same spot until it is time to lift the foot off the ground. Since a number of software packages use nulls to manipulate IK chains, the following technique for creating a walking sequence refers to the

Fig. 12-20 The hips swing in the opposite direction of the shoulders during the walk cycle.

IK manipulators as nulls. As you work through the walking sequence, you can use the poses in Figure 12-19 as a general guide.

The following exercise is for a thirty-three-frame walking cycle, which means that it will take one second to complete all the body motions. Everything begins to repeat at frame 33. Note the pose at frame 33 is the same as the one at 0. The final walking animation can be viewed on the accompanying CD-ROM as CD12-19.

Before working with sticky IK handles or nulls at the feet, the repeating motions of the upper body should be set. The rotation of the shoulders and hips are taken care of first. Notice the angle of the shoulders and hipbones in Figure 12-20. The hips swing in the opposite direction of the shoulders. When one foot comes down and the hip rotates down, the shoulder on that same side goes up. This hip sway is especially noticeable in female walks.

In our thirty-three-frame cycle, the keyframes for the hips and shoulders are 0, 12, 18, 27, and 33. Frames 0 and 33 are always identical. Starting at frame 0 the left and right hips are set in their normal positions. At frame 12, the left hip is rotated down while the right hip is rotated up. Moving to frame 18, both hips are set back to their normal positions. At frame 27, the left hip is rotated up while the right hip is rotated down. Frame 33 is the same as 0, so the hips are back to their normal positions. Once you have keyframed the left and right hips at the specified frames, be sure to turn on "repeat" for them so that their motions will continue. Figure 12-21 has a chart summarizing the hip motions.

As mentioned before, the hips and shoulders rotate opposite each other. Therefore, using the same keyframes, 0, 12, 18, 27, and 33, rotate the shoulders in the following manner. At frame 0 the right and left shoulders are in their normal, relaxed positions. Go to frame 12 and rotate the right shoulder down and the left shoulder up. The shoulders are set back to their normal state at frame 18. At frame 27 rotate the right shoulder up and the left shoulder down. Frame 33 has the same, normal relaxed position for both shoulders as does frame 0. Figure 12-22 sums up the keyframes for the shoulders.

Rotating the shoulder bones might place the arms in some odd positions. This will be remedied through the correct placement of the left and right arms. The lower part of the arms from the elbows to the fingers are posed separately. The keyframes for the upper arms are at frames 0, 12, 18, 27 and 33. As before, the upper arms are positioned identically at 0 and 33. The left upper arm is rotated back at frames 0 and 33. At frame 12, rotate the left upper arm forward. Moving to frame 18, the left

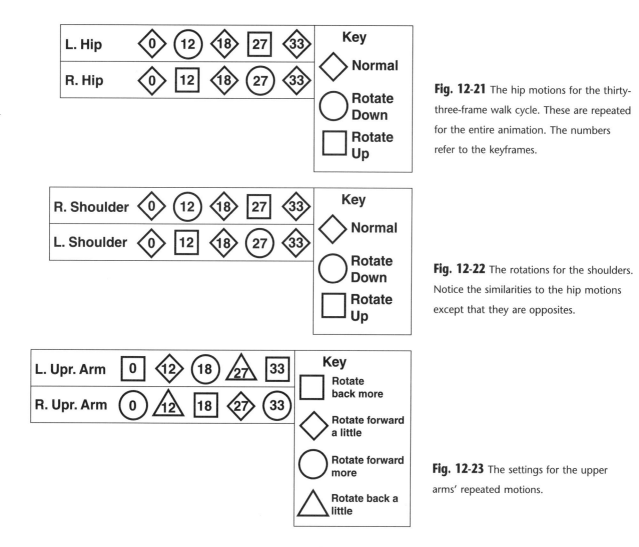

Fig. 12-21 The hip motions for the thirty-three-frame walk cycle. These are repeated for the entire animation. The numbers refer to the keyframes.

Fig. 12-22 The rotations for the shoulders. Notice the similarities to the hip motions except that they are opposites.

Fig. 12-23 The settings for the upper arms' repeated motions.

upper arm is rotated forward even more. When you go to frame 27, rotate the left upper arm back a little. You can use the chart in Figure 12-23 and the poses in Figure 12-19 as guides for keyframing the left and right upper arms correctly.

The right upper arm rotates forward to the greatest extent at frames 0 and 33. At frame 12, it is turned back a little and at 18, it is positioned back the most. Rotate the upper arm forward a little at frame 27. Refer to the chart in Figure 12-23.

The swing of the lower part of the arms makes

the secondary motions. Only three keyframes are set for their repeating cycles. The left lower arm is placed at frames 0 and 33 in its normal relaxed position. At frame 21, rotate the left lower arm forward. This serves as the follow-through and lag-time motion because the left upper arm had already moved forward three frames before. Figure 12-24 shows a chart with the lower arm movements.

The right lower arm starts out at frame 0 in a forward position and finishes that way at frame 33.

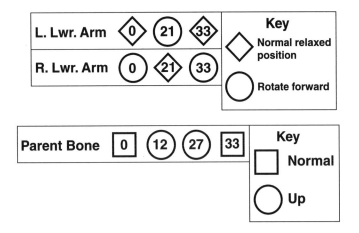

Fig. 12-24 The keyframes and rotations for the lower part of the arms.

Fig. 12-25 The parent bone moves the body up and down.

At frame 21, place the right lower arm back to its normal relaxed position.

During the walk, the body proceeds forward in an undulating up and down motion. Since the up and down wave motion repeats itself, the parent bone is assigned this movement. This makes it easier to move the body various amounts during the cycle. The keyframes for the parent bone's up and down motions are 0, 12, 27, and 33. The parent bone is set in its normal position at frames 0 and 33. It is the down position for the body. At frames 12 and 27, the parent bone is keyframed in an up position. This moves the entire skeleton up, which in turn places the body at its highest point. The motion graph between 12 and 27 should have a curve giving the body a little bit of a bounce. Figure 12-25 shows the chart for the parent bone.

Other secondary actions can also be repeated. For example, the head can bend forward at specific keyframes. The cycle is 0, normal position; 15, bend forward a little; 21, normal position; 30, bend forward a little; and 33, normal position. The ponytail in the sample animation has repeating motions. At frames 0 and 33, all three bones are in their normal positions. At frame 12, the first bone is rotated up. Frame 15 shows the second bone

rotated up. Finally, at frame 18, the last ponytail bone rotates up. The lag time of three frames creates a waving motion that works itself through the entire object like the motion of a chain.

When you finish setting the repeating motions for the upper parts, make some test animations. Correct any problems. The movements should have a natural and relaxed appearance. The next part of the walk involves the movement of the legs and the body. As mentioned before, IK manipulators used to move the feet, as well as lock them to the ground at certain points, are referred to as nulls. Since the feet also move in repeating cycles, we can set these nulls according to a pattern. Motion graphs can then be utilized for each recurring event.

In order to make the repeating motions less complex, our goal is to complete every null and body movement at frame 33. Every part finishes at the same point. To simplify the animation process, we will work on one leg at a time for the entire thirty-three-frame cycle. Since the nulls are anchoring the feet, this makes the body pose look awkward at times, but it will be resolved eventually. Make sure that whenever a null (IK handle) hits the ground, it locks at that point or becomes sticky. It unlocks or ceases to be sticky when you reach a frame where it is specified that the null be moved.

Pose the body similar to the first position in Figure 12-19. Keyframe all the nulls and the body at frame 0. The legs will be moved using only the four toe and knee nulls. The body and the four nulls are keyframed at frames 0, 12, 18, 24, and 33.

At frame 12, move the right toe and right knee nulls forward until the right leg looks posed like the leg at frame 12 in Figure 12-19. Since we haven't moved the body yet, the leg does not look quite right. Later, when the body is moved, you can go back to this keyframe and make whatever minor adjustments are necessary. Keyframe the right toe and knee nulls at frame 12.

Move to frame 18 and position the right toe and knee nulls forward. Again, do not worry about distortions caused by the body being left behind. You are only trying to approximate the general placement of the right leg according to frame 18 in Figure 12-19. Keyframe the right toe and knee nulls at frame 18.

Go to frame 24 and move the right toe null straight down to the ground. Adjust the right knee null and keyframe it and the right toe null at frame 24. At this point, the foot will most likely look distorted. This will be adjusted when we move the body in the next step.

Now, it is time to move the body forward. Since each person has a different size character, the amount of forward movement will vary. Measure the length of your body from the toes to the lower chest. This will give you the approximate distance you need to move the body. For example, if your character is five feet eight inches tall, then you would move it three feet eight inches. At frame 33, move the body forward using your calculated distance.

While you are at frame 33, move the right knee null forward until the right leg looks like it is in the same pose as it was at frame 0. The right toe null stays anchored at this frame in the same place as it was in frame 24. Keyframe both the right toe and knee nulls at frame 33.

Even though the left leg may look a little odd at frame 33, it will be fixed soon. Before starting on this leg, it is important to go back and adjust the right leg at frames 12, 18, 24, and 33. Check to make sure that the leg matches the position of the right leg in Figure 12-19.

At frame 33, drag the left toe and left knee nulls forward until the left leg looks identical to its position at frame 0. Keyframe both nulls at 33. The entire pose of the body should now look the same at frames 0 and 33.

Go back to frame 0 and lower the left toe null down to the ground and keyframe it at frames 12 and 18. Do not keyframe it at 0. We are only using its position at 0 as a reference point. At frames 12 and 18, adjust and keyframe the left knee null.

Move to frame 24 and raise the left toe null up and forward a little. Move the left knee null forward. Keyframe both at frame 24.

It is time now to check keyframes 0, 12, 18, 24, and 33. If you need to make adjustments to the left and right toe and knee nulls, use Figure 12-19 as a guide. If you have extra controls such as ankle nulls, you might utilize them to make minor modifications. Play back the animation between frames 0 and 33 while checking for odd-looking poses. Try to adjust any mistakes only at keyframes 0, 12, 18, 24, and 33. Remember, the body has to look identical at frames 0 and 33.

Run some test animations. Once you are satisfied, you can continue the animation by repeating the process. This can be done by working with motion graphs or repeating the previous steps. If you decide to do it by hand instead of mathematically with motion graphs, then instead of keyframing at 0, 12, 18, 24, and 33, you will keyframe at 33, 45, 51, 57, and 66. The body pose at 33 and 66 is the same. The next set of keyframes is 66, 78, 84, 90, and 99. Frames 66 and 99 have the same body poses.

Since walking is basically a repeating cycle, you may decide to speed up the process by working with motion graphs. Although motion graphs are useful for speeding up repetitive tasks, you will most likely have to make minor adjustments afterward. Relying on them totally will make your walking movements look a little too mechanical. Therefore, it is a good idea to go back and make adjustments here and there to give the walk little variations.

Every software package with motion graphs utilizes them in a different manner. Generally, what you are doing is calculating the distance of the body at it walks from point A to point B. You can do this by using the algebra distance formula:

$$| \text{ frame } 0 - \text{frame } 33 |$$

Now you can copy the motion graph from frames 0 to 33. Paste it in starting at frame 34. Your motion graph now extends from 0 to 67. The next step, starting at frame 34, is to shift the values by the distance that you calculated with your algebra formula. The slope of your motion graph should continue moving up or down between frames 0 and 67. The only thing left is to delete the extra frame, frame 34. You can continue this process with all the leg nulls and the body for whatever distance you want your person to walk.

The following is an example of using motion

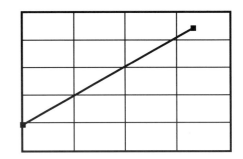

Fig. 12-26 The 33-frame motion graph for the body moving along the x-axis.

graphs in this manner. The software package utilized is LightWave 3D.

Select the body and open its "Graph Editor," which might look somewhat like Figure 12-26. Find the difference between the current value of frames 0 and 33. Use the old algebra distance formula:

$$| \text{ frame } 0 - \text{frame } 33 |$$

What this does is to take the absolute value of the difference between frames 0 and 33. It will be used later to determine how much to "Shift Values."

Click the "Copy/Paste Keys" button and type in the following settings: *Low Frame 0, High Frame 33, Paste Frames at 34.*

Your motion graph will now look somewhat like the one shown in Figure 12-27. The values of the duplicate frames now have to be adjusted.

Click the "Shift Keys" button and type the following: *Low Frame 34, High Frame 67, Shift Frames by –1.*

Shift Values by? (This setting is the absolute value from your previous algebra formula. Be sure to type the measurement next to the number: inches, feet, etc.).

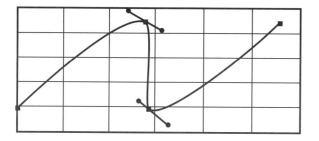

Fig. 12-27 After copying and pasting, the thirty-three frames at frame 34, the motion graph extends to frame 67.

If the slope of your motion graph is downward, type a negative value for "Shift Values By." For example, if your distance formula value is 50 cm and the motion graph slopes downward, enter 50 cm in the "Shift Values by" box.

After shifting the values, delete the extra frame 34. The motion graph might look like the one shown in Figure 12-28.

Open the motion graph for the left knee null and calculate the absolute value of the difference between frames 0 and 33.

Click the "Copy/Paste Keys" button and type in the following settings: *Low Frame 0, High Frame 33, Paste Frames at 34.*

The values of the duplicate frames will have to be adjusted. Click the Shift Keys button and type the following: *Low Frame 34, High Frame 67, Shift Frames by –1.*

Shift Values by? (This setting is the absolute value from your previous algebra formula. Be sure to type the measurement next to the number: inches, feet, etc.).

After shifting the values, delete the extra frame 34.

Repeat all of the previous steps of copying, pasting, and shifting keys for the rest of the nulls.

Drag the frame slider back and forth to test the movements. Create a preview animation and watch the character move forward and backward. Correct some of the minor flaws without setting new key frames for the nulls. If the body lags behind or moves ahead too far at certain points, then adjust its position by moving it and adding new keyframes.

If your animation extends beyond frame 67, repeat the previous steps for the body and all the nulls.

Using motion graphs to repeat the movements might make your walking sequence look a little too mechanical. Therefore, it is a good idea to go back and adjust some of the keyframes to give the walk a little variation.

I hope that this process helps you create a better walking animation. There are many other avenues to explore when doing this type of movement, like scaling keys to vary the speed of the walk. Once you feel more comfortable with this procedure, you might want to add other nuances like moving the head, shoulders, fingers, and other parts.

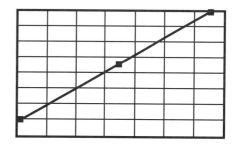

Fig. 12-28 The corrected 67-frame motion graph after shifting the keys starting at frame 34. The extra frame 34 is then deleted.

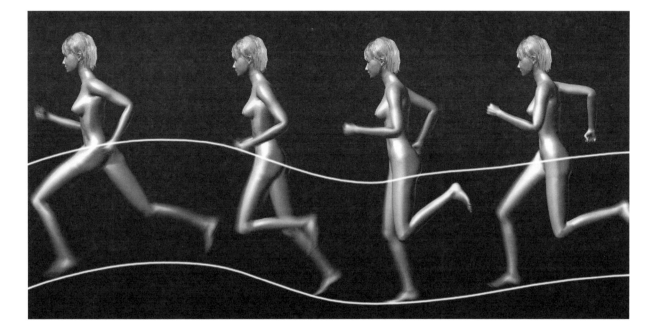

CHAPTER 13

Movements of the Figure

One of the most challenging tasks that the computer animation artist faces is conveying mass or weight. Working in a virtual environment where the rules of physics do not apply, the animator has to be resourceful in convincing viewers that his characters and the objects they interact with have weight. His creatures and the things that they manipulate have to exhibit the ability to rebound in response to specific actions.

Recording the Motion of Body Masses

One way to communicate weight is through delayed secondary action. When a character lands on a surface, a chain reaction takes place. The impact starts at the point of contact and travels upward through the body causing certain limbs to move in a time lag. A good follow-through is achieved when various parts arrive at a certain point at different times. Other methods for achieving weight are proper timing, ease in, ease out, arcs, anticipation, exaggeration, weight and recoil, follow-through, staging, and overlapping actions.

An example of weight and follow-through can be seen in Figure 13-2. The character walks up to a chair and sits in it. This animation may appear simple at first, but to do it right, a number of extra movements have to be keyframed. When the character sits down, the chair has to respond to his weight. Other parts of the character's body also react. The arms have a little bounce to them and the head snaps back somewhat and then recovers its stable position. This animation can be viewed on the accompanying CD-ROM as CD13-2.

The following exercise takes you through the steps of animating a character sitting down in a chair. You can use the models that you created

Fig. 13-1 Several views of the skeleton set up in a chair. The arrows point to the parent bone.

from previous chapters. Before starting, add bones to the chair so that it can react to the character's weight and also bend back as the character leans backward. Figure 13-1 shows the skeleton for the chair. The parent bone begins at the base and the rest of the bones radiate outward from it for the wooden supports and wheels. The shaft of the chair has a series of bones moving upward toward the seat. These are part of the spring system and are rotated to bend the chair back and forth. The seat cushion follows with radiating bones and the back of the chair and the support cushion have bones for extra flexibility.

Once you have set up your lights and camera position, place your character next to the chair (Figure 13-2). Because there is a little walking sequence involved before your character can sit down, you may decide to lock or anchor the feet to the ground. If you are working with Forward Kinematics, use nulls or an object that will not render to mark the location of the feet. To make it easier for the character to sit down, position it at about a 45-degree angle to the chair.

At frame 7, move one of the legs forward. The

Fig. 13-2 Weight and gravity is conveyed by the movement of the chair as it reacts to the character's mass. The secondary actions of the figure, like the arms bouncing up and the head snapping back, also communicate body weight.

upper arm opposite that leg should also swing ahead in a delayed secondary motion at frame 10. The lower arm completes the secondary swing forward at frame 14. An extra keyframe for this lower arm is inserted at frame 26. It has the same setting as frame 14. The motion curve for the lower arm between frames 14 and 26 should have a slight arc. This gives it a little bounce so that the arm doesn't appear to come to a dead stop. When you add an extra keyframe like this after a specific move, it keeps the movement from looking too mechanical. In real life no object can come to a dead stop without first reacting to its original force.

The leg that was moved forward lands on the ground at frame 14, while the opposite leg that stayed behind should be locked to the same spot. This does not mean that it stays flat on the ground, but instead, rotates between frames 1 and 14 from the heel to the base of the big toe.

Between frames 14 and 28, the leg that stayed behind is now moved forward. It should land on a spot in front of the chair. Be careful not to let the leg intersect the chair. You may have to insert a frame or two between frames 14 and 28 to keep this from happening.

After frame 28, the foot will no longer be

moved except to rotate into position later, when the character sits down. The other foot that had been moved previously remains locked on the spot where it landed at frame 14. This locked foot rotates from the heel to the base of the toes between frames 14 and 28.

In the meantime, the arm opposite the leg that was moved ahead also rotates forward a few frames later and is followed by its lower arm. To give the arm a little bounce at the end, keyframe the lower arm twice with the same setting spaced approximately seven frames apart. If necessary, edit the motion curve's arc.

Starting at frame 28 and ending at frame 43, move the locked leg forward so that its foot is also in front of the chair. The other foot already in front of the chair rotates forward without lifting up. This occurs during the process of sitting down. When viewing the animation, notice how the arms come forward and together to help with balance so that the body does not fall into the chair. The head, neck, and spine also bend forward to keep balance.

At frame 43, the body lands on the chair and both feet face forward. The spine straightens out while the head snaps back between frames 37 and 43. The head is given an extra bounce by keyframing it with the same setting at frames 43 and 50. The arms spring up a little. To give the body a little bounce, keyframe it the same at frames 43 and 50.

So far, you have created delayed secondary actions on the body by moving extremities in reaction to the force of other body parts as they move or meet resistance. Now it is time to show how the character has mass and weight by making the chair react to the body's force. Starting at frame 43 and ending at 50 the bone(s) in the shaft of the chair underneath the seat are moved down a little. At frame 57 move the bones back to their original position by keyframing them the same as frame 43. For that extra little bounce, frame 67 is given the same keyframe as 57.

The spine bends back as the body settles into the chair between frames 43 and 80. In response to the body's force, the chair's bones in the shaft are rotated back between frames 67 and 80. From this point on, you may decide to initiate a whole new cycle of actions. Of course, it helps to have a good reason for each action.

Pacing and Impact

Just like music, animations are time-based. Music has a certain tempo or beat. This holds true for animation. Animators regulate the pace of animation. They develop an instinct for acting at the right moment to change the pace or speed of their characters and the entire flow of events. Dramatic impact is measured by the right timing. Every circumstance should have a meaning. Even occurrences that appear random have a purpose behind them. Timing is the arrangement of temporal events. It is probably the most important skill an animator can develop. The audience needs a certain period of time to comprehend each circumstance. If a character picks up something, it should be performed at a rate that gives people a chance to see what was lifted up.

The pattern of actions can be planned before beginning the animation. However, the animator develops the structure intuitively during the animation. At first it may appear awkward to interpret seconds as numbered frames, but after a while you develop a second sense for patterns of spacing. A thirty-frame animation lasts one second. The viewer normally does not register one frame consciously. At least three to five frames are needed to

Fig. 13-3 Pacing and impact play an important role in animation. This sequence begins peacefully, builds up to a climax with an impact, and ends quietly.

read a scene. A quick gesture requires between four and ten frames, depending on the length of the motion. Figure 13-3 illustrates some scenes from an animation in which the pacing changes several times to convey the right feeling and impact. The animation can be viewed on the accompanying CD-ROM as CD13-3.

The animation opens with a quiet pastoral scene. A Frisbee flies overhead toward the horizon and disappears among the trees. Before the audience has a chance to question the reason for the Frisbee's presence, a bull chasing the Frisbee thunders onto the scene and above the camera—which is at ground level—and disappears among the trees. What started out as a quiet and slow event quickly became a fast-paced occurrence. Motion blur is used to enhance the illusion of movement.

A cut to a different view of the bull chasing the

Frisbee is seen next. This gives the audience time to comprehend the circumstances. The fast pace is maintained by showing the background as a blur. One way to accomplish this is to have the character run in place while the background is moved.

The tempo slows down in the next cut, which gives the audience a little respite from the hectic pace and sets up the next occurrence. This helps them comprehend the following shot, which anticipates the climax of the running scene. Anticipation is created by the rooster's panic. The leisurely pace of an idyllic scene is disrupted suddenly by the appearance of the bull.

Impact is seen literally when the bull collides with the car. This results in a series of connected secondary events that reinforce the magnitude of the crash. The camera is jittered violently by rotating it left over the course of two frames, then right for the next three frames, and back again to its original position two frames later. The rocks in the scene fly straight up and down over the course of ten frames. The rooster is hurtled out of the scene by the impact. The bull flies backward and his form is compressed into an accordion shape. The car rolls several times in the opposite direction. Both the bull and the car are hurtled out of the shot in opposite directions. The setting now reverts back to its former peaceful view. A few of the rooster's feathers float down to the ground as a reminder of what just occurred.

Equilibrium

Balance refers to a situation in which the masses of the body work to create a stable condition. Usually, the body's base of support is in the feet. Thus, the center of gravity moves toward the ground and rests between the feet. Whether a figure is stationary or in motion, the muscles work to maintain equilibrium. The animator is often faced with the challenge of making the characters appear to be influenced by gravitational forces. By depicting elements in the body striving to maintain equilibrium, the artist shows tension generated by opposing fields of energy.

Balance can be either symmetrical or asymmetrical. A symmetrical pose (Figure 13-4) means an equal distribution of body mass. The figure appears stable and the center of gravity falls between the feet.

Asymmetrical balance is a result of the unequal distribution of body weight. Figure 13-5 illustrates the resulting tension when all the weight rests on one foot. The center of gravity is no longer between the feet, but now rests in front of the foot. Notice how the arms and head attempt to uphold equilibrium by assuming new positions. These sec-

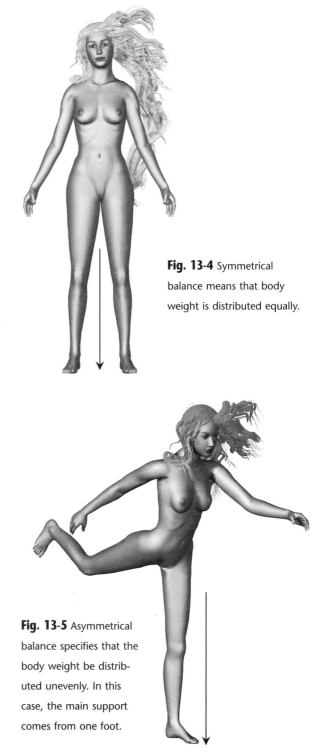

Fig. 13-4 Symmetrical balance means that body weight is distributed equally.

Fig. 13-5 Asymmetrical balance specifies that the body weight be distributed unevenly. In this case, the main support comes from one foot.

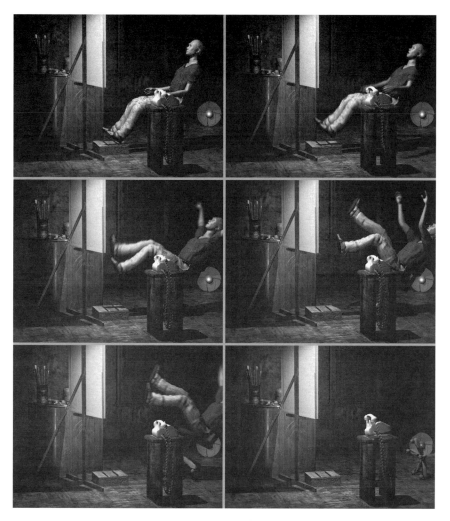

Fig. 13-6 Equilibrium and disequilibrium in an animation indicate the presence of physical forces.

ondary movements of the limbs have to occur almost simultaneous and appear spontaneous. When a person stands and shifts body weight from one foot to the other, the center of gravity moves. It may start out centered between the two feet but switches to one foot during the weight transfer.

A very effective method for learning how to depict gravitational forces is to create an animation in which the body starts out in a stable posture, begins to lose equilibrium, tries to regain it, and either fails or succeeds. Figure 13-6 shows an example of this type of animation. The animation

itself can be viewed on the accompanying CD-ROM as CD13-6.

Figure 13-6 shows an opening shot with an artist sitting in a chair contemplating his next painting. At this point his position is fairly stable. When the phone rings, he suddenly jumps out of his half-awake state. Animations that are more cartoon-like give life to objects that are normally inanimate. In this case, the phone becomes the obnoxious intruder.

His startled reflex triggers a state of instability, making him and the chair fall backward. Compared to the opening shot, we now see a dramatic shift in weight distribution. The only stable point left is on one or two of the wheels on the chair.

An important part of this animation occurs when the character tries to gain stability. This must look like a reflex action without any conscious effort by the digital actor. It occurs over the course of approximately fifteen frames.

In the animation, we see that any effort to counteract the effects of force and gravity are futile and the artist continues to fall. Sometimes, it is better to let the audience imagine the result of an action. Therefore, rather than letting it see the artist fall, the camera remains stationary and the figure lands outside of the shot. It also makes the animator's job easier. Remember, one of the most important rules of animation and movie making is to show viewers only what you want them to see. If it gets the point across, there is no need for anything else. The final parting shot shows an empty scene with the phone showing the only sign of life.

Expectation and Action

Expectation or anticipation forms a mental picture about the future. It carries a feeling that something is about to happen. In animation, it is a powerful method for setting up an event or series of activities. Figure 13-7 shows a few frames from an animation that can be viewed on the CD-ROM as CD13-7a. It depicts a cartoon character winding up like a coil before running off screen and leaving a puff of smoke behind. A version of the animation without expectation or the result of the action can be seen as CD13-7b. Notice that this animation without anticipation and resolution lacks interest and is more difficult to comprehend.

The first part of a motion prepares the viewer for what is to follow. It adds drama to the animation. Other examples of this are crouching before jumping, stretching before crouching, pulling an arm back before punching, and so on.

The go part of the animation (action) can take any number of forms, but it is usually the fastest component of the animation. If your character makes contact with something during this stage, try skipping the actual moment of contact. Since it happens within a split second, it does not have to be seen and will make the action appear more concise and less awkward.

The follow-through or reaction that comes after an action brings about resolution. It tells the viewer the effect of a specific cause. In the case of the sample animation, a smoke cloud in the shape of the character is left behind and gradually dissipates. Other responses to actions can involve weight and recoil after a character crashes into a wall, or a return to a relaxed position, a throbbing fist after a punch, and so on.

Most of the time, it is a good idea to let the viewer know what is about to occur, followed by what takes place, and finally showing what has happened. Physically, characters require a kind of preparation before doing something. This could be in the form of shifting weight before running or walking, taking a deep breath before shouting, moving the eyes before turning the head, or winding up before pitching a ball.

Spacing and Timing Patterns

Characters move according to the space between keyframes. A fast walk means that the arms and legs move back and forth within a shorter span of frames. These motions can be timed according to a certain beat. It is similar to the ticks of a

Fig. 13-7 Expectation followed by action and finally, the result are seen in this cartoon character's preliminary wind up before running. It can be compared to tightening the spring of a wind-up toy before setting it loose. The result is a puff of smoke left behind.

metronome helping a beginner play the piano at a certain pace. Intuition and experience are the determining factors for knowing how fast or slow to move a character.

Figure 13-8 illustrates some scenes from a CD-ROM animation (CD13-8a) in which a woman picks up a bucket. The animation moves too quickly, making the bucket appear insubstantial. The entire sequence is only thirty-two frames long. The CD13-8b animation moves at medium speed and lasts for ninety-eight frames. This time, the bucket has a stronger presence but seems to be empty. The slowest animation on CD13-8c lasts 198 frames. The woman appears to have a harder time picking up the bucket. Greater spacing between keyframes brings about the manifestation of a full bucket.

A clock's ticks are evenly spaced. Walking and running movements are evenly spaced. Figure 13-9 depicts a highway line-painting truck. It serves as an analogy to a character's movements and how far apart they are spaced. The spray mechanism on the truck paints stripes on the road at the same

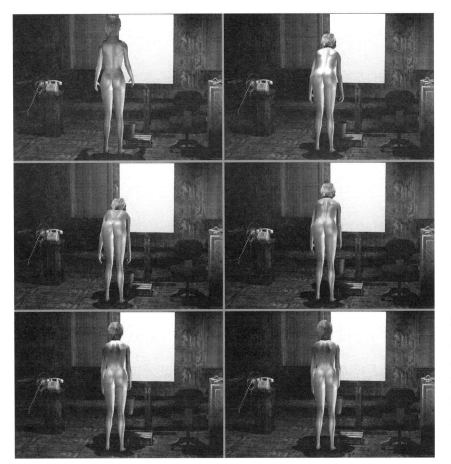

Fig. 13-8 Timing and spacing are based on content. The intent of an action defines its duration. In the example above, the weight of a bucket determines how long it takes for the woman to pick it up.

even pace. When the truck moves slower covering less distance, the lines are spaced closer together. As it speeds up to cover more distance, the stripes become more separated.

Let us assume that each stripe represents a character's keyframed movement and the rate of spray is similar to the even rate that its limbs move. When the duration of the animation is set too quickly (CD13-8a, the 32-frame sequence of the woman picking up the bucket), each body part's motion is spaced too closely together. This can result in jerky movements that are often difficult to discern, just as stripes that are too close together appear to almost blend into one long strip. If the

overall animation is spaced out for a longer period of time as seen on CD13-8c, each body movement—which is still the same amount as before—is now spaced further apart and appears smoother and more distinct. This is similar to the truck covering more distance on the road and with the painted stripes becoming separated from each other and much more distinct.

Oftentimes, characters' movements appear to have a light or buoyant feeling. This can happen when the space between movements is too far apart or the motion graph for a moving part curves up too much. Imagine a deer jumping and landing. If the keyframes for the creature are too close

Line Painting Truck

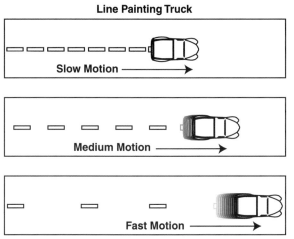

Fig. 13-9 Pacing can be seen in the above analogy of a paint truck painting white stripes on a road. Each paint stripe represents a keyframed motion. The truck sprays paint at the same rate no matter how fast it goes. Similarly, a character might have a specific set of movements that it performs during a run cycle. If the character runs slowly, each of its leg and arm motions are keyframed close together. The further it runs, the more ground is covered and the keyframes for its other motions, which are still going at the same rate, are spaced further apart and thus appear smoother.

together, it appears to land hard and take off quickly. When they are spaced further apart, it seems to almost float and land lightly on the ground. A situation like this needs more uneven spacing of frames. When the deer is in the air, more keyframes are set than when it lands on the ground. This puts the accent on the upward motion of the creature and less emphasis on the landing. A heavy character such as an elephant would need the opposite, with more keyframes as it lands on the ground because it spends more time trying to overcome mass and gravity. Proper timing requires a balance between movements that

are too snappy (spaced closely together) and floaty (spaced far apart).

Ease In, Ease Out; Fast In, Fast Out; and Arcs

Objects, when acted upon by another force, tend to speed up and then slow down. The larger the mass of the body, the longer it takes to accelerate. In animation, most movements start gradually, speed up, and then come to rest. This is referred to as ease in (or slow in) and ease out (or slow out).

Whenever a muscle or set of muscles contracts to pull a limb, other opposing muscles become active to oppose and slow down the contracting

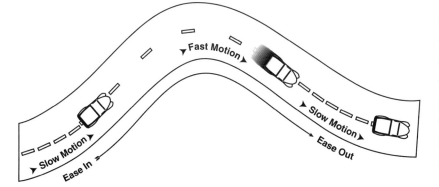

Fig. 13-10 Ease in, ease out means that an object starts slowly, gradually overcomes inertia to speed up, and then slows down again. Using the line painting truck analogy, you can see that during the acceleration stage, keyframes are spaced out further since more distance is covered.

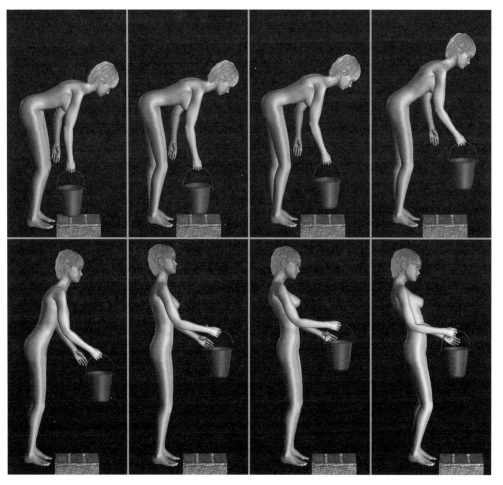

Fig. 13-11 Some scenes from the ease in, ease out animation. At first, the woman has to overcome the inertia of the heavy bucket. After picking it up slowly, her motions become faster. In the end, she slows down to stabilize her movements.

muscles. This works to regulate and fine-tune the body's actions. In addition, all bodies have to overcome the attraction of the earth's mass. When applied to animation, characters that appear to move according to the actions of the muscles and the influence of gravity have more convincing motions.

Figure 13-10 continues the analogy of the line-painting truck as it relates to ease in, ease out. Closely spaced frames shown as stripes painted near each other are the result of the initial slow motion. The slow movement covers less distance, and therefore, the beginning actions are packed close to each other. As the truck accelerates and passes over more area, the space between actions (stripes) becomes wider. Ease out can be seen in the truck slowing down and the space between frames becoming tighter again.

An animation of slow in, slow out can be seen on the CD-ROM as CD13-11. Figure 13-11 illustrates some of the image sequences from the CD-ROM animation in which a woman picks up a heavy bucket. Her movements are slow at first as she overcomes the weight of the bucket's contents. Approximately halfway through the animation, her movements pick up tempo and at the end, slow down again as she struggles to hold up her burden. You can see how ease in, ease out play an important role in communicating weight.

This animation can also be viewed as an example of arcs or curving movements. The spinal cord, ball and socket, and hinge joints are the determining factors for pivotal motion. The woman in the animation bends back when the joints or bones in the skeleton's spinal column are turned. When these motions are combined with the entire body's rotation, they create a 45-degree arc moving in a counterclockwise revolution. The secondary movement of the lower arm holding the bucket also follows a curving path. The other overlapping action of the head trying to stabilize the body makes a small arc at the end in the opposite direction. One thing to remember is that, except in the mineral world, straight lines do not exist in nature.

A graphic depiction of the movements involved in picking up a bucket can be seen in Figure 13-12. When bending over, the frames are spaced evenly apart. As the character begins to pick up the bucket, the struggle to overcome its heaviness

slows down her movements. The pattern of her actions at this point is closely spaced. Once inertia has been overcome, the spacing is wider between motions as she speeds up. At the end, she slows down, creating a tightly packed pattern.

Ease in, ease out does not always mean slow. It can mean medium speed that picks up tempo gradually and then returns to a slower rate. Sometimes, the opposite happens when a character is caught in the middle of an action going at full speed, slows down, and again speeds up. This is generally referred to as fast in, fast out.

Exaggeration, Action, and Reaction

For viewers to register certain actions, animators will resort to amplifying characters' motions. Sometimes, this can take the form of anticipation and take. A fat man spots a delicious looking cake. His eyes pop out in anticipation of a feast followed by the take in which he flies up, smacks his lips, claps his hands together, and then lunges toward the cake.

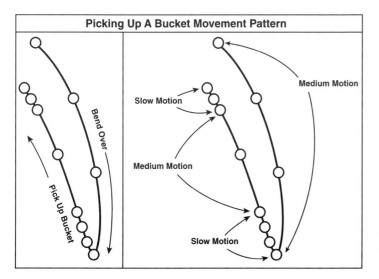

Fig. 13-12 A graphic depiction of the ease in, ease out motion during the picking-up-a-bucket action. The circles show how movements are spaced further apart during faster movements and closer together during slow movements.

Fig. 13-13a The first set of frames from the animation showing exaggeration. The walking motions are very measured and display the overstated shifting of weight. When the tentacle appears, there is a brief anticipation followed by a subtle take.

When you use exaggeration, it has to make sense. Whatever takes place should have a meaning or reason behind it. Once you have decided on the objective of a scene, figure out which motions are to be amplified to reinforce meaning.

Emotion plays an important role here. It helps to get inside a character and act out a scene first before trying to animate. Ask yourself what would you be thinking and feeling in this circumstance. Even though you may think that the movements are overblown, you should notice that the animation becomes more fun to watch and often more realistic.

Figures 13-13a and 13-13b contain some excerpts from an animation found on the CD-ROM

as CD13-13. The color versions of the images can also be found on the CD-ROM as CD13-13a and CD13-13b. The animation shows the artist's character having a daydream about Botticelli's *Birth of Venus*. As he approaches, his steps are exaggerated. You can see this in the deliberate manner in which he shifts his weight each time one of his feet touches the ground. He is a little self-conscious in her presence, so his movements are somewhat stiff. Her movements, on the other hand, are languid and slow.

The highlight takes place when this pastoral scene is suddenly disrupted by the appearance of a giant tentacle that bashes the artist on the side of the face. He freezes for a brief moment before col-

Fig. 13-13b The action becomes more amplified when the tentacle strikes the character who then reacts with an overdone take showing him frozen for ten frames before collapsing.

lapsing. This is referred to as a motion hold. It occurs when a character interrupts a motion by pausing for an instant before resuming the rest of the action. It gives the audience a little time to comprehend what has happened and also indicates that a new action is about to begin. Usually, motion holds have a few minor movements like the twitching of a limb or blinking of the eyes.

The struck character is an example of action followed by reaction. Anticipation and the take become more noticeable when the tentacle appears. The tentacle is also given a personality, which becomes more apparent when it pauses briefly to observe the artist collapsing before disappearing underwater. In cartoon animation, inanimate objects as well as creature parts can be given a life of their own. It is another example of exaggeration.

Exaggeration is an important element in animation that should not be ignored. Whether you are using motion capture, rotoscoping, pose to pose, or straight-ahead animation, be sure to add those important accents at key times.

Liveliness and Personality

The 3D modeler and animator are forced to overcome the mechanical nature of computer graphics. Hardware and software place a barrier between the artist and the creative process. Traditional tools like a pencil and paper offer less resistance and a

Fig. 13-14 A lively character with personality. The bull exhibits certain characteristics unique to his personality.

more direct approach to making art. If computer artists can make characters appear to be full of life, they have achieved a great deal.

A vital character conveys appeal. It communicates a personality, which the audience responds to in a positive or negative way, but not in an apathetic way. Charisma is that elusive trait which draws interest to a character. It has been said that the best compliment you can give an animation is that it makes you feel something about a character.

Figure 13-14 illustrates a scene from an animation found on the CD-ROM as CD13-14. The color version of this illustration is found as CD13-14a. It serves as an example of a creature that expresses temperamental characteristics. The bull's behavior distinguishes it from the other characters that appear later in the animation.

When working on a script and drawing storyboards, think about each character's identity: How will each of them communicate an emotional and mental constitution?

Paths of Action

Most characters move in paths of action that curve. When keyframing, be sure that each action follows an established path or moves sequentially toward a specific goal. Any keyframes that do not follow that route can appear out of place. The action might look unsteady, unreal, or jittery.

Most of the time, it is difficult to spot out-of-place actions until a preview is made of the entire sequence. If you find any movements that seem inappropriate to the entire arrangement, try deleting that keyframe. This should smooth out the angle of the curve in the motion graph, resulting in a more fluid action. If the motion appears to be too soft and floating, then change the motion graph's curve. Try making the angle sharper or insert another keyframe in place of the deleted one. This time, the frame's settings might be closer to the previous and following frames. Another solution is to place the keyframe closer to either the previous or following frame rather than in the middle of the two.

Figure 13-15 shows the path of action that a figure creates when running. You can see how it curves up and down like a wave. Weight and recoil are usually the determining factors for the angle of this motion curve. A lighter character will create a higher curve while a heavier character's motion curve will be lower.

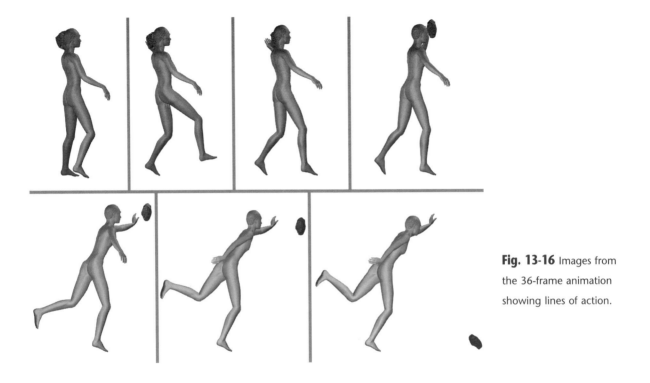

Fig. 13-16 Images from the 36-frame animation showing lines of action.

Lines of Action

Experienced animators can see beyond the visible form to observe the movements of the lines of action. They can usually spot clumsy and ill-timed motions. Therefore, it is important to visualize an imaginary line that extends through the main action of a figure. Secondary movements, like those in the arms and legs, can also be visualized as lines of motion.

such as those of the arms, hands, head, legs, feet and so on, form the basis for other lines of action. When planning an animation, it is often advantageous to sketch the main lines of action first. Drawing your figures comes after this. Details are meant to accentuate the line of action.

Animations created without a conscious effort to delineate a line of action often appear to be drifting aimlessly. They lack the dynamic quality,

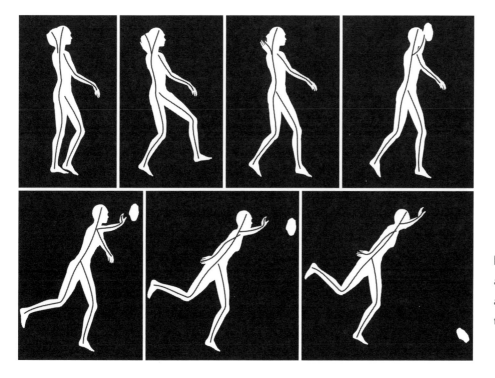

Fig. 13-17 Lines of action are illustrated for the body and secondary motions for the arms and legs.

consists of various objects and their parts moving at various speeds, times, and directions. Needless to say, the majority of character animations involves complex actions. Characters with multiple joints have primary and secondary movements.

Figure 13-8 shows images from the CD13-18 animation in which the primary movement consists of the character dancing, spinning, and eventually falling. His body carries the action forward. The secondary movements are found in the clothes, legs, feet, arms, hands, and head. Since their motions do not occur independently of the body, nor of each other, they are called overlapping actions. A more detailed color illustration can be found on the CD-ROM as CD13-18a. It gives a clearer view of the facial expressions, which are just as important as the movements of the limbs.

The expressions tell the viewer what he is thinking and make the performance more emotional.

Overlapping actions can precede as well as follow the main action. These lesser motions relate to or are the result of the main action. Overlapping action enhances the animation. As one movement ends, another begins.

Follow-through is another kind of overlapping action. It is usually associated with elastic objects, which adjust readily to different conditions. These are prescribed by the primary object to which they are attached. In Figure 13-8 and on the CD13-8 animation, you can observe the movements of the cape, which follows the actions of the character it is connected to. Follow-through indicates the completion of a motion. In the animation, the cape is the last object to move as it flutters up and settles on the prone man. Other common objects that

Fig. 13-18 Objects like the cape, that are flexible, behave in accordance to modifications in the primary entity they are attached to. These loosely waving artifacts change a split second after the action of the primary object. In animation, this is referred to as follow-through.

have a certain amount of give and thus exhibit follow-through, are hair, tails, floppy ears, loose fitting clothes like a skirt, and so on.

The movement of loose objects can be animated in a variety of ways. Natural-world characteristics, such as soft bodies, can be applied to them, or they can be animated manually by placing bones inside. The skeleton can have goal objects or IK handles on certain parts to make their manipulation easier. In a case like this, it is usually a good idea to parent all the handles or goal objects to one cluster handle or null. This makes it easier to move or rotate the entire object as well as to manipulate parts of it.

Overlapping action and follow-through illustrate an important principle of animation: Not all parts of a character arrive at the same time. If every action ended at the same frame, the character's movements would look too mechanical. The skeletal hierarchy can be compared to a chain. Force and drag cause each part of a limb to move and stop with slight time lags. When one part is beginning to end its motion, a second attached object might be in its beginning movement stage. This works its way up or down the hierarchy in a whip-like action. For example, when a character bends over, you can rotate the lower back bone, then after a few frames, rotate the following back bone located above the first one, wait another few frames to rotate the next back bone, and so on. The same applies to the arm. After rotating the upper arm, the lower arm's rotation can follow a few frames later, after which the hand is moved. The motion can continue down to the fingertips. An IK chain with several handles or nulls as goal objects gives you more control to simulate this kind of action.

As mentioned previously, whenever a limb comes to a complete stop before changing its direction, be sure to keyframe it twice. The two identical keyframes can be spaced anywhere between three and twenty or so frames. The motion graph's natural curve between these two frames make the limb appear to have a slight adjustment or settling down movement at the end.

Rhythm

Repetition of similar characteristics of any kind produces rhythm. Lines of action that form a pattern have a certain tempo. These can be discerned among unlike elements. Contrasting lines of action can make an animation appear more dynamic and interesting. It is similar to contrapuntal music, where two or more independent but harmonically related melodic parts work together.

Action that has a specific direction can be perceived as having a beat. Rhythm becomes stronger when it is reinforced more frequently. Overlapping actions form an integral part of rhythm. The rhythmic accents in lines overlap each other. Normally, the lines form curves that wave back and forth.

Walking and running cycles are examples of rhythm. A dancing character is another representative of rhythm. Figure 13-19 illustrates some views from an animation found on the CD-ROM as CD13-19. The color images are seen as CD13-19a. A man performs a dance in which he leaps and spins. The counterpoint occurs when he whirls in the opposite direction.

The impetus of the body controls the limbs and head. You can see how the head responds to the movement and impact of the body as it lands. It can be compared to a flag as it waves in response to the rhythmic motions of the stick it is attached to. This was referred to earlier as follow-through.

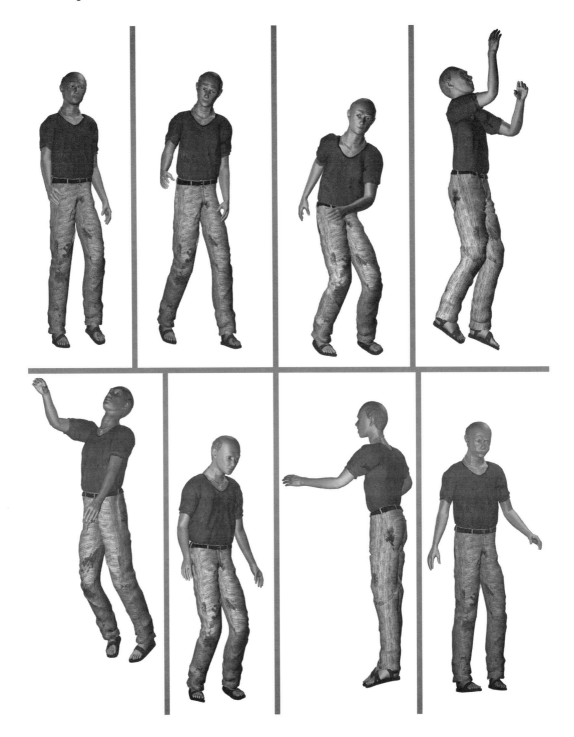

Fig. 13-19 The spirited dance illustrates one form of rhythm in animation. The sweep in the contrasting and repeating lines of action twist together to form rhythm and movement.

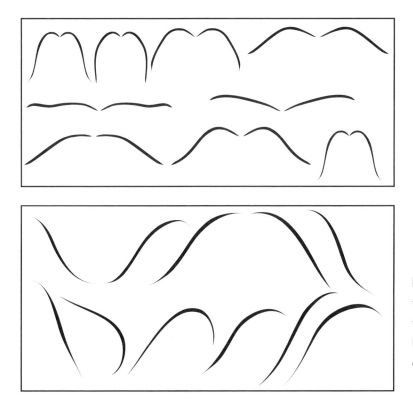

Fig. 13-20 Some basic lines of action illustrating rhythmic motion. The top set shows the steady beating of a bird's wings. The bottom group depicts the tempestuous opposing lines of a bucking bronco.

In their most basic forms, lines of rhythm wave back and forth and up and down like a whip. Figure 13-20 depicts a few of these. The top illustration shows the rhythmic lines of a bird's wings while the bottom set shows the curving actions of a bucking bronco. The bird's wings have a steady rhythm while the horse illustrates opposing lines full of accents.

Conclusion

As you become more experienced in animation, you may start to perceive how all the underlying principles overlap each other. It is difficult to concentrate on one aspect without making use of others. All of them play an important role in the overall animation.

A conscious awareness of the basic ideas of animation is the first step. Experience moves this awareness to an unconscious level where it becomes instinct and no longer subject to argument and reasoning. The subconscious mind acts. It accepts the conclusions of the conscious mind as final. This is the reason great art, music, and literature appear to have been created effortlessly. Through experience, these artists radiate courage, confidence, and power in their work.

CHAPTER 14

Composition and Cinematography

The arrangement of a character's environment entails knowing what makes a good composition. All the objects seen through the camera should relate to each other and to the whole in a cohesive manner. Since animation is not a static art form, a basic understanding of cinematography is another element in the process that should not be ignored. A discussion of some basic techniques for composition or design of a scene and an overview of digital cinematography should assist you in establishing the proper staging.

Composition

An animator's goal is to keep the work fresh and spontaneous. This can sometimes be difficult when screen redraws and previews have a sluggish response time. The entire workflow becomes disjointed when you have to wait several seconds or minutes for an outcome after each action.

Blocking

To speed up screen redraws, block in most of your objects and later substitute them with the actual high quality versions. One way to do this is to have a set of low-polygon substitute objects. When animating use these low resolution characters and their basic surroundings. This should help your work appear more natural because you will get faster feedback after each move. When you are ready to do a final rendering, substitute each low-resolution object with its equivalent in high-resolution.

Spatial Arrangement

Composition is the ordering of forms, colors, lines, values, and textures in a picture. Expression is the emotive effect of these conditions as they occur in an image. A good design is one in which all the relational parts form a balanced unity. A 3D image or animation shares many of the abstract principles of design. Different parts exist to tell a story or express a dramatic mood. There are several considerations when examining composition. These are the arrangement of forms, balance, direction, and rhythm. Even though this discussion treats them as separate entities, in reality they influence each other to the degree that none could exist without the others.

The way in which forms are arranged is the foundation of a scene. Some of the more commonly known arrangements are oval, vertical, horizontal, diagonal, triangle, and their combinations. An effective use of these organizing principles can bring forth specific feelings in a viewer. This type of focus makes the work very powerful. Many artists learn about composition in school and then forget about it. Their design judgment becomes an intuitive function. They no longer rely on reasoning and deduction. Their instincts tell them what works and what does not.

Oval Composition

Composition based on the oval can be seen in Figure 14-1. The direction of the arms, the two heads, and the child's back form a kind of egg shape. Oval structures tend to be unified and harmonious. They often convey a sense of well-being.

Vertical Composition

Vertical design (Figure 14-2) implies strength, stability, and sometimes, spirituality. Early religious paintings employed vertical design to show a holy person reaching upward. The person or groups of people appeared to be in this world but not of it. Even though the pose in Figure 14-2 shows mostly vertical direction, it is broken up by the diagonal line of the arms. This makes the image much more interesting than if the character had her arms down at her sides.

Horizontal Composition

Horizontal composition (Figure 14-3) usually denotes calm and steadiness. Landscape art is often composed of strong horizontal lines. Nature appears constant with its continually recurring seasons. Compositions based on the horizontal line appear grounded and secure. They can also convey a sense of speed as evidenced by the ship in Figure 14-3.

Diagonal Composition

Diagonal designs (Figure 14-4) often show a state of instability with dynamic forces at work. The direction of the line leads the viewer immediately into the picture. Crossed diagonal lines are a very effective method for portraying action in a scene (Figure 14-5). The patterns formed create tension and disorder. The angles of arms, legs, a tail, spears, and so on express feelings through gesture. It is no wonder that crossing lines are often found in battle scenes.

Fig. 14-1 Composition based on the oval.

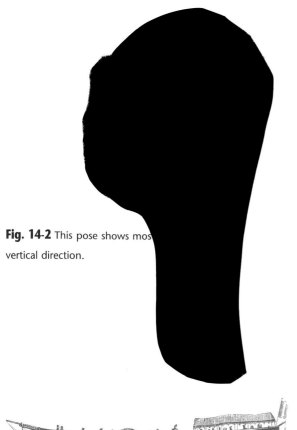

Fig. 14-2 This pose shows most vertical direction.

Fig. 14-3 Composition based on horizontal lines.

Fig. 14-4 Diagonal design.

Triangular Composition

The triangular composition (Figure 14-6) can be thought of as a symbol of unity. Based on a firm foundation, it forms a harmonious relationship that is always striving upward. In the Christian faith it symbolizes the Trinity. Renaissance artists often painted the Madonna and child in a triangular composition.

If you are so inclined, you can find other composition forms such as the rectangle, spiral, radial, and so on. Most designs utilize a combination of the various line arrangements.

Balance

Balance is the equilibrium of visual weight, in seesaw fashion, on either side of an imaginary fulcrum and lever. When matching weights are placed equidistant from the center, we have symmetrical balance (Fig   ). Asymmetrical balance in a compos   ts of varying weights distri   center fulcrum. Equ   the elements cou   ain a unified who   rical balance. The   weight somewhat   ugh the hand and flo   t of her, their positio   ances the image.

Fig. 14-5 Crossed diagonal lines can make an image more dynamic.

Fig. 14-6 The triangle conveys unity and stability with an upward striving to reach a lofty goal.

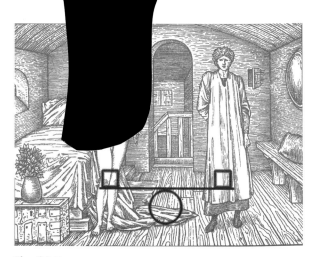

Fig. 14-7 Symmetrical balance means that visual elements even out identically on both sides of a central axis.

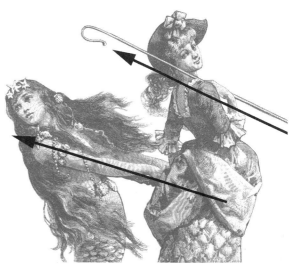

Fig. 14-9 Direction means that a picture's components can be arranged to guide your attention toward specific areas of a scene.

Fig. 14-8 Asymmetrical balance achieves equilibrium through the unequal distribution of visual weight.

While symmetrical balance conveys stability and serenity, asymmetrical balance can express tension and restlessness.

Direction

Direction is the orientation of various elements with the express purpose of guiding the viewer's observation to specific points in the picture. Abstract parts of an image line up to point toward a center or lead the viewer's gaze around the entire scene. Figure 14-9 shows two bodies posed in a way that pulls toward the upper left of the composition. The staff's orientation in the woman's hand substantiates the direction toward which the main elements point. In animation you can also have objects or their parts move toward certain areas of a scene. The use of motion blur indicates faster movement.

Fig. 14-10 Rhythm is the repetition of a picture's elements directed in a pattern of movement.

Rhythm

Rhythm is produced from elements placed in a way that establishes a pulsation. When colors, shapes, lines, values, textures, and forms are placed in a reoccurring fashion, or in a discernable pattern, a certain beat is established. Movement becomes more pronounced when the rhythm of a piece is reinforced. Figure 14-10 shows a pattern that is established by similarly posed figures.

Camera Techniques

The placement and movement of the camera takes on an important role in determining the composition of a scene. In essence, the animator can think of the camera as the spectator's eyes. Novice animators are often guilty of improper or exuberant use of the camera. Lacking the skills of motion picture photography, they will move and rotate the camera excessively. The result is a bewildering array of images that can baffle viewers or even make them dizzy and nauseous. The first thing beginners might want to learn is to exercise some restraint. The audience should not even be aware of the presence of a camera.

Movies often create the illusion that there is no camera between the scene and the viewer. Aspiring animators may find it beneficial to study the cinematography employed in the best movies. Over the years, filmmakers have developed certain techniques that are applicable to animation. Unlike traditional movie making, 3D cinematography is

Fig. 14-12 An image from the animation shot through a 15mm wide lens.

not restrained by physical limitations. Therefore, animators often achieve a greater degree of control and creativity with the camera.

Field of View

The field of view on a computer graphics camera mimics the lenses in a real camera. A long lens means that the camera has a narrow field of view (Figure 14-11). A wide-angle or wide lens has a large field of view. Figures 14-12, 14-13, and 14-14 illustrate images from two animations. One was shot through a 15mm wide-angle lens while the second one was filmed with an 85mm long lens. The 15mm and 85mm animations can be found on the CD-ROM as CD14-12 and CD14-14.

When you compare the two animations, notice how the shot gives the impression that the woman is running faster and covering more ground in the 15mm, wide-angle lens version. The long lens animation makes it seem that she is running slower. As you can see, an effective use of long lenses is having the camera appear to linger longer over a scene of characters moving across the screen.

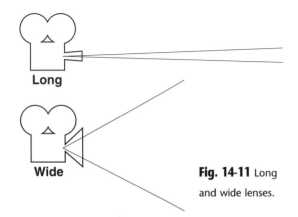

Long

Wide

Fig. 14-11 Long and wide lenses.

Fig. 14-13 The same scene shot through a medium 50mm lens.

Fig. 14-14 This animation was filmed with an 85mm long lens.

Another application of the long lens might be to show a person walking or running and seemingly going nowhere. If you want the shot to appear more frenzied, consider utilizing a wide lens.

The way objects appear in scenes shot with wide and long lenses can be radically different. Figure 14-15 illustrates a scene rendered with a 100mm long lens. All the elements appear to be brought

closer together. Depth seems shallower and there is less distortion. The field of view is compressed. Characters that are distant from each other can be brought closer together with the long lens. When you are shooting a scene that is very large, then a long lens will work fine. Wildlife pictures are often shot with long lenses so that the photographers can remain far away from their subjects.

Fig. 14-15 This scene was shot through a 100mm long lens. Objects appear to be flattened, less distorted, and the background seems to be closer to the camera.

Fig. 14-16 The exact same scene when shot through a 15mm wide lens. This time the foreground objects appear to be distorted and the background seems farther away.

On the other hand, when you are in an enclosed space and do not have the luxury of moving the camera far away from the subject, then a wide-angle lens can be used. Indoor pictures are often shot with a wider lens so that the photographer can take in more of the scene. Figure 14-16 shows the exact same scene as the previous illustration. This time the field of view has more depth and the background objects appear to be farther away. The space between objects expands and the wider field of view amplifies perspective. The foreground objects are more distorted. The lens seems to make a figure more rounded as if seen through a magnifying glass. This may be useful for having a scene look more three-dimensional, but it is at the expense of accuracy. Wide lenses can make characters close to each other appear to be distant. If you move a wide-angle lens through a scene, you should notice a distortion at the edges as if space were bending around the camera.

Most people are used to the 50mm standard lens when viewing movies and photographs. Realistic scenes are usually shot with a 40, 50, or 60mm lens. For more variety, you may want to consider switching between lenses. An animation might be filmed mostly with a standard lens, and switching to a wide or long lens could emphasize certain parts. For example, an evil character could be shot with a wide lens and the good guy with a standard lens. Objects that are usually filmed from far away, such as sporting events, wildlife, airplanes, and so on, can be shot with a long lens. Since people are used to seeing these activities filmed with long lenses, they may find your animation more credible. If you want a shot to appear somewhat strange, then try using a wide-angle lens.

Depth of Field

Depth of field measures the amount of area that falls within the range of focus. Lenses have a point of focus that is usually set on the subject. Other parts of the image that fall outside of the focal range are blurred. Figure 14-17 and the CD-ROM color image CD14-17 depict the same scene and subject matter as the previous two illustrations, except that this time, a standard, 60mm lens and depth of field were used. The f-stop was fixed at 8. A lens's f-stop determines the amount of light that is allowed into the camera. Higher settings represent smaller lens openings and therefore, less light enters the camera. Lens f-stops at higher numbers also widen the depth of field and ensure that more elements are in focus.

In computer graphics, everything in a scene can be in focus. Even though software does not have the limitations of a physical camera, many artists utilize depth of field to draw attention to the main subject. In addition, people are used to seeing depth of field in photographs and movies. Depth of field becomes important when animation com-

Fig. 14-17 Depth of field blurs the objects that are outside of the camera's focal point. This time the scene was shot with a standard 60mm lens.

panies have to match computer graphics to actual filmed footage.

Because computer artists do not operate under the same constraints as cinematographers, the option to use depth of field becomes an aesthetic one. The two main concerns are the area you focus on and the depth of your area of focus. When animating several characters, you might want to switch depth of field among them. Whoever is talking or doing something can be the focal point.

Using depth of field can increase rendering time significantly. If the camera in a shot is not moved, then consider rendering the background as one image with depth of field. The characters and any objects in front of them can be shot without depth of field separately with alpha channels. The blurred background and foreground images can be composited in a movie-editing program. This method also works when the camera moves. Shoot the background separately from the foreground. Instead of using depth of field, you can blur the background images in the movie-editing program.

Dolly, Truck, and Boom

In cinematography, cameras are often moved about on traveling platforms. Specific mechanical rigs are designed to create smoother camera movements. A wheeled cart that propels the camera along a track is referred to as a dolly. Many cinematography terms stem from the devices used to manipulate the camera.

Dollying the camera refers to its movement along the *x*-axis (Figure 14-18). For example, the camera may keep pace with someone walking. Truck-in and truck-out means that the camera moves along the *z*-axis. Truck-in refers to the camera moving in closer to the subject and truck-out moving away from it. Sometimes, truck-out is

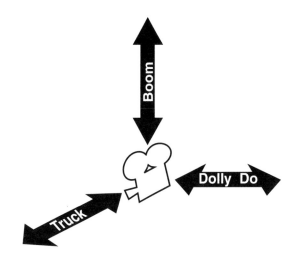

Fig. 14-18 Camera movements along the *x*-, *y*-, and *z*-axes.

called a reveal. Boom denotes the up and down movement of the camera on the *y*-axis.

Figure 14-19 illustrates some images from the CD14-19 animation in which the camera moves closer to the subject. This truck-in action is a very common method for drawing near the point of focus. The field of view remains the same while the distance between the camera and subject narrows.

Zoom

Zooming the camera means changing the camera's focal length. The result is a shot in which the field of view expands or contracts. Figure 14-20 shows some scenes from the CD14-20 animation. The character and background are identical to the previous animation that used a truck-in action. This time the camera does not move, but instead, the focal length of the lens becomes narrower. It changes from a 60mm standard lens to a 160mm long lens. The result is that the scene compresses to bring the subject closer to the viewer. When you compare the two animations, notice how the back-

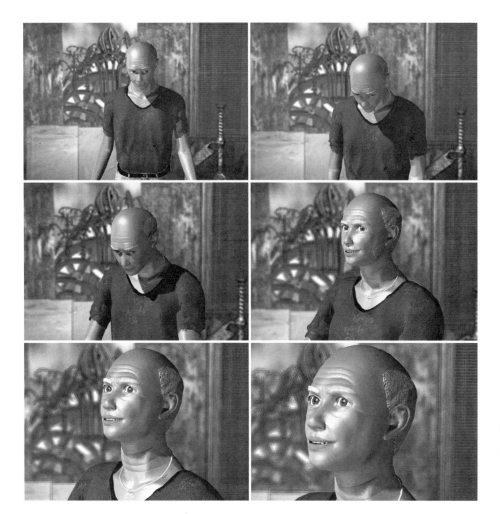

Fig. 14-19 A truck-in movement of the camera.

ground expands with the zoom. This distortion is one of the reasons why movies do not use zooming as often as moving the camera. The shot tends to look somewhat flat. Because television shows are often filmed from fixed camera positions, they utilize zooming. The choice of whether to use camera movements or zooming depends on the effect that you are after. If you want to emulate the fluid and coherent camera movements of films, then move the camera. On the other hand, if your animation is done in the style of low budget movies, documentaries, nature films, or TV shows, you might as well use zooming.

Pan, Tilt, and Roll

Pan, tilt, and roll are all methods for rotating the camera around a specific axis. Figure 14-21 illustrates the manner in which the camera revolves around the x-, y-, and z-axes. Panning is a commonly used method for scanning a scene from side to side or following an action. CD14-21 depicts an animation utilizing the pan. The camera rotates around the y-axis while remaining in one place. It can be compared to the direction that an airplane flies in, its heading. Pan is sometimes identified as yaw. The top, front, or camera views are the windows used for this action.

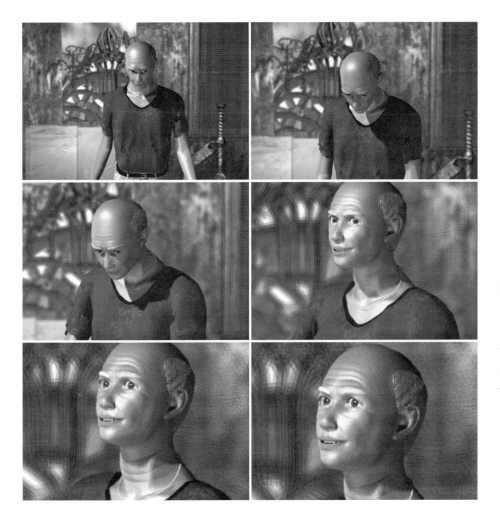

Fig. 14-20 A zoom-in lens change. Notice the difference in the background from the previous illustration. The field of view flattens out as the lens changes from a standard 60mm to a 160mm long lens.

Tilt means the camera is turned on the *x*-axis. Continuing with the analogy of an airplane, when it takes off or turns its nose down to land, this action is referred to as pitch. It can also be called a pivot. A common use of tilt is having the camera scan someone up and down. Tilting works best in the side or camera views.

Roll is the rotation of the camera around the *z*-axis. Using the airplane analogy, when its wings are tilted up and down, this action is called a bank. Rolls can be seen in fly-through animations. The front and camera views are the most commonly utilized windows for executing a roll.

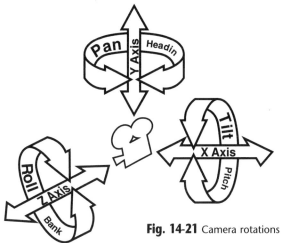

Fig. 14-21 Camera rotations around the *x*-, *y*-, and *z*-axes.

313

Fig. 14-22 Truck-in combined with zoom-out creates a disconcerting effect. The subject appears to remain the same distance from the camera, but the background seems to move away. When the lens becomes wider, a greater amount of the background appears.

Pan, tilt, and roll are more easily associated with the way people look at things. When they are watching something, they do not usually get up and follow it. More likely, their heads will turn, lean to the side, or tilt up and down. This is one reason for using camera rotations. Since they mimic our behavior, they feel normal to people. A common use of camera rotations occurs in movies or TV shows where the camera is used to introduce us to a cast of characters and the environment they live in. It may start by panning across a scene as it follows one person. When the person crosses paths with someone else, the camera shifts to follow this new character. When the person stops to kick a ball, the camera follows the ball to the youngster it belongs to. Of course, this can continue for a long time.

Truck-in Combined with Zoom-out or Truck-out Combined with Zoom-in

A combination of the truck and zoom can bring about some unsettling effects. The camera is moved closer to the subject in a truck-in, while the lens is made wide with a zoom-out. The result is that the subject appears to remain consistently the same distance from the camera, but the space

Fig. 14-23 Truck-out combined with zoom-in creates a disconcerting effect. The subject appears to remain the same distance from the camera, but the background seems to move forward. When the lens is made long, less background is visible.

around the person warps. Figure 14-22 illustrates some images from the truck-in/zoom-out animation found on the CD-ROM as CD14-22. Notice how the space enlarges due to the widening of the lens. Normally, making the lens wide would create greater distance between the camera and subject. To compensate for this, the camera is moved closer to the person.

Truck-out with zoom-in reverses the process. While the camera moves away from the subject, the lens is made narrow to keep the person at a constant distance from the camera. Figure 14-23 shows some images from the CD14-23 animation.

You can see that the background appears to move closer to the camera. Unlike the previous truck-in/zoom-out animation, the space compresses.

Truck combined with zoom is sometimes referred to as a rack focus or vertigo shot. Used correctly, it can convey a disorienting effect. It is commonly used to show a character's state of mind. Often, it is used to indicate changing circumstances. Since this is a very dramatic move, one has to be careful before deciding to use it. If there is no meaning behind this action, then the audience will only be confused by it.

Fig. 14-24 The crane or boom shot moves the camera up or down. In these images from the animation, it is used to open the first scene and to reveal the main character.

Crane or Boom

This shot derives its name from a camera attached to a moveable crane or pivoted boom. It is used when the camera needs to be moved up or down. Rarely is the camera moved only on the *y*-axis. The crane or boom is usually combined with a dolly or truck shot. Figure 14-24 shows some images from the CD14-24 animation using the crane or boom with a truck shot. Its purpose is to reveal the scene and swoop down on the main character.

The crane or boom shot can be very useful at the beginning of an animation when you want to display an overview of the environment or the characters. It can also be used to communicate distance between your characters and the viewer. For example, a person who has lost his family and friends, is seen as a lonely person in an alien environment. When the camera pulls up and away, the person appears as a small speck in his surroundings.

Hand-held Camera

Movies that show ordinary people in actual or fabricated activities sometimes have a bold look to them. These are usually shot on a low budget with hand-held cameras. Often, they are not even controlled by a director.

In computer graphics, you can imitate the hand-held camera style by having it shake, tilt, and roll while following the action. Figure 14-25 displays some frames from the CD14-25 animation in which the camera acts as if it were hand-held. There is no effort to hide the presence of the camera. Mistakes are visible as when the camera loses track of the subject or is jolted. The idea is to make it look as if an amateur is running the camera and that the animation was not planned.

Transitions

Transitions are a way to blend or skip from one image to another. They can be simple or complex. Some can be performed during the action, while others require video editing software. Transitions can be used to add variety to an animation, depict the passage of time, anticipate upcoming events, slow down a scene, and so on. They are mostly used to define time and space between shots. The most common transitions are the fade, dissolve, cut, and wipe.

Fade

A fade occurs when a shot disappears gradually. If the shot fades to a still frame of a solid color, it is referred to as a fade-out. A more common transition is the fade-to-black. Figure 14-26 shows a few clips from a short fade-to-black animation (CD14-26). Instead of creating the fade in a post-process-

Fig. 14-25 Images from the hand-held camera animation.

Fig. 14-26 Fade-to-black images from the animation.

ing program, it was performed directly during the animation.

Figure 14-27 illustrates a method for creating the fade-to-black. The camera is placed inside a black box. The box has a dissolve envelope making it 100% transparent for the first thirty frames. Between frames 30 and 60, the dissolve envelope changes the opacity of the box until it is 100% opaque (0% dissolve). During the fade-to-black sequence, the dissolve envelope gradually enshrouds the camera with the black box. This method also works for fading to white or any color simply by making the box of that color.

The process can also be reversed. The box can start with a 0% dissolve, which changes over time to a 100% dissolve. This is called a fade-in transition. A still black, white, or color frame starts the sequence and gradually disappears to reveal the scene.

Dissolve

A dissolve or cross-dissolve is a transition effect where one shot blends into another. The first shot disappears revealing 100% of the second shot. Figure 14-28 illustrates this type of transition. The animation is labeled CD14-28. Midway into the dissolve, both images appear at 50% opacity.

Dissolves are an effective way of linking two separate scenes. They work very well when two sub-

jects from different scenes are similar in some way. They can be alike in physical terms like shape or pose, or similar in mental or spiritual outlook. An example of psychological and physical similarities is having a person become a werewolf in one scene. The camera can then move in close to show the change in the person's eye. The cross-dissolve gradually turns the eye into an image of the full moon.

Other uses for dissolves are to give the audience

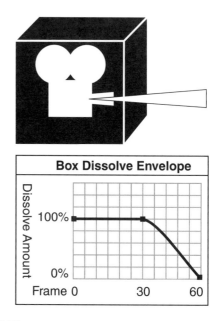

Fig. 14-27 A camera inside a black box can make a fade-to-black transition. A dissolve envelope on the box sets the interval for making the box opaque.

Fig. 14-28 Images from the cross-dissolve animation.

time to ponder an event that occurred, to show a flashback, a future event, or to simply state what is in a character's mind. Dream sequences can be made up of a series of cross-dissolves layered on top of each other. Short dissolves are called soft cuts. Longer ones can be used to slow the pace of the action.

Cut

A cut is an immediate change from one shot to another. The transition occurs so rapidly that it is usually not noticed. Commercials and music videos use cuts extensively to set up a rapid pace and build up some excitement in the viewer's mind. The cut derives its name from movies in which two separate strips of film are cut and spliced together.

If your software limits you to only one camera, you can create a cut by moving the camera from one view to another over the course of only two frames. For example, the first shot can show the interior of a house until frame 60. At frame 61 the camera is moved outdoors to show the outside of the house. The one-frame interval occurs so quickly that the viewer does not perceive the motion of the camera. Another purpose for the cut is to simply start a new scene. When two separate sequences are put together in a final animation, it is seen as a cut.

Wipe

Wipes occur when a second shot slides over the first one and replaces it. The transition can take on a variety of configurations and can come from any direction. Some of the more common forms of wipes are the page turn and page peel where the corner of an image curls to unveil the next shot underneath. The curtain has one image draw back to display the second. The flip over has the first image turn over to reveal the second one underneath. The cube spin shows the first image spinning around to show the second one. The pinwheel has multiple wipes from the center of an image to uncover the second one under it. If you use a video editing program, you are probably aware of the numerous wipe transitions available.

Conclusion

As you can see, the art of 3D animation is a complex but highly interesting field of study. You have to invest many years of hard work to bring modeling, surfacing, lighting, and animation skills to perfection. New technologies and discoveries by other artists continually challenge the most experienced animators. The adage, "Roads were made for traveling not destinations" is applicable here. No matter how much you think you know, there is always something to make you take the next step.

Since this is a book about computer graphics, it might be of benefit to discuss the parallels between a computer and the mind. Some minds are more powerful than others. They may have more memory and are better equipped. A certain number of them are more flexible and find it easy to interface with others. No matter what aptitude the mind displays, it has the basic capability to grasp what the senses tell it, to comprehend the information, and then to act on it.

The diagram in Figure 14-29 illustrates the four faculties of the mind. The aesthetic part recognizes beauty, harmony, form, color, rhythm, and perspective. It is limited by its likes and dislikes. People who do not know this can mistake reality for what is actually their narrow state of awareness.

The sensory faculty of the mind absorbs impressions through smell, taste, hearing, and feeling. Its judgment is also colored by what it likes and dislikes. Thus, the two sensory parts of the mind can cloud your judgment. A person may think he or she is unique, but often this is based on selective limitations.

Reasoning and intellect form another part of the mind. This is a higher level that receives information from the sensory abilities. It assesses the opinions of the first two mental faculties, makes its decisions, and passes its judgment on to the final evaluator, which is the ego.

The ego is the executor of the mind. Based on the opinions of other parts of the mind, it carries out the judgment of the reasoning and intellect faculty. The ego is the part of the mind that asserts itself. It differentiates itself from others and recognizes what is in its self-interest. Its chief concern is self-preservation. Conceit is the result of an overblown ego. A person with strong likes and dislikes can easily become self-righteous and inflexible.

Artists may find it more desirable to develop a sense of randomness. Rather than being incapable of adapting or changing to meet new circumstances, you might think of becoming more flexible. Creating with computers may be a boon, but it can also train us to work under fixed conditions. A possible future could be that the more we work with machines, the greater the chances that we will become a part of them.

Even though computer animation is created mostly for commercial reasons, its roots are in the fine arts. There is no reason why computer graphic artists, who now possess the most remarkable tools a creative person could ask for, cannot produce work as great as that made with traditional tools. Perhaps, with some, their first step is to become aware of the creative force within.

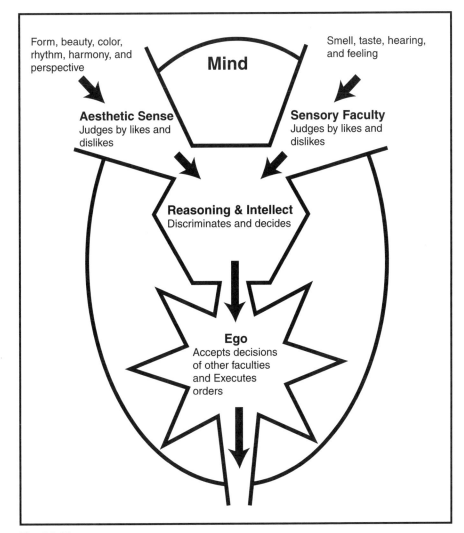

Fig. 14-29 The four parts of the mind.

Glossary

Absolute value: A value or a change in the value of a property that is made with respect to the original value.

Alpha channel: The information that is embedded in an image that describes empty space around rendered pixels. It is used for compositing or transparency mapping.

Ambient light: The overall light that saturates an entire scene. Unlike radiosity, rendering which calculates the effect of light bouncing off objects, ambient light only simulates this process.

Anti-aliasing: The process of smoothing edges of forms in a rendering by blending pixels with background colors and values. It removes the stair-casing effect that is often referred to as jaggies. Sometimes, textures can have the option of being rendered with anti-aliasing to prevent flickering and moiré patterns from occurring during an animation.

Area light: An array of lights, illuminating in all directions, whose size can usually be scaled.

Axis: The coordinate system of 3D space. *X*-axis means side to side or movement along the horizontal plane. *Y*-axis refers to top and bottom or vertical movement. *Z*-axis is front to back or in and out movement.

Back-facing polygons: Polygons whose normals face away from the viewer or camera.

Bevel: Extruding an object to produce an angled or shaped cut. It can produce the kind of shape found on the edge of ledges, computers, moldings, and so on.

Bezier curve: A curve that contains all its control points on the line itself.

B-spline: A spline that rarely goes through the points that created it. The curve tries to find a way between the points in a smooth manner.

Bitmap: An image that is composed of pixels.

Booleans: Refers to the joining or removing of one object from another.

Boom: The up-and-down movement of a camera on the *y*-axis. Its name originates from a moveable crane or pivoted boom that carries a camera.

Bounce lights: Colored lights that are placed next to objects in a scene to simulate radiosity.

Bump map: A procedural or bitmap image that is used to perturb the surface normals to create the illusion of bumps on a surface. The values of the image are treated like a height field.

Cardinal spline: A curve that passes through the points that created it.

Contact shadows: A technique for creating shadows

through the use of negative and positive lights. Two lights of the same intensity values except that one is positive and the other negative are placed in the same space and directed at a subject. The result is that the object casts a shadow but the surface illumination remains the same.

Cubic mapping: A method of placing a texture map on an object so that the map is duplicated six times. Cubic mapping does not distort the bitmap but seams can often be seen on the object.

Cut: An immediate change from one shot to another.

Cylindrical mapping: A method of placing a texture by wrapping it into a cylindrical shape around the object.

Diffuse: The manner in which light is scattered across a surface. The surface appearance is governed by its shape and the location and angle of the light source(s).

Dissolve: A transition effect in which one shot blends into another.

Distant light: Sometimes referred to as directional light, it is light whose effects do not diminish over distance. This type of light is often used to simulate the phenomenon of sunlight.

Dolly: Camera movement along the *x*-axis. Its original name stems from a wheeled vehicle called a dolly that carries a camera along a track.

Ease-in/Ease-out: The manner in which an animation is interpolated between keyframes. Ease-in gradually accelerates the animation from zero velocity. Ease-out gradually decelerates the animation to zero velocity.

Extrude: Creating a surface by extending it in space.

Fade: A transition in which a shot disappears gradually.

Fall off: The point at which a light's illumination degrades with distance.

Fillet/Blend: Builds a surface by forming a blend between two boundaries defined by a set of curves.

Frame: An individual image contained in an animation.

Front-facing polygons: Polygons whose surface normals face toward the viewer or camera.

Front projection image map: A method of projecting the image seen through the camera and applying it to a surface.

Gimbal lock: A situation in which an object no longer rotates correctly around one or more of its axes. With some software packages, gimbal lock can occur when the object is rotated past 90 degrees.

Interpolate: The calculation performed by the software to determine the values between two keyframes.

Isoparm: Flow lines or constant U or V parameter curves on a surface.

Keyframe: The specific property along a timeline that is set by the animator.

Layer: The manner in which objects are organized in certain programs so that they can be hidden or shown in specific groups. Layering can also refer to placing multiple textures on objects.

Lathe: A method for creating a surface by rotating a profile around an axis.

Linear light: Similar to a row of lights, these lights can usually be scaled in size.

Linear spline: A straight spline that passes through all its connecting points.

Loft: Often referred to as skinning, it is a method of stretching a surface over a series of profiles composed of splines or polygons.

Luminosity: The brightness or value of a surface.

The total amount of light emitted by the object's surface.

Model: An object that is created with 3D tools.

Negative light: A light with an intensity less than 0.

Normal: The direction that indicates which way a polygon is facing. It tells the viewer which is the front side and which is the back.

NURBS curves: The most complex and flexible of curve types. The points can be weighted unequally so that some portions of the curve can bend more than others, hence the name Non-Uniform, Rational B-Spline (NURBS).

Object: Any 2D or 3D surface that can be manipulated in 3D space.

Pan: Rotating the camera on the *y*-axis so that it scans a scene from side to side.

Penumbra: A fringe region of partial shadow around an umbra.

Pitch: Rotation around the *x*-axis.

Pivot point: Sometimes referred to as the center or rotation point, it is the coordinate around which an object rotates. The pivot point can be moved, and its location determines how an object will be linked to another.

Pixel: One of the small dots or squares that constitutes a computer image.

Planar mapping: A method for texturing a surface by projecting an image on the object similarly to a slide projector.

Point light: Illuminating equally in every direction from a central source, it can be compared to an incandescent light bulb.

Polygon: A plane that is defined by points connected with straight edges.

Procedural textures: Sometimes referred to as shaders, they are image maps based on mathematical functions or short programs that create abstract patterns.

Radiosity: A renderer that calculates the amount of light that is transmitted from one surface to another. The renderer continues to follow the light until it is fully absorbed by all the surfaces or dissipates in space.

Ray tracing: A method of rendering that creates a ray for each pixel in a scene and traces its path, one at a time, all the way back to the light source. The value for each ray is calculated as it travels through and bounces of various surfaces.

Reflection: The phenomenon of a propagating wave (light) being thrown back from a surface.

Refraction: The manner in which light is bent as it passes through a surface of varying density.

Render: Producing an image or series of images from a 3D scene.

Roll: Rotating the camera around the *z*-axis. Often used in fly-through animations, the camera banks from side to side.

Roughness: The material attribute that determines the amount and quality of specular reflection from a surface.

Saturation: The degree of intensity in a color.

Scale: Making an object larger or smaller in any of the three *x*, *y*, and *z* directions.

Scene: The 3D world that can contain models, lights, cameras, and materials.

Shaders: Sometimes referred to as procedural textures, they are image maps based on mathematical functions or short programs that create abstract patterns.

Shadow maps: Shadows that are calculated by how far they are from the light(s) that are casting them. The renderer uses this information and the position of the light source to determine which items produce shadows. Shadow maps are sometimes called Depth map shadows.

Skin: Often referred to as lofting, it is a method of stretching a surface over a series of profiles composed of splines or polygons.

Specular: The manner in which light is reflected off a surface. The angle and location of a light(s) creates highlights on the surface.

Spherical mapping: A technique for wrapping a texture around an object and pinching it closed at the two ends.

Spline: A curve that is defined by points or vertices.

Spotlight: A light whose beam is emitted as a cone of light in varying degrees.

Sweep: A modeling procedure that creates surfaces by pulling a profile along a specified path.

Tangent line: A line that passes through the control vertices of a spline but does not touch the curve itself. A tangent line is used to adjust the angle of the curve.

Tessellations: A series of joined polygons forming a tiling pattern. Semi-regular tessellations are tiling patterns composed of a combination of regular and semi-regular polygons.

Texture map: An image that is applied to a surface. The size aspect ratio of the image is matched to the object's surface coordinates by various methods, such as planar, cylindrical, spherical, cubic, front projection, or UV mapping.

Tilt: Turning the camera on the x-axis so that scans the subject up and down. Its action is sometimes referred to as pitch.

Timeline: The time continuum of an animation as calculated by frames-per-second values.

Translucent: Almost transparent; allowing light to pass through diffusely so that objects cannot be seen clearly on the other side of it. Frosted glass has translucent surfaces.

Truck: The movement of a camera along the z-axis. Truck-in moves the camera closer to the subject while truck-out moves it away.

Trim curves: A curve drawn on an object's surface after a profile has been projected onto it or another object has intersected it. Trim curves allow one to trim away parts of a surface.

Umbra: A region of complete shadow resulting from total obstruction of light.

UV coordinate mapping: A precise method for mapping textures on curved surfaces. Unlike other mapping features, which treat all objects as if they were simple shapes, UV coordinate mapping allows one to match a texture to the structure of the geometry.

Vertex: A point along a spline, mesh, or polygon defined by x, y, and z coordinates. A series of points are called vertices. Control vertices are found on tangent lines.

Wipe: When a second shot slides over the first one to replace it.

Yaw: Rotation around the y-axis. This type of motion can also be defined as heading or pan.

Z-buffer: Depth information that is stored in a buffer and made available during the rendering process. The distance of each pixel from the camera plane (z-distance) is calculated in the order of proximity to the camera. Pixels closest to the camera are rendered last.

Zoom: Changing the focal length of a camera so that the subject appears closer or further away.

Index

W

water, *see* liquid

weight, 256, 259–261, 262, 280, 282, 284, 285, 286, 290, 291, 292, 295

weight and recoil, 259–261, 280, 286, 295

wind, 88, 92, 104, 106

wipe, 319–320

wrinkle, 7, 8, 14, 68, 69

X

x-ray, 232

X-ray Shade, 121

x, *y*, and *z*

location, 44

value of, 4

Y

yaw, *see also* pan

Z

zoom, 311–312, 314–315

Zygomatic Major, 119

Books from Allworth Press

The Education of an Illustrator
by Steven Heller and Marshall Arisman (softcover, 6 × 9, 288 pages, $19.95)

Business and Legal Forms for Illustrators, Revised Edition
by Tad Crawford (softcover, 8½ × 11, 192 pages, includes CD-ROM, $24.95)

Legal Guide for the Visual Artist, Fourth Edition
by Tad Crawford (softcover, 8½ × 11, 272 pages, $19.95)

Licensing Art and Design, Revised Edition
by Caryn R. Leland (softcover, 6 × 9, 128 pages, $16.95)

The Business of Being an Artist, Third Edition
by Daniel Grant (softcover, 6 × 9, 352 pages, $19.95)

AIGA Professional Practices in Graphic Design
The American Institute of Graphic Arts, edited by Tad Crawford
(softcover, 6¾ × 10, 320 pages, $24.95)

Business and Legal Forms for Graphic Designers, Revised Edition
by Tad Crawford and Eva Doman Bruck
(softcover, 8½ × 11, 240 pages, includes CD-ROM, $24.95)

The Fine Artist's Career Guide
by Daniel Grant (softcover, 6 × 9, 224 pages, $18.95)

**Careers by Design: A Headhunters Secrets for Success and Survival in Graphic
Design, Revised Edition** *by Roz Goldfarb* (softcover, 6¾ × 10, 224 pages, $18.95)

The Fine Artist's Guide to Marketing and Self-Promotion
by Julius Vitali (softcover, 6 × 9, 288 pages, $18.95)

The Artist's Quest for Inspiration
by Peggy Hadden (softcover, 6 × 9, 224 pages, $15.95)

**Artists Communities: A Directory of Residencies in the United States That Offer
Time and Space for Creativity, Second Edition**
by the Alliance of Artists' Communities (6¾ × 10, 240 pages, $18.95)

Please write to request our free catalog. To order by credit card, call 1-800-491-2808 or send a check or money order to Allworth Press, 10 East 23rd Street, Suite 510, New York, NY 10010. Include $5 for shipping and handling for the first book ordered and $1 for each additional book. Ten dollars plus $1 for each additional book if ordering from Canada. New York State residents must add sales tax.

To *see* our complete catalog on the World Wide Web, or to order online, you can find us at *www.allworth.com*.